A WOMAN'S PLACE:
MANAGEMENT

A WOMAN'S PLACE: MANAGEMENT

CONNIE SITTERLY

BETH WHITLEY DUKE

PRENTICE HALL, Englewood Cliffs, New Jersey 07632

Library of Congress Cataloging-in-Publication Data

Sitterly, Connie.
  A woman's place.

  Includes bibliographies and index.
  1. Women executives. 2. Women middle managers.
I. Duke, Beth Whitley. II. Title.
HD6054.3.S67 1988   658.4'09'024042   87-25746
ISBN 0-13-961954-2

Editorial/production supervision: *Harriet Damon Shields*
Cover photo: *Connie Frady*
Manufacturing buyer: *Ed O'Dougherty*

MONOPOLY® game equipment used with permission
from Parker Brothers, © 1935, 1985.

Printed in the United States of America

10 9 8 7 6 5 4 3 2 1

ISBN 0-13-961954-2 01

Prentice-Hall International (UK) Limited, *London*
Prentice-Hall of Australia Pty. Limited, *Sydney*
Prentice-Hall Canada Inc., *Toronto*
Prentice-Hall Hispanoamericana, S.A., *Mexico*
Prentice-Hall of India Private Limited, *New Delhi*
Prentice-Hall of Japan, Inc., *Tokyo*
Simon & Schuster Asia Pte. Ltd., *Singapore*
Editora Prentice-Hall do Brasil, Ltda., *Rio de Janeiro*

To our parents,
Claude and Virda Sitterly
and
Golden and R.N. Whitley,
and to Ralph Duke and Connie Frady

CONTENTS

PREFACE

About five years ago, two women in widely varying fields began to realize that they were living in the midst of change. The women they knew, who were entering the work force in ever-increasing numbers, suddenly wanted more than merely a job. They wanted a career with responsibility, relevance, and rewards.

As a professor, Connie Sitterly observed women in her classes preparing to meet new and demanding challenges. She perceived that the answer to these challenges lay in academic training, and implemented her perceptions by pioneering courses on women in management at the college/university level and offering continuing education classes and seminars in business skills. Her marketing attracted not only traditional college students who required another course in business but also women who were already in the business world, who wanted to move ahead. Through her research in developing a meaningful curriculum for the classes, she realized that a need existed to help bridge the information gap for women who desired a career in management.

As a journalist, Beth Whitley Duke was covering women's news as it moved from the tea room to the board room. New organizations, such as women's professional networks and political caucuses, were joining the ranks of more traditional community organizations. Now, in addition to columns directed to the needs and problems of women in general, readers wanted advice for working women, stories on day care, and updates on legislation affecting women's rights. Week after week, the headlines and the women behind them proved that the 1950's concept of a male breadwinner and a female homemaker now described a minority of families. Instead, women wanted to achieve their greatest potential both at home and at work.

This book, then, was a natural outgrowth of many in-depth discussions on issues facing women who wanted to explore new roles. Drawing from autobiographical events as well as from the experiences of students and readers, the authors hope to provide a practical guide for women in management. Those experiences, combined with research and readings in the latest literature, encourage us to learn from each other as women continue to break new ground in the business world. Although few role models exist for women in business, women no longer have to learn solely by personal experience. By drawing on the experiences of others, in both formal and informal education, women can build skills to form a foundation for their future careers.

The college students, seminar participants, colleagues, and newspaper readers who inspired this book represent the same varied audience as those who will read it. With this in mind, the chapters in this volume include information for women at all different stages of their careers and education.

If our efforts smooth the path for just one woman to achieve her goal as she starts her career or save another woman from a serious mistake as she makes a career move, then we feel that all our efforts have been well rewarded.

The authors wish to acknowledge the help and encouragement of friends and colleagues who helped to make this book possible. We express special thanks to Kristin Fabro, Robyn Ford, Don Moore, Alison Reeves, and Willie Weaver.

A WOMAN'S PLACE: MANAGEMENT

1

WOMEN IN MANAGEMENT

OBJECTIVES

- Trace the changing roles of women and the advancements women have made
- Compare unfounded and well-established beliefs about sex differences
- Trace registration and executive orders that have helped to reshape the rights of women
- Compare attitudes of women and men in the late 1980s and note changes that have occurred
- Contrast stereotypes and facts about women
- Address current issues of day care, comparable worth, sexual harassment, flextime, flexplace, job sharing, and the compressed work week
- Provide guidelines to keep in mind when making career decisions

As long ago as the 1800s, Stendhal wrote: "Granting women complete equality would be the surest sign of civilization and it would double the intellectual power of the human race."

Yet more than 20 years after Betty Friedan wrote *The Feminine Mystique*, women are still struggling with issues of equal pay, equal roles, and equal opportunities. In the latest United Nations 10-year study on equality, reported in the July 8, 1985 issue of *U. S. News and World Report*, statistics showed that

- ❑ Women do two-thirds of the world's work.
- ❑ Women receive one-tenth of its income.
- ❑ Women own one one-hundredth of its property.

Women have always worked, either as part of the family responsibilities of maintaining a home and rearing children or as part of a family enterprise such as farming or some other small business. However, most American women never received a paycheck for work until World War II when a shortage of adult male workers enabled women to fill the factory jobs necessary for the war effort. After the war, many women returned home to raise the children who would become known as the baby boom generation. A few discovered that they enjoyed the independence and challenge of working outside the home. Those women became the early role models for women who grew up in the 1950s, 1960s, and 1970s hoping to "have it all." Having it all—a career, a family, and a comfortable life-style—remains the goal of many women. More and more women are finding that, although progress has been made in the last decade, they still face cultural and economic obstacles.

In "Working Women in the 80s and Beyond" (Sitterly, 1987, pp. 201-202), the author states the following:

> Astonishing is a fair word to describe women's advancements in the last decade. In 1963, Betty Friedan inspired the modern woman's movements with her book, *The Feminine Mystique*. Between 1963-1970, the lines of sex discrimination were drawn. Lawsuits abounded. Today the lines are still being defined, particularly in subtle attitudes, and lawsuits are still abounding. "Equal pay for equal work," the slogan of the 70s, is still more myth than reality: women earned 52 percent of what men earned in 1968 and only 68 percent in 1986.

In approximately the same time span, the number of women in management has doubled to more than 3 million. The top female managers, however, are in mid-management positions, earning $30,000 to $50,000. Of the 33 percent of women who reach the management level, only 6 percent are at the top of their professions and fewer than 1 percent hold senior-level corporate directorships. Less than 4 percent of the women in the work force earn $25,000 and 80 percent of working women are concentrated in clerical, sales, or service jobs. An occupation in which more than 60 percent of the jobholders are women can be defined as *female intensive*.

As one former nurse expressed it, "When I was growing up, the only options were to be a secretary, a teacher, or a nurse." Together these jobs comprise what some analysts have termed the *pink ghetto* of employment, with disproportionate numbers of women in lower paying professions. Although many of these jobs offer little opportunity for promotion, some women have been able to reach the tops of their professions within the ranks of jobs traditionally termed *women's work*. These types of jobs, designated for women, were based on a sexist, stereotypical, traditional classification according to sex or role rather than qualifications or abilities. For example, both Estée Lauder and Mary Kay Ash turned their knowledge of cosmetics and beauty into multimillion dollar corporations. Liz Claiborne Ortenberg, who designs fashions as Liz Claiborne, founded and heads a company on the Fortune 500 list.

NATURE VERSUS NURTURE

Trying to explain the gaps between women's and men's accomplishments and salaries in the working world has added another dimension to the *nature versus nurture* debate. This debate questions whether we inherit certain qualities that make us different from birth (nature) or whether we come into the world with equal capabilities, but environmental factors cause us to develop different abilities (nurture).

Practically speaking, each of us is a product of both the traits we inherit, such as intelligence or physical appearance, and our environment, such as our home life or educational opportunities. Because men were larger, they were perceived as stronger; because women bore children, they were thought to have a greater capacity as nurturers, and so on.

Many parents, either consciously or unconsciously, express these assumptions when rearing their children. Qualities that are reinforced in boys tend to be achievement, independence, self-reliance, and responsibility, the qualities needed to mold them into tomorrow's executives. In girls, adults tend to reinforce qualities of attractiveness, kindness, lack of selfishness, and good behavior, the qualities needed to mold them into tomorrow's wives and mothers, even though most studies now conclude that, except for a brief time around childbirth, most women will work outside the home until retirement.

These assumptions carry over into societal stereotypes that are difficult to overcome. *Stereotypes* are beliefs about a group's predictable characteristics that allow us, based on these beliefs, to categorize the group and generalize about its behavior without looking at the individuals. Stereotypes about race, sex, and religion are reflected throughout society. Although individuals can overcome stereotypes, myths may become deeply ingrained, leading the individual to act in the expected way and make the self-fulfilling prophecy come true.

Parents are not the only people perpetuating stereotypical myths. Authors of children's literature often do too. Fortunately, more and more children's books are showing that girls as well as boys can be doctors and boys as well as girls can be nurses. Allowing boy characters to be more sensitive and girl characters to be tougher helps reinforce children's beliefs that they can be anything they want to be.

Women who now aspire to become managers may provide the answers to the differences that remain to be proved or disproved. Competitiveness, dominance, and compliance are all skills that come into play in a working world in which women are just now gaining an equal opportunity to achieve results.

THE CHANGING WOMAN

One of the most popular advertising campaigns to come out of the women's movement was the Virginia Slims cigarette slogan, "You've come a long way, baby."

The advances women have made can be attributed to a number of demographic and psychological changes that occurred in the 1960s and 1970s.

Education. In the 1960s, more and more women entered colleges to continue their education. Middle class and affluent parents saw a college education as a worthwhile goal for their girls as well as for their boys. Additionally, new federal and state programs offered scholarship money, grants, and student loans to lower income and minority students who sought higher education.

Reproductive freedom. Historically, women married and had children during the time their husbands were becoming established in careers. If a woman entered the work force, she waited until either her children enrolled in school or economic need necessitated working outside the home. Advanced birth control methods gave women the freedom to plan their child-bearing future. Many women opted to establish a career first and have children second. Other women limited the number of children they wanted or even elected not to have children.

Tolerance of different life-styles. In 1957, 80 percent of the population felt that "a person who does not want to get married is sick, immoral, selfish or neurotic." By 1976, only 25 percent of the population still held this view. Women who used to be defined by their roles as someone's wife, mother, or daughter are now defined on their own terms, with different choices of life-style more widely accepted.

Higher divorce rates. The number of divorces doubled between 1965 and 1980. Government statistics predict that 4 out of every 10 marriages will end in divorce. This trend abolished the traditional American family profile of the husband as the chief support of the family and the wife as the chief caretaker of the home and children. Higher divorce rates led to establishment of new family units for single people, single parents, and stepfamilies.

The feminization of poverty. When women become single heads of households, their earning power drops. Almost 75 percent of fathers stop child support payments within a year of separation. With many women in the work force, some divorce settlements are based on the assumption that the woman will be able to find suitable employment, although she may in fact lack the skills or opportunities to do so. Almost half of the 5 million women who live alone have yearly incomes of $3,000 or less; for black women that amount decreases to $2,000.

Female longevity. Women generally live longer than men, which means that many women will face their last years as widows. The average age for widowhood in the United States is 56. Two-thirds of all widows live alone and one-third live below the poverty line. Three-fourths of all nursing home residents are women. The average nonmarried working woman retires with less than $1,000 in the bank.

GOVERNMENT REACTION AND INTERVENTION

During the 1960s, feminist activists campaigned to include women under legislation that established equal rights for minorities. Although the Equal Rights Amendment never became part of the Constitution, other legislation and executive orders helped reshape the rights of women which many of us take for granted today (Table 1-1).

Felice Belman (1986), in an article titled "How Working Women Won Their Rights," outlined key governmental action that opened opportunities for women.

- ❑ In 1963, Congress passed the *Equal Pay Act*, which prohibited employers from paying women less than men for the same work (defined as jobs with equal skills, effort, and responsibility).

- ❑ In 1964, Congress passed the *Civil Rights Act* in which Title VII banned employment discrimination based on "race, color, religion, sex or national origin" and created the *Equal Employment Opportunity Commission* to enforce antidiscrimination laws.

- ❑ In 1967, President Lyndon Johnson added women to the groups protected under a previous executive order by President John Kennedy requiring contractors to take affirmative action to recruit, hire, and promote more minorities among their employees. That same year, Congress passed the *Age Discrimination in Employment Act*, protecting employees between 40 and 70 years of age from discrimination in hiring, firing, and other terms of employment.

- ❑ In 1972, Congress passed *Title IX of the Education Amendments of 1972*, prohibiting sex bias in institutions receiving federal money. Although this was originally interpreted to mean that if any part of an institution received money, the whole institution was held to this standard, a 1984 Grove City Supreme Court Case limited the Title IX protections to cover only the program or activity receiving federal funds.

Table 1-1   Key Governmental Action That Opened Opportunities for Women

1963	Equal Pay Act
1964	Civil Rights Act
1967	Age Discrimination in Employment Act
1972	Title IX of Educational Amendments
1973	Rehabilitation Act
1978	Pregnancy Discrimination Act
1979	Equal Employment Opportunity Commission
1983	Executive Order (requiring federal agencies to increase employment of minority-owned subcontractors by at least 10 percent)

❑ In 1973, the *Rehabilitation Act* banned discrimination against qualified individuals with handicaps who can perform the essential functions of the job with "reasonable accommodation."

❑ In 1974, the *Equal Credit Opportunity Act* (later amended in 1976) gave women access to the same financial services as males by prohibiting discrimination against women.

❑ In 1978, the *Pregnancy Discrimination Act* extended the protection of Title VII to pregnant employees.

❑ In 1979, President Jimmy Carter unified the enforcement of *Title VII,* the *Equal Pay Act,* the *Age Discrimination in Employment Act,* and the *Rehabilitation Act* under the *Equal Employment Opportunity Commission.* Responsibility for federal contract-compliance programs was transferred to an office in the Labor Department.

❑ In 1983, President Ronald Reagan signed an executive order requiring federal agencies to increase their goals for employment of minority-owned subcontractors by at least 10 percent.

❑ In 1986, the Supreme Court upheld a California law requiring employers to grant leave for pregnant workers even if leaves are not granted for other health conditions.

While women now enjoy legal protection from many injustices of equality, these same protections are constantly being challenged in court cases. In addition, if a woman believes she has experienced discrimination, her only alternative may be to hire an attorney and face court costs and drawn out litigation in order to test the law.

WHAT WOMEN THINK

With the background of major societal changes over the past two decades, women's attitudes have experienced major changes. In an attitude survey titled "A Woman's Choice," researchers printed a questionnaire in the October 15, 1985 issue of *Woman's Day* magazine. More than 60,000 women responded to the 77-question survey. Of the returned surveys, the poll sampled every ninth basis yielding 3,009 returns. The typical respondent was a wife and mother under 45 years of age who either worked or was planning to go to work soon.

Some of the survey's findings, as released by *Woman's Day* and Yankelovich, Skelly & White (June 10, 1986), included the following:

❑ Women think life is tougher than ever but don't want to retreat or go back to the way things were.

❑ Women think men are the big winners over the past 20 years and children are the big losers.

❑ Most women feel that they must work, but only one-third would quit if they could.

❑ Only one-half of the women say they would marry the same man again.

❑ Women feel that men do not do their fair share of work and that men underestimate women's abilities in the workplace.

❑ Women think neither men nor society is giving them the support or flexibility they need.

WHAT MEN THINK

Men along with women have experienced societal changes. The results of a survey of 180 men conducted in a regional Texas magazine showed that 78 percent of the respondents felt confused about what women really want (Sitterly, 1985).

Other significant findings included the following:

❑ 52 percent thought women were paid less because they were women.

❑ 55 percent said women had less opportunity for promotion.

❑ 58 percent felt women were discriminated against.

❑ 79 percent said women could make decisions as well as men.

Concerning the homefront

❑ 91 percent said men should help with household chores.

❑ 80 percent thought women should not choose a career over a family.

The gap between theory and practice may be greater in certain areas of male-female relationships. Although men may state that they should take greater responsibility for household chores, few actually split the duties equally. Although 79 percent of the respondents in this survey thought women could make decisions as well as men, another survey showed that 40 percent of 8,000 men surveyed had misgivings about working for a woman boss

(Baron, 1982). Some of the reasons men gave for not wanting a woman boss were

❑   Women are not as confident.
❑   Women have less clout or power.
❑   Women do not know how to play the game.
❑   Women sometimes come on too strong.
❑   Men do not know how to treat a woman boss.
❑   Having a woman boss makes a man look bad.
❑   Women are more likely to be promoted as a gesture of tokenism rather than based on competence or other factors.

These stereotypical judgments of women's behavior have created a "Catch 22" for women entering business. That is, when women exhibit behavior generally associated with a successful executive, they may be judged on women's stereotypes rather than objective evaluations of their actions. For example:

❑   A man is serious—A woman lacks a sense of humor.
❑   A man is persistent—A woman is nagging.
❑   A man is assertive—A woman is aggressive.
❑   A man is objective—A woman is cold hearted.
❑   A man is straightforward—A woman is abrasive.
❑   A man is thoughtful—A woman is scared.
❑   A man is demanding—A woman is picky.
❑   A man is decisive—A woman is masculine.

THE FACTS

When many people think of a family, they may get a mental picture of a 1950s situation comedy such as "Father Knows Best" or "Ozzie and Harriet," in which the father worked outside the home as the sole wage earner and the mother's major responsibilities centered on homemaking and child rearing. Although less than 7 percent of families in the United States now fit into this category, much of our behavior is still predicated on the so-called nuclear family.

Today, 49 million women are employed in the United States. Even if people admit that women now comprise 54 percent of the work force, they may not realize that women work for many of the same reasons men work: money, financial security, and self-fulfillment. By 1995, 81 percent of all women aged 25 to 34 years are expected to be in the labor force, compared with 70 percent in 1986.

COMMON SENSE AND STATISTICS DISPEL
MYTHS ABOUT WOMEN WHO WORK

- ❏ Although women are considered to be poor economic risks because of excessive sick leave, studies show that age, occupation, and salary are more important influences on time lost from work.

- ❏ Although women are somewhat more concerned than men that their co-workers are friendly and helpful, they attach more importance to competence than to niceness.

- ❏ Women and men are equally interested in getting promotions and in doing interesting work. Although women express slightly more interest in having a clean place to work, few men or women would trade a challenging job for better working conditions.

- ❏ Although some people think women are too emotional to make decisions, women have historically made life-and-death decisions in homes and hospitals.

- ❏ Although some employers may think women work only until they get married or have children, statistics indicate that the majority of working women are married and many of those women have children. The number of working women with children under 1 year of age increased by 70 percent in the last decade.

- ❏ One of the most pervasive myths is that women would not work if they did not have to. The fact is that some men and some women would not work if they did not need the money, but most people express apprehension when faced with not having a purpose or meaningful task in their lives.

STEREOTYPES AT HOME

In addition to stamping out stereotypes in the workplace, women face a disproportionate share of responsibility at home. The first woman in a nontraditional job is likely to be asked how she juggles a family and a career, even though men in similar positions can have families and careers without ever addressing this question. Women face other issues that impact on the family in ways that traditional business policies are just beginning to address. Two of the major issues facing working women today are dual-career marriages and child care.

Dual-Career Marriages

When most corporate executives were men whose wives did not work outside the home, certain business and social customs were taken for granted. Cartoons joked about unexpectedly bringing the boss home for dinner or calling home to report the need to work late. Many families are now facing new situations in their relationships as both husband and wife work each day at demanding jobs.

In these situations, how would you decide which choice to make for the partners?

- ❑ If a company offers a transfer to a woman, will her husband leave his job as she might have been expected to do for him in a more traditional era?
- ❑ If a child is sick, which working parent takes time off from work to stay home or meet a doctor's appointment?
- ❑ If an important out-of-town corporate visitor arrives unexpectedly and needs to be entertained, which spouse assumes the duty of host or hostess?
- ❑ If a couple has to attend two equally important business functions for their respective jobs during one evening, how do they decide which one takes precedence?

Some of these situations may seem extreme, but more and more couples are facing or have already faced similar predicaments. As with most complex problems, there are no simple solutions. For example, if you decide to take a transfer or a sick day based on which partner earns the most money, you may be neglecting other important factors such as future job security or long-range promotional potential based on accepting a transfer or a strong attendance record. Money is only one indicator in making family decisions, and in some cases, it doesn't seem to matter who earns the most. In *A Profile of Women Senior Executives*, from Korn/Ferry International, the study found that 49 percent of the women take primary responsibility for housekeeping although in 75 percent of the cases they provide at least half of the household income.

Every family develops different coping skills when trying to combine two careers and a marriage or two careers, a marriage, and rearing children. The extent to which these coping skills are successful may help determine which career-marriage partnerships succeed and which fail. One of the primary things to remember about dual-career marriage is that there is no one right way to manage all the variables. Second, as long as both partners respect the other's job and commitment to the family unit, they can generally meet on common ground to discuss family issues. Most working people say they put family first and job second, but occasionally the job will have to come first. In some cases, a couple may find that professional help is needed to overcome a particular obstacle or to gain an objective opinion about a pending decision.

SIX GUIDELINES TO REMEMBER WHEN MAKING
CAREER/MARRIAGE DECISIONS

1. *Communicate as openly as possible without resorting to old arguments when trying to make a decision.* Not expressing thoughts may lead to resentment later. Allow both parties to air their feelings before coming to a decision.
2. *Compromise rather than issue an ultimatum.* Life is a trade-off in many ways. The perfect home, the perfect marriage, and the perfect jobs are all ideals that we may never reach. Selecting a compromise based on the best of all possible choices is a more realistic way to approach life.
3. *Decide what is really important to you and stick with it.* Many couples find that they can live in a house that is less than military-inspection clean or eat a few less home-cooked meals in order to enjoy more leisure time together.
4. *Realize that you may have to schedule time together or plan activities more when both of you are working.* If you wait until you have time to have fun, you may be too tired to enjoy yourself.
5. *Leave work at work and leave home at home.* If you are frustrated because of a bad day at work, try not to let that carry over to time at home. Likewise, if a personal problem is distracting you, it should not affect your behavior at work.
6. *Be as creative at home as you are at work.* Apply all the creative problem-solving techniques of business to home situations. If both parties hate housework, for example, consider cutting back on the entertainment budget to find money to hire a housekeeper. If both parties agree that they need a vacation trip, research inexpensive alternatives to get a change of scenery without adding to the stress of staying within a budget.

Day Care

Day care is a specialized problem that affects both married working women with children and women who are single parents.

Working women raise more than one-half of the children in the United States. Almost 85 percent of working women will bear children during their careers.

Just as housekeeping duties have traditionally been assigned to women, so have responsibilities of rearing children, arranging day care, seeking medical care when needed, and serving as a liaison between the child and school or other institutions. Ideally, when a husband and wife share parenting duties, either could be on call for emergencies or take an occasional day off to babysit a sick child at home. However, many couples find this situation unworkable for a number of reasons:

- ❏ One partner may not have a job flexible enough to allow telephone calls or emergency errands.
- ❏ One partner may lose face with a boss (of either sex) because of time lost from work in dealing with children or child care problems.
- ❏ One partner may not feel an equal commitment to either child rearing, the other partner's job, or the marriage itself.

For single parents, the problems are compounded by the lack of a marriage partner and by a single income that has to stretch to cover day care costs. One out of two marriages will end in divorce. Single and divorced women who are heads of households already account for almost one-fifth of the homes in the United States. Many of these women receive no help from the former husband, the employer, or the government. In fact, the average child support payment in the United States is about $34 a week, which is far less than the average day care fee of about $50 for one child.

In any case, a dependable, safe child care arrangement is a priority for many working women. Without this, a woman cannot get to her own job on time or meet the demands of her day. Strategies to help avoid a day care crisis include the following:

Build a support system.   Find neighbors or family members who will agree to help in an emergency if the regular sitter is unavailable or the child is sick.

Investigate company policy and attitudes about children before a situation arises.   Some companies allow parents to use their own sick leave to care for children. Other companies prohibit this practice. Find out in advance so as not to jeopardize your position.

Shop around for day care. Prices in many communities vary widely, from private day care centers and private homes to nonprofit community centers and church programs. Services vary from simple babysitting to preschool programs that prepare children for school. Many *United Way* offices offer an information service that can refer you to day care centers in a certain area or within a certain price range. The state welfare department or department of human resources generally is responsible for day care regulations and evaluations. These offices are listed with other state offices in the white pages of the telephone book.

Ask for help even if you are not sure you are entitled to it. Many centers have scholarships for certain special cases. Others reduce fees when more than one child is enrolled from the same family. Check to see if your center charges for holidays or other times when your child is not attending. You may be able to cut costs by paying by the month rather than by the week.

Remember, peace of mind is worth the investment when it comes to day care. Working mothers often report feeling guilty at having to leave small children with a stranger. Buy the best care you can afford at the most convenient location so that you can concentrate on your job during the day. Leave clear rules about who is to be called in case of emergencies and know procedures to follow if you must be late or if someone else will pick the child up to avoid any unforeseen problems.

The United States lags far behind most industrial nations in developing a child care or family policy to address the needs of working parents. More than 100 countries have laws that provide paid maternity leave for women, but not the United States. More than 50 countries have day care provided by the government or a policy that employers must provide day care, but not the United States. Fewer children are getting day care today than 5 years ago, even though the number of children in need of child care keeps growing.

Some communities and employers have found new solutions to the problem of day care. Companies may offer on-site day care that allows parents and children to come to the office together in the morning and leave together at night. Some facilities have extra space to allow parents to eat noon meals with their children. Other companies have begun issuing child care vouchers to employees as a company benefit. Still others have opted for a cafeteria-style plan of benefits, which allows employees to select the benefits they most need. For example, a dual-career couple might choose her retirement plan, his health insurance coverage, her stock purchase option, and his day care subsidy instead of duplicating benefits at different companies.

In companies that do not offer day care benefits, groups of concerned employees may opt to research different alternatives and recommend a plan of action to management.

Some highly progressive companies now allow paid paternity leave as an option for men who are taking care of newborns or some form of parental leave for employees who adopt children.

Since children are sick more often than adults, one hospital recently opened a Sick Bay that sets aside part of a pediatric floor to care for sick children during the day. The children get periodic attention from the nurses and are divided according to symptoms rather than being taken to regular day care where healthy children might be exposed to their germs.

For older children, many communities offer a latch-key program aimed at providing supervision for children between the time they get out of school and the time their parents arrive home from work. These programs may operate from a YWCA or YMCA, a church, or even the school itself under special arrangements with volunteer groups.

STEREOTYPES AT WORK

Just as women face new challenges at home as they try to succeed, they will also face new challenges at work. Two important issues for working women are *comparable worth* and *sexual harassment.*

Comparable Worth

Comparable worth is not simply equal pay for equal work. As we have noted, the *Equal Pay Act of 1963* required employers to "provide equal pay for substantially equal work regardless of sex." In other words, when a man and a woman hold the same position, they must receive equal paychecks by law. Since many salary schedules are confidential, most women working side by side with men never know if they receive equal pay. Although studies show that most Americans believe in the intent of the law, some employers still think a man must receive a larger paycheck since "he has a family to support."

Comparable worth is the concept that asserts that women should be paid as much as men for performing tasks in other jobs requiring comparable but not identical skills, education, responsibilities, and effort. The comparable worth argument goes beyond equal pay for the same job. It forces some entity, such as the government or an employer, to make a value judgment on the relative importance of the work being done. For example, should a janitor or maintenance worker receive more or less pay than a housekeeper or a nurse? Since the former are generally regarded as "men's jobs" and the latter as "women's jobs," advocates of comparable worth want to reduce many historical incidences of discrimination in female-dominated jobs.

Comparable worth, also known as pay equity, may be an alternative strategy to help women close the salary gap. Comparable worth faces a strong opposition from employers who see a structured salary guide as an intrusion into the private enterprise system. By raising salaries in lower paying jobs to match salaries in higher paying jobs of equal responsibility, employers face higher employment costs during the transitional years until salaries are equivalent.

Three main issues that must be resolved before comparable worth will become a reality are

1. Who decides which jobs are comparable?
2. How do you measure the comparability of jobs?
3. How do you implement comparable pay?

Historically, most changes affecting equal rights have begun with government intervention before becoming accepted into private business. For example, government orders requiring consideration for minority contractors helped pave the way for equal commerce rights throughout society. Since government salaries are usually graded based on education, experience, and performance, government jobs would be a logical place to begin implementation. The idea is that once the government defines comparable job categories, private business will follow.

Factors to be considered in evaluating comparable worth situations include the level of education necessary for the job, the relative responsibility within the job description, and the length of on-the-job training for competence or seniority within a company. As advocates of comparable worth point out, employers would still retain full discretion about how much to pay each employee. The major difference would be that employees on certain levels would be guaranteed the same amount of remuneration.

Although the fate of legislation adopting pay equity remains to be tested in the courts, the issue itself will force employers to rethink practices that have resulted in unfair pay scales.

Sexual Harassment

Another important issue for working women is sexual harassment in the workplace. *Sexual harassment* is any unwanted behavior, whether verbal or physical, that either creates an implicit or explicit condition for employment or interferes with an individual's ability to work in an atmosphere free from intimidation.

Sexual harassment can take any of five forms:

1. *Verbal.* Dirty jokes or sexually explicit statements.
2. *Abuse.* Verbal put-downs that try to demean work efforts because of sex.
3. *Subtle pressure for sexual activity.* Flirting behavior that implies a promotion or reward for favors.
4. *Rape or attempted rape.* Violent sexual assault.
5. *Coercive pressure for sexual activity.* Threats of job loss or other punishment if favors are not granted.

Although there are degrees of sexual harassment, any form should be taken seriously. Sexual harassment is not a compliment and is not a laughing matter. It can lead to feelings of guilt, a tarnished reputation, anxiety, and economic losses. Men as well as women have reported experiencing sexual harassment. In some cases, the only solution may be to find another job. Other companies have stated policies against sexual harassment. A few victims have sued successfully in court and have won civil actions against employers who were guilty of sexual harassment or companies that knowingly allowed the practice to continue. However, in many cases, victims forego costly litigation and try to deal with the problem through other channels. Too often, women fear losing their jobs or reputations and endure the harassment in silence.

Sexual harassment grows out of an environment of sexism, that is, treating people differently because of their sex. Because women have only recently assumed positions of power in corporations, they generally hold jobs in which their bosses are male. In many cases, men at work relate to women along traditional roles they have learned in families. They might treat an older woman as they would treat their mother. A younger women might be viewed as their daughter. Some men relate to working women as sexual beings rather than as colleagues or co-workers. Sometimes sexual harassment begins with sexist comments. A man might call a male clerk by his first name but refer to a female as a "girl."

Some strategies for combating sexism and harassment include the following (see also Table 1-2):

1. Avoid situations that encourage a high level of familiarity; maintain professionalism at all times.

Table 1-2 How to Stop Sexual Harassment

1. Tell him to stop—talk privately, confront early
2. Ask yourself if the harassment is linked to employment
3. Determine how it interferes with your work.
4. Keep a diary to document incidents
5. Tell others
6. Write a letter(s); follow-up notes
7. Contact EEO or outside agency or both
8. Tell your supervisor or union
9. Look at *your* personnel file
10. Solicit statements from witnesses

2. Privately tell the offender to stop the offending action in an assertive, direct manner.
3. Know the company policy about sexual harassment.
4. Document any incidents in case you need to file a grievance or eventually provide evidence.

OPTIONS IN THE 1990s

Not all the issues of working in the 1990s are negative. There are some positive options.

Flextime. This is a condition in which employees may, within prior approval, alter their working hours or decide their work schedule. In flextime, a worker can select an 8-hour shift within the company hours such as 7 AM to 4 PM or 9 AM to 6 PM rather than working 8 AM to 5 PM. Some firms allow employees to take a 30-minute lunch break and leave a half-hour early instead. Flextime addresses the needs of changing families. It can allow one parent to take a child to school and the other to pick the child up after work.

Job sharing. This is an approach to job enrichment in which two employees share a full-time position, splitting one job into two part-time jobs. Two people hold one position and share the responsibilities and the paycheck. This arrangement may allow two people to stay in the work force while still having time for children or other commitments. Job sharing may mean that one person works in the morning and one person works in the afternoon or one person works the first half of a week and the other person completes the week, with a small overlap of time for continuity and communication.

Flexplace. This is an employment practice in which employees are allowed to work at home rather in the office or plant. Personal computers and advanced telecommunications enable many people to work out of their homes without ever going to the office. Data entry, word processing, bookkeeping, and other jobs can be performed from a work station that may be miles from the company headquarters. Working at home cuts down time and money spent on commuting to work and allows parents to cut day care costs if they can effectively work at home and watch their children at the same time. It also allows a more flexible schedule, since the work can generally be done late at night or during the day to meet specific needs.

Compressed work week. This is the shortening of the work week so that the number of hours increases per day and the number of days decrease, such as a 4-day, 40-hour week. Many firms offer the option of working four 10-hour days instead of five 8-hour days to reach 40 hours. Companies save utility costs and other overhead expenses, and employees gain a 3-day weekend on a regular basis, which can lead to a higher level of productivity on working days.

SUMMARY

Through a combination of societal and political change, women have entered the work force in record numbers since the 1970s. Legislation aimed at curbing discrimination on the basis of race and sex has enabled women to move ahead in many areas that used to be traditional male domains.

However, women still tend to earn less and have less representation at the highest levels of management than men. Some obstacles to full rights include sexual harassment and discrimination.

As women continue to make strides in the executive world, they will face the issue of comparable worth as they demand equal pay not just for equal jobs but for equally important jobs as well. Dual-career families and working mothers are also changing the way Americans think about families and family needs. To meet these needs, new concepts such as flextime and job sharing are being developed.

TERMS AND CONCEPTS

age discrimination	harassment
Civil Rights Act	job sharing
compressed work week	nature versus nurture
dual-career marriages	pink ghetto
Equal Credit Opportunity Act	Pregnancy Discrimination
Equal Employment	Act
Opportunity Commission	Rehabilitation Act of 1973
Equal Pay Act	reproductive freedom
female-intensive occupation	stereotypes
female longevity	Title IX of Education
feminization of poverty	Amendments of 1972
flextime	working at home

REVIEW QUESTIONS

1. What was the Equal Pay Act and why was it important to the women's movement?
2. Define sexual harassment.
3. How does comparable worth differ from the equal pay for equal work issue?
4. What stereotypes must women overcome to compete in traditional male fields?
5. What avenues are open to a woman who feels she has been a victim of sexual harassment?
6. How are companies dealing with family issues such as child care?
7. What are cafeteria-style benefits and how do they affect dual-career marriages?

SUGGESTED READINGS

Baron, A. "How We're Viewed by the Men We Boss." *Savvy* (July 1982).

Belman, F. "How Working Women Won Their Rights." *Working Woman* (November, 1986).

Berch, B. *The Endless Day: The Political Economy of Women and Work.* Harcourt Brace Jovanovich, Orlando, FL, 1982.

Colwill, N. L. *The New Partnership, Women and Men in Organizations.* Mayfield, Palo Alto, CA, 1982.

Editors. *Working Woman* Magazine. *The Working Woman Report.* Simon & Schuster, New York, 1984.

Editors. *Working Woman* Magazine. *The Working Woman Success Book.* Ace Books, New York, 1981.

Eichenbaum, L., and Orbach, S. *What Do Women Want.* Berkley Books, New York, 1983.

Fox, M. F., and Hesse-Biber, S. *Women at Work.* Mayfield, Palo Alto, CA, 1984.

Friedan, B. *The Feminine Mystique.* Dell Books, New York, 1977.

Friedman, S. *Men Are Just Desserts.* Warner Books, New York, 1983.

Horn, P. D., and Horn, J. C. *Sex in the Office.* Addison-Wesley, Reading, MA, 1982.

Hunter College Women's Studies Collective. *Women's Realities, Women's Choices.* Oxford University Press, New York, 1983.

Hyatt, C. *Women and Work.* Warner Books, New York, 1980.

Kerber, L. K., and Mathews, J. D. *Women's America, Refocusing the Past.* Oxford University Press, New York, 1982.

Lainson, S. *Crash Course. The Instant M.B.A.* Fawcett Crest, New York, 1985.

LaRouche, J., and Ryan, R. *Strategies for Women at Work.* Avon Books, New York, 1984.

Lee, N. *Targeting the Top.* Ballantine Books, New York, 1980.

McElroy, W. *Freedom, Feminism and the State.* The Cato Institute, Washington, DC, 1982.

Ryan, M. F. *Womanhood in America* (3rd ed.). Franklin Watts, New York, 1983.

Sitterly, C. "Do Men Know What Women Really Want?" *Accent West* (February, 1985).

Sitterly, C. *Learning Guide for Kossen's Human Side of Organizations* (4th ed.). Harper & Row, New York, 1987.

Stead, B. A. *Women in Management* (2nd ed.). Prentice-Hall, Inc., Englewood Cliffs, NJ, 1985.

Tarvis. C., and Wade, C. *The Longest War* (2nd ed.). Harcourt Brace Jovanovich, Orlando, FL, 1984.

Wyse, L. *The Six-Figure Woman and How to Be One.* Linden Press, New York, 1983.

2

MANAGEMENT OVERVIEW

OBJECTIVES

- Define management
- Compare old and new managerial assumptions
- Compare old and new societal trends
- Identify at least five barriers to women's progress
- Evaluate different beliefs, perspectives, and attitudes of men and women and how they impact on women's careers in management
- Compare skills and levels required for management
- Contrast Theories X, Y, and Z
- Consider entrepreneurship as an alternative to a corporate career
- Define primary functions of management

Management is the effective utilization of human and material resources to achieve the organization's objectives. *Managers*, then, are the people charged with carrying out the responsibilities of management. In the past two decades, business has seen many changes in the profile of a manager. We now know that managers come from a wide variety of educational and interest backgrounds. The numbers of women in management are growing as more and more women set their goals at achieving higher career levels. In addition to demographic changes, management has also undergone changes in philosophy. One of the best ways to understand the philosophical changes is to contrast the old and new assumptions about business (Table 2-1).

OLD ASSUMPTIONS VERSUS NEW ASSUMPTIONS

Old: Businesses thrive when workers are tightly controlled. This assumption fostered an entire generation of authoritarian managers with little room for flexibility or management by consensus. This model continues the schoolroom stereotype of the teacher as a disciplinarian, dispensing bad grades and punishment for poor performance.

New: Positive reinforcement and rewards motivate workers to higher levels of productivity. The manager is more of a coach, helping employees achieve their potential. Employee interaction leads to better quality control and the generation of new ideas.

Old: Machines will never replace people. Machines are fine for repetitive, routine tasks, but require human interfacing to be effective.

Table 2-1 Seven Old versus New Assumptions about Business

OLD	NEW
1. Managers must tightly control workers	1. Manager coaches, rewards, reinforces
2. Machines will never replace people	2. People do what machines cannot
3. Managers rely on power and authority	3. Managers must lead and build a strong team
4. Managers need technical skills	4. Managers need human social skills
5. One problem at a time	5. Systems theory: events affect other people and departments as a part of the whole
6. Status quo	6. Forecast change
7. United States	7. International

New: Technology generates new machines every day that are capable of handling more and more tasks formerly performed by humans. Robots already ensure a consistent quality of assembly line functions, whereas humans might become bored with the repetition. Computers driven by voice or video telecommunication already exist. The emphasis should be on creative tasks that only people can do; basic functions should be assigned to machines.

Old: Managers can rely on power and authority so that their decisions will not be questioned. Once a supervisor makes a decision, that is the final word.

New: Managers should strive to become leaders rather than forces pushing employees who may or may not want to move ahead. Building a strong team based on the talents of team members may prove more effective than relying solely on one authority.

Old: Managers need technical skills to get and retain their jobs. Technical skills give managers the edge needed to supervise other employees.

New: Managers need human social skills. Technical skills can be found in hired employees or consultants. Human skills must be the basis for a successful organization.

Old: Businesses should deal with one problem at a time. Managers need to take things in order.

New: Time and events combine to be part of a whole. Seemingly isolated events may have an impact on other departments or other people in the company. A linear timeline oversimplifies the complex interaction of a business cycle.

Old: Maintaining the status quo is a primary goal. Change and uncertainty may prove unprofitable and should be avoided.

New: No business can be immune to change. Therefore, managers must learn to forecast trends and be on the leading edge of those trends to achieve profitability. Just as stockbrokers make a living advising people on how long to hold a stock, managers make their living by advising companies when to adopt a new strategy and change or when to follow through on existing plans.

Old: The United States offers enough opportunities to keep any business busy for generations.

New: The world has become smaller because of telecommunications and travel. The world is the new marketplace in which businesses will have to be competitive. Foreign languages and cultures will become part of doing business in an international field.

ADAPTING TO TRENDS

These assumptions are based on emerging trends that can be predicted statistically from available data on population and attitudes. John Naisbitt has become a pioneer in the concept of planning for the future. In the book *Re-inventing the Corporation* (Naisbitt and Aburdene, 1985), Naisbitt expands on his earlier work, *Megatrends* (Naisbitt, 1982), in which he identifies 10 trends that are forcing managers to analyze different facets of corporate life (Table 2-2).

1. The strategic resource will shift from industry to information. Information is the new natural resource and people are the reservoir for this creative energy and knowledge.

2. Companies may experience a labor shortage as the baby boomers give way to a generation with lower birth rates. Beginning in 1990, some jobs will experience a crunch as the job market turns into a seller's market for top employees.

3. Middle management will erode as a class. Budget cuts and a tendency to transfer certain functions, such as compiling and processing information, to computers will continue as businesses strive toward higher productivity and efficiency.

4. Entrepreneurs will revolutionize traditional corporate thinking. More and more people want to trade the security of working for someone else for the chance to be their own boss and have unlimited earning potential. As corporations try to retain these entrepreneurial spirits, they may turn to intrapreneurism or

Table 2-2 Ten Trends for Corporate Life in the Future

FROM	TO
1. Industry	1. Information
2. Baby boom	2. Baby bust—shortage
3. Middle management	3. Management cutbacks
4. Organization	4. Entrepreneurs
5. Stereotypes	5. Minorities and women advancing
6. Male work force	6. Women—dual careers
7. Duplicate another company's success	7. Competition, risks, vision, creativity, and intuition valued
8. Separate—business and education	8. New partnerships
9. Rising health care costs	9. Corporate health and wellness
10. Conservative generation	10. Social liberalism, independence, health consciousness

the cultivation of entrepreneurship through projects or teams within the company.

5. The emerging work force will continue to break away from the stereotypical patterns of the post-World War II era in which men were the primary breadwinners and women stayed home to raise children. The work force is younger, better educated, and more varied with regard to gender and ethnic heritage.

6. Women will continue to comprise a growing segment of working adults. In previous generations, women may have held jobs to help a spouse through school or to meet family expenses before children were born. Typically they dropped out of the work force for several years during child rearing. Women in the 1990s will generally work until retirement with only brief leaves of absence for childbirth. Dual-career families and working mothers will bring changes in the ways companies relate to employees' families.

7. Intuition and vision will be used more creatively. As old solutions outlive their usefulness in companies striving to compete in a changing world, companies will increasingly value the people who take creative risks to come up with new ideas and plans ahead of the competition. If companies wait to duplicate another company's success, they may find themselves in a position of never being able to catch up or close the technological gaps.

8. Education and business will have to form new partnerships to meet the needs of industries. The need for skilled, well-educated employees has overcome the need for marginally educated people who are trained to do a limited number of tasks.

9. Corporate health will continue to be an issue. Companies will encourage better health as a way to invest in human resources while cutting back on health care costs.

10. The baby boom generation, which will account for 54 percent of all workers by 1990, will implant its values on the work force. Baby boomers grew up with more material luxuries. An affluent generation, they formed their lifelong values during a period that stressed social liberalism, self-reliance, independence, and health consciousness.

A Place for Women

Naisbitt's sixth trend speaks directly to the growing number of women seeking career opportunities rather than simply jobs. Women are making gains in a number of professions, but the statistics they face are staggering. A report from the U.S. Department of Labor, Employment Standards Administration

Women's Bureau, "The Myth and the Reality," indicates that women constitute 5 percent of top management, an increase from less than 1 percent in 1950. Women held 26 percent of managerial and administrative positions in 1980; almost 3 million out of a total of 10.25 million managers were women. However, women still represent 80 percent of all clerical workers.

Women are making gains but they face cultural, statistical, and even psychological obstacles as almost half of the work force competes for half of the management opportunities.

Barriers to Progress

One of the obstacles women face is the *lack of role models* for women in business. Until recently, jobs were mentally classified as men's work or women's work. Teachers and nurses were women, so children associated these jobs with women. Doctors and lawyers were men, so boys selected these professions for their careers. Now parents, counselors, teachers, and even the media are trying to remove sexual stereotypes from jobs. Children are encouraged to pursue jobs according to aptitude or earning power rather than gender.

The lack of role models directly impacts on another obstacle, the *absence of a track record* for people to measure in corporate circles. People tend to hire people most like themselves because they believe they can trust the performance record of these people to meet certain standards. Since women were excluded from hiring and promotional responsibilities, they had no opportunity to extend opportunities to other women. In addition, the fears and doubts of *sexually biased people* worked to keep women out of management.

Psychological barriers include *feelings of isolation* and *lack of peer support structure* that would encourage success among women. Men have had support networks such as clubs, alumni of fraternal or collegiate groups; however, women have had to form networks outside traditional areas. Women who have achieved their goals are just learning the skill of helping other women get ahead.

The final factor women must overcome is the *statistical time lag between entry-level jobs and management.* Traditionally, it takes about 20 years for a manager to rise to the top. Because women were less well represented in business classes 20 years ago, they are in a minority among the group of candidates able to compete for these jobs today. With more and more companies finding it economical to merge and acquire rather than create new companies, the number of company executive officers (CEOs) will also dwindle, making fewer positions available to either men or women.

MANAGEMENT BY GENDER

As women make significant gains in career fields previously dominated by men, certain behavior patterns become apparent. Some studies attribute the behavior to the way each group was programmed to react by parents, teachers, and society. Whatever the reason, men and women bring different beliefs, values, and assumptions to a job.

In the *Managerial Woman*, Hennig and Jardin (1979) explore the ways in which these beliefs impact on women's careers in management. For example, when asked to define a job, most men related their current position to a larger picture of career advancement. A job was an important component of their career as a whole. Women, however, supplied different definitions for job and career. For them a job was more likely to be seen as a nine-to-five obligation enabling them to earn money to make a living. However, career was a means of achieving personal growth and self-fulfillment. Having a career meant making a contribution to others and doing what one wants to do.

Men and women also exhibited different attitudes toward risk and risk taking. Men tended to be gamblers, viewing the risk as a chance to win or lose and a chance to trade security for a greater opportunity. Women were more likely to view risk as negative, seeing instead of potential gain, only loss, danger, injury, hurt, or ruin.

By understanding these basic differences, a woman manager can prevent the possibility of misunderstandings and miscommunication between herself and men who may have different points of view as well as come to terms with her own inner conflicts that may pose obstacles to her success. For example, if a woman can learn to mesh the idea of her current job with her long-term career goals, she may be happier with her present circumstances, knowing that a career is really a series of different jobs within one company or within several different companies. If a woman knows that security is an important ideal which causes her to stay away from risks, she can practice taking small risks to build confidence before making a major job change or career decision. (See Exercise 2-1.)

Differing Paths

Just as women bring different perspectives to management positions, they also arrive at those positions from different paths. Many successful women report taking an entry-level job and working up to a more responsible job.

Charlotte began her career as a secretary for a foundation in a city with a population of about 75,000 people. She enjoyed the office but was not content to remain in a clerical job. She began learning different facets of the office work and taking management courses at a local community college in the evenings. Soon she was campaign director in charge of raising almost $1 million. That success enabled her to transfer to another city where she became director of development for a private health organization.

Men are more apt to be recruited into a management training program or placed in a job with a recognizable career path. Women have to train themselves to concentrate on doing the best possible job in their current position while looking ahead to the next position.

Ironically, the very qualities that make women outstanding in their jobs may hinder them from taking advanced management roles. Women tend to emphasize technical skills, task completion, and job performance. A major criticism of women as managers is that they are too preoccupied with details. Yet when we consider their work background in clerical or support positions, in which details for other managers are handled, we can understand why a new female manager might have trouble letting go of her detail-oriented perspective.

To succeed as a manager, women must begin to see their work commitment as part of a larger career picture rather than as an end in itself.

A MANAGER'S JOB

A manager's job goes beyond technical skills. Skills in dealing with people as human resources are vital to the new roles of managers. A manager must do the following:

1. *Relate to environment.* Whether the environment is the business itself, the community in which the business is located, or the national or international business community, the manager must be able to relate day-to-day incidents to the larger environment.

2. *Set objectives and plans.* Managers cannot afford to be satisfied with completing tasks during 8-hour days and 40-hour weeks. They must see beyond the day's work to look at the short- and long-term impact of business cycles, demographics, profits, sales, and trends. After analyzing these data, they must make plans to adapt current business needs.

3. *Solve problems.* Managers are paid to solve problems. Effective managers must handle questions from clients and subordinates to the best of their ability without constantly seeking assistance from the next higher level of management. Making decisions is a vital part of a manager's job.

4. *Control the work load.* Managers delegate tasks to accomplish objectives and meet deadlines. Deciding who will do which assignment or who is best suited to a certain aspect of the project contributes to the overall success of the venture. Distributing work evenly and fairly with an eye to developing new leadership and training new employees comprises part of any manager's agenda.

5. *Manage human relations.* People are the major resource of businesses. Group dynamics, personality clashes, competition, and cooperation all determine how effectively a group of people will work together to accomplish a given purpose. The manager must deal with problems and build on strengths in order to make the most of human resources.

6. *Communicate.* Many workers are outstanding technicians or skilled craftsmen, but they lack a key element no manager can be without. Communication, both to subordinates and superiors, forms the bridge that links all levels of corporate structure. Communication skills also make the difference between which employee is chosen to interact with customers and which is kept behind the scenes.

7. *Lead.* People can be pushed to gain eventual results but the authoritarian personality of management is changing. Companies want individuals who will lead others to higher productivity, quality, and accomplishment.

THEORIES OF MANAGEMENT

Theory X is an autocratic and traditional set of assumptions about people. Theory X management relates directly to the push–pull analogy. As described by McGregor (1960) in *The Human Side of Enterprise*, Theory X is based on three assumptions about people:

1. People basically dislike work and want to avoid it.
2. People will not strive to achieve within an organization without threats of punishment, either overt or implied, and must be directed and controlled to achieve management's ends.
3. Most people crave security over ambition and want to avoid responsibility.

Theory X as a way to manage people can be seen as the prevailing theory used in the past. An educated class of people controlled the actions of all those people below who had little opportunity to rise out of the governed class. Negative rewards in the form of coercion, punishment, or threats are used to motivate people externally.

Theory Y management is a human and supportive set of assumptions about people. From the bleak viewpoint of Theory X, McGregor moves on to describe Theory Y managers. These managers may more nearly seem to fit the ideal of the contemporary manager. Theory Y makes six basic assumptions about people:

1. People are motivated from within as well as from without. Internal motivators include self-direction, self-control, and commitment.
2. People naturally use physical and mental energy in work as well as at play and at rest.
3. Workers can learn to accept and even seek responsibility under certain conditions.
4. The ability to function creatively using mental skills is not limited to a small segment of the population.
5. People enjoy achievement. Achievement motivates people toward constantly higher goals.
6. Most people do not use their full intellectual potential; they have a capacity for learning and achievement beyond their current level.

Theory X managers push stubborn employees to do work largely against their natural will. Theory Y managers, on the other hand, work to make conditions conducive to tapping the unused human resources in a corporation. If Theory X managers are autocratic rulers who exert control by threats of punishment, then Theory Y managers are supportive coaches striving to help employees achieve their potential.

Although the two theories seem worlds apart, most managers have adopted a blend of these two basic styles in reacting to management situations.   A third theory, Theory Z, addresses these conflicting philosophies.

Theory Z is a model that adapts elements of Japanese management systems to the culture of the United States and emphasizes cooperation and consensus decision processes.

Theory Z assumes that some employees have been trained under the Theory X scenario. They know exactly how much work they have to do to continue to earn their paychecks and stubbornly refuse change or additional responsibilities. They see no additional rewards for extra effort and are content with the status quo. On the other hand, some employees want to achieve more. They feel motivated from within whether negative external controls exist or not. They want the additional interpersonal interaction between management and employees that Theory Y provides.

Theory Z is a hybrid that combines the strengths of Theories X and Y to meet the needs of a particular situation. Using Theory Z enables a manager to study the background of particular employees or the history of different departments to analyze previous successes.   If the employee or department seems to require a more authoritative approach, the manager can modify Theory Y to include some components of Theory X. In *Theory Z*, Ouchi (1981) suggests that involved workers are the key to increased productivity.

Theory Z merges both a democratic style and a participatory style of management. Questions of productivity are solved by coordinating individual efforts in a productive manner and giving employees the incentives to do so with a cooperative long-range view. For example, to involve a group of employees in Theory Z, a supervisor might say, "I believe that I understand your point of view" or "I believe you understand my point of view" rather than making autocratic pronouncements or handing down demands.

Sometimes different theories will apply in one department, particularly when managers supervise employees from different age groups or educational levels. Older workers who have grown accustomed to being told what to do may require a Theory X manager. Younger workers who want to test their ideas or want to have input into the organization may perform better in an atmosphere that allows a degree of experimentation along looser guidelines.

Systems Theory

The *Systems Theory* also takes into account the different situations that managers face and their effect on the organization.

This theory states that all parts of a system are interrelated and a change in one part affects all other parts.

This is useful in analyzing the potential effects of a decision. Since an event that appears to affect one individual or one department may have significant influences elsewhere in the organization, managers must look beyond the immediate situation in order to determine the effects on the larger system. Top managers must see the big picture, conceptualizing and analyzing their decisions to see how each piece "fits" with the others. Managers should avoid *tunnel vision*, the tendency to view a situation or idea in shortsighted, self-centered, immediate terms. When a decision is made, the systems theory can help a manager decide who will be affected and what the effect will be.

SKILLS OF MANAGEMENT

Management skills can be organized into three levels: *technical, human,* and *conceptual* (Table 2-3).

Technical Skills

Technical skill implies the understanding of and the ability to perform a specific kind of activity or task. Specialized knowledge, such as computer literacy, or the ability to use special resources and tools, such as a drafting machine, could fall into this category. Technical skills are most important to entry-level management.

Table 2-3 Comparison of Three Skill Levels of Management

TECHNICAL	HUMAN	CONCEPTUAL
Ability to perform specific tasks	Team–group	Analyze
Special skills and tools	Social skills	Conceptualize
Know jargon	Build cooperation	Play forecast
Entry-level management	Motivate, guide, and counsel feelings	Long term
	Resolve conflicts	See organization as a whole
	Communicate	Systems theory
	Middle-level management	Interpret ideas and concepts
		Top-level management

Human Skills

Human skills comprise the largest part of a manager's job. Technical skill may enable a manager to move up from an entry-level job, but human skills will determine the success as a manager who is directing others to use their skills. Human skill is an individual's ability to work effectively as a group member, to build a cooperative effort within the unit, and to motivate, guide, and counsel. Components of human skill include an awareness of one's own beliefs and attitudes as well as an awareness of other people and their backgrounds.

Being aware of these feelings is not enough. The manager must extend the awareness to an analysis of how these feelings work in a group and then must work to resolve conflict or mesh perceptions so that the ultimate goal is met. Communication skills in bringing parts of a group together or bridging conflicting ideas are examples of human skills. Human skills are most important to the middle-level manager.

Conceptual Skills

Although human skills take up most of a manager's time, *conceptual* or *idea skills* may have the most impact. Conceptual skill is the ability to see the organization as a whole. It allows the manager to see how parts of the organization are interdependent on each other and how changes in one area will affect another. Conceptual skills reach beyond the internal organization to see how changes affect the social, political, and economic forces in the larger community of the outside world. Conceptual skills are most important to top-level managers and include the ability to coordinate and interpret ideas, concepts, and practices and to analyze, forecast, and plan.

LEVELS OF MANAGEMENT

Although we tend to categorize all jobs as either entry or CEO level, business actually provides a continuum for positions up and down the corporate hierarchy. Within any company, three levels of management exist: entry, middle, and top (Table 2-4).

The three levels of management indicate the different roles a manager fills at different stages of a career. Entry-, middle-, and top-level management share a blend of skills but in strongly varying proportions.

Table 2-4   Three Levels of Management

TOP

Makes policy, creates and develops plans, evaluates progress, conceptualizes ideas, analyzes data, makes decision, solves problems, outlines long-term plans, sees organization a whole. Spends 90% of time delegating and 10% doing.

MIDDLE

Translates policies, reviews employees, checks progress, resolves conflicts, trains subordinates, interacts with levels above and below, assigns duties, balances overall picture with day-to-day technical demands. Spends 50% of time delegating and 50% doing.

ENTRY

Carries out policies, applies technical skills, organizes tasks, enforces rules, develops group cohesiveness, solves daily problems, motivates workers, discharges individual responsibilities. Spends 30% of time delegating and 70% doing.

Entry-Level Management

An entry-level job and an entry-level management job are not the same. To be a manager, you must have the responsibilities that come with management. Generally this will mean supervising the work of at least one or more persons and having authority over a certain range of decisions. An entry-level job may evolve into an entry-level management job, but most employees start by working for someone before they have someone who reports to them.

Jane took a job at a marketing department for the city's largest bank. Her primary job was to produce a bimonthly newsletter that was sent to bank shareholders and a monthly newsletter that was sent to bank employees. Shareholders responded positively to the newsletter, which soon grew to a full-fledged magazine format. When the magazine expanded to a monthly publishing schedule, Jane was allowed to hire an assistant. This is an example of an entry-level job evolving into an entry-level management job.

Entry-level managers carry out policies, implement projects, organize and direct tasks, train employees, and enforce rules. They are the leaders who have the most direct contact with non-managerial employees. They require a greater proportion of technical skills than mid- or upper-level managers, but about the same proportion of human skills as their mid-management counterparts. Their conceptual skills do not come into play unless they reach the next levels of management.

For these managers, 74 percent of the day is spent communicating, 8 percent on the telephone, 17 percent writing, and 9 percent reading. Their world is full of interruptions and day-to-day problems that require immediate attention. Their style of leadership must reflect this close contact with subordinates to be effective.

Most companies have a chart that shows corporate organization. By following the lines of command, an employee can see how any job fits in the corporate hierarchy. A company can further delineate lines of command by assigning specific titles to jobs. An assistant sales director or an assistant cashier obviously reports to the sales director or the cashier. Depending on the number of people in certain departments, these jobs may or may not carry management responsibilities. Most likely, these jobs will be assigned certain characteristics associated with mid-management.

Middle-Level Management

Mid-managers, at the middle level of administration, coordinate the work of subordinates and report to managers. These mid-managers comprise the bulk of the jobs considered within the general title of managers. Generally mid-managers supervise at least two or three people directly and may supervise others indirectly. Yet they are mid-managers because one or more corporate levels separate them from top management. They have authority over more decisions, but they do not enjoy the final say in certain financial or personnel matters. Most of these mid-managers aspire to upper management. However, with dwindling numbers of mid-management jobs, this may be as high as some people will progress in certain companies. Faced with that reality, mid-managers with higher aspirations will often start their own businesses.

Mid-managers bring their technical skills to the next higher level of management. They translate policies into objectives, review and evaluate employees, and serve as a buffer zone between top management and entry-level positions. They use their technical skills less often, but need more human skills in reserve as they fill their role. Their need for conceptual skills grows as they translate the policies of top management into projects for subordinates.

They spend 81 percent of the day communicating as compared to entry-level managers (74 percent), yet they are still on the telephone 8 percent of the time. They spend 14 percent of their time writing and 10 percent reading. They face a demanding style of leadership that must relate not only to peers but also to people above and below their management levels on the corporate chart.

Top-Level Management

Upper managers, at the top level of the administrative hierarchy, coordinate the work of managers but do not report to managers. They include CEOs as well as general managers, executive directors, and a host of other titles. Generally a person in upper management is accountable only to the stockholders or the business owner. The company annual report indicates how well management has performed. With the sweeping authority to make a full range of decisions comes the responsibility for fiscally sound policies and the necessity of turning a profit on sales and investments for the company.

Top managers form the smallest percentage of managers. They make policy, develop and implement business plans, conceptualize data, outline the future for the company, and organize the entire concept. As they have climbed up the corporate ladder, their need for technical skills has been reduced, as they are in a position to be paid more for their conceptual skills. Even their need for human skills diminishes as they concentrate on the ability to see the organization as a whole and plan for the future of the company.

They spend 87 percent of their time communicating with managers in the company and people in the outside business community. They are more likely to have frequent demands on their time outside the office. They spend 8 percent of their time on the telephone, 13 percent of their time writing, and 12 percent reading as they carry out their duties.

Skills Required of Effective Managers

ENTRY LEVEL

- ❑ Carries out policies and implements projects
- ❑ Organizes tasks
- ❑ Directs, motivates, and trains
- ❑ Enforces rules
- ❑ Develops group cohesiveness
- ❑ Is busy, encountering frequent interruptions
- ❑ Deals with hour-to-hour and day-to-day problems
- ❑ Has direct contact with nonmanagerial employees and close contact with subordinates
- ❑ Spends 74 percent of the workday communicating, 8 percent on the telephone, 17 percent writing, and 9 percent reading
- ❑ Possesses technical skills
- ❑ Has an understanding of and an ability to perform a specific kind of task or activity

MIDDLE LEVEL

- ❑ Translates policies
- ❑ Possesses fewer technical and more human skills
- ❑ Acts as a buffer
- ❑ Reviews, checks, and selects
- ❑ Translates top managerial decisions into projects
- ❑ Spends much time alone

- ❑ Spends 81 percent of the workday communicating, 8 percent on the telephone, 14 percent writing, and 10 percent reading
- ❑ Communicates with peers as well as with those above and below
- ❑ Translates policies and projects
- ❑ Has the ability to work effectively as a group member and to build a cooperative effort
- ❑ Accepts different viewpoints
- ❑ Resolves conflicts
- ❑ Is aware of beliefs and attitudes, and is aware of other people
- ❑ Uses human skills

TOP LEVEL

- ❑ Makes policy
- ❑ Creates, evaluates, develops, conceptualizes, and analyzes
- ❑ Makes decisions and solves problems
- ❑ Is involved with futuristic, long-term plans based on the systems theory and the "big picture"
- ❑ Possesses conceptual and human skills
- ❑ Spends much time away from the office with peers and outsiders
- ❑ Spends 87 percent of the workday communicating, 8 percent on the telephone, 13 percent writing, and 12 percent reading
- ❑ Creates and develops projects
- ❑ Has the ability to see the organization as a whole
- ❑ Sees how changes and functions of one part of the organization affect all the other parts
- ❑ Primarily uses conceptual skills

"MANAGERS MUST MANAGE"

In *Managing*, Geneen, with Moscow (1986), writes that "Management must have a purpose, a dedication, and that dedication must be an emotional commitment. It must be built in as a vital part of the personality of anyone who is truly a manager. He or she is the one who understands that 'management must manage.'. . . manage means to accomplish something that you or your management team sets out to do." Using the analogy of reading a book, Geneen says that running a business is the opposite of reading a book. In reading a book, you start from the beginning and read to the end. In business you start at the end and do everything you can to reach that end.

Geneen lists these hard-learned lessons about management:

❑ You must play by the rules but you do not have to think by the rules. In other words, you may not be able to avoid channels of communication or shortcuts, but you do not have to limit your thinking to the way it has always been done before.

❑ Avoid all pretensions. Doing anything for show allows room for the worst disease of business executives: egotism.

❑ Facts from paper are not the same as facts from people. The reliability of facts may be determined from the source.

ENTREPRENEURSHIP

CEOs and company presidents represent one form of upper management. Few employees will ever become a CEO of a Fortune 500 company. Because of the competition for a few top management slots, more and more women are taking a direct approach to gaining top-management jobs as entrepreneurs. A full 25 percent of all small businesses are owned by women. In 1986, nearly one-third of the delegates at a White House Conference on Small Business were women. In a cover story on the conference in October 1986, *Nation's Business* predicted that by the year 2000 women will own half the nation's small businesses if current trends hold.

With more than three million female entrepreneurs and more than two million home-based businesses, the projections do not include businesses with female partners or co-owners. One theory as to why women have left traditional corporate structures in such numbers is that women who have climbed the corporate ladder for a decade now elect to climb their own ladder instead. Entrepreneurs can tie their rewards directly to their own efforts rather than seeing others reap profits from their ideas and concepts. When advancement opportunities seem too slow, they become the risk takers, moving their orientation toward success to the self-confident world of owning their own businesses.

The typical female business owner is motivated by the need for achievement. She is self-confident and has a high energy level. Many times she has traded a dependable salary and solid corporate benefits for greater job satisfaction in providing a new product or service. Statistical profiles of women business owners show they are likely to be the first-born child of middle-class parents in a home where the father was self-employed and the mother was a full-time homemaker. The average women business owner has a bachelor's degree in liberal arts, is married, and has children. Her work experience includes administrative, teaching, or secretarial experience, and she started her first business venture between the ages of 35 and 45.

Women business owners face unique challenges in starting their own businesses. They may find it difficult to raise capital or arrange financing. Although the Equal Credit Opportunity Act prohibits discrimination in the granting of credit based on the sex of the applicant, these protections are generally thought to extend only to personal credit. A woman whose background has been primarily in the liberal arts may not have the financial background to convince a loan officer to finance start-up costs. If the loan is granted, the female business owner may receive less favorable repayment terms than her male counterpart.

Because the growth of female-owned businesses is a recent trend, these businesses lack a long-term track record of performance, which banks often research to determine a business owner's ability to repay a loan. For this reason, many women business owners often borrow from their personal savings or from friends and relatives.

The small business owner also faces more subtle sex discrimination because although she may be the boss, she may have less experience in dealing with subordinates or business associates outside the firm. Many women business owners report incidents of business callers who demand to speak to "the man in charge." Male-dominated business groups such as Chambers of Commerce or executive clubs may not be willing to include women business owners on an equal basis. In addition to supervising employees and delivering a service or product, she must also be able to gain the respect of her suppliers, manage a payroll, maintain a positive cash flow, and plan for the future growth of the company.

For women considering starting their own business, a good exercise is to interview a woman who currently owns her own business (see Exercise 2-2). For this exercise, contact the Small Business Administration (SBA) office nearest your city or check the files of the local newspaper for stories about women who have been successful in their own businesses.

Traits of Successful Enterprises

The Small Business Administration estimates that over 25 percent of all small businesses fail within the first 5 years of operation. Although this may signify the risk new business owners face, it also means that 75 percent of new businesses are still operating after the first crucial years.

Success in a small business stems from planning: planning the concept, planning the financing, planning the short- and long-term goals, and planning a commitment.

KEY QUESTIONS FOR SOMEONE THINKING OF
STARTING HER OWN BUSINESS

- ❏ Am I willing to trade security for the risk of starting a new venture?
- ❏ What is the current competition for my idea or service?
- ❏ How are those businesses succeeding or meeting the current market needs?
- ❏ Can I commit to investing profits back into the business until the business reaches a break-even point?
- ❏ What are my goals?
- ❏ Do I want to provide a specialized service and keep my business small or do I want to start a new company from scratch that will eventually grow to many offices or retail outlets?

With answers to these questions in mind, an entrepreneur must begin research into all areas of the business idea. The current business climate may be an indicator on the timing of starting a new business. The SBA is a valuable source of information on business trends geared to fledgling businesses. The SBA can help suggest ways to finance a new venture, either through loans from friends and relatives or from traditional financial institutions. Using their resources, you can develop a business plan with projections as to where you want your business to be after certain intervals.

A business plan is vital as you try to market yourself and your new business to the public. The business plan should incorporate personal, financial, and company goals, providing a road map of where you want to be in 3 to 5 years.

PRIMARY MANAGEMENT FUNCTIONS

The *primary functions of management* can be summed up with the letters POSDC for plan, organize, staff, direct, and control (Table 2-5).

Plan. A plan allows the manager to define objectives and to determine the appropriate means of achieving the objectives. It indicates what, when, and how things will be done in view of the organization's capabilities and the surrounding business environment. Planning sets the stage for all other management functions.

Specific planning activities might include forecasting or estimating the future, writing objectives to measure accomplishments, developing policies for efficiency and interpreting rules on new decisions, allocating resources through budgets, and creating standardized methods of performing specific tasks.

Organize. Organization results in the design of a formal structure of tasks and authority. Using a combination of flexible and authoritarian approaches, managers organize workers by making schedules, delegating tasks, and structuring the office so that work will be accomplished under the original plan.

Organizational activities include identifying the work to be done related to the available staff, delegating authority to staff members once work proceeds, developing relationships among peers, subordinates, and superiors so that cooperative efforts are possible, and monitoring progress through timetables or measurable objectives as work continues.

Staff. The staff, which includes advising and supporting personnel, contributes indirectly to the organization's output. Filling jobs with qualified people, and hiring, firing, and promoting are all functions of staffing.

Activities related to staffing include training new and current employees for the required performance, evaluating individual and group performance, administering a plan of rewards, including salaries and bonuses for workers, applying a system of negative rewards when appropriate, such as reprimands or disciplinary action, and developing potential leadership among employees.

Direct. Directing takes organizing one step further by developing rules and specifications for effective operations. This

Table 2-5 Five Primary Management Functions: POSDC

1.	*Plan*:	Set goals, forecast, develop, allocate
2.	*Organize*:	Structure tasks, make schedules, delegate
3.	*Staff*:	Hire, fire, promote people, train, evaluate
4.	*Direct*:	Motivate, inspire, communicate, develop rules
5.	*Control*	Measure performance, gain feedback, assure actual operations

might include adjustments in staffing or asking groups for regular reports on the progress of the plan.

Activities under direction involve making decisions by accumulating data with which to make judgments, motivating and inspiring employees to complete the required action, and establishing communication among employees and departments for better understanding.

Control. With control, managers establish ways to measure performance and to gain feedback on their plan's progress, thereby ensuring that actual operations go according to plan.

Control begins with establishing standards of quality that are the criteria against which future work will be measured. Other activities include measuring work in progress and completed projects for effectiveness, evaluating the end results against overall goals or ideals, correcting problems that impede effectiveness, and obtaining feedback for current and future projects.

Each of these five functions is interrelated with the others. It would be unrealistic to characterize one managerial function alone. For example, the staffing activity of training new employees overlaps with the directing function that motivates employees to improve their work or productivity. Anytime a manager deals with subordinates, the control function will be active along with staffing functions.

Management can be seen as a synthesis, in which the starting product includes a set of management, labor, materials, and capital. These resources are processed by planning, organizing, staffing, directing, and controlling. The end product is the achievement of objectives, which is the true test of a manager's performance. (See Exercise 2-3.)

SUMMARY

Assumptions about management are changing. Moving to a participatory style of management instead of the authoritarian style and adapting to rapidly changing technology are all ways in which management is adapting to these trends. Women are an important part of the demographic profile of workers as they continue to comprise a growing segment of working adults and business owners. Management theories have changed, too, moving from Theory X, which assumes workers need strict control to be productive, to Theory Y, which states that people are motivated internally to do a good job. More and more managers are using Theory Z, which uses a combination of styles for different situations.

Management uses three types of skills, human, technical, and conceptual, to deal with people, tasks and ideas. All levels of management (entry, middle, and top) use these skills, although to varying degrees, as a manager moves up the corporate ladder. Finally, the functions of management may be summarized into the POSDC model: plan, organize, staff, direct, and control.

TERMS AND CONCEPTS

conceptual skills	plan
control	staff
direct	systems theory
entrepreneur	technical skills
human skills	Theory X
management	Theory Y
managers	Theory Z
middle management	top management
organize	tunnel vision

REVIEW QUESTIONS

1. What population trends will affect managers of the future?
2. What are role models and how do they relate to people aspiring to higher management jobs?
3. What fundamental assumptions about people set Theory X apart from Theory Y?
4. Of the three general skills used by managers, which is more important to a CEO's daily challenges?
5. Where does an entry-level manager spend the majority of time, according to percentage?
6. What motivates people to start their own businesses?
7. Describe activities involved in planning as a management function.
8. According to Geneen, how does running a business contrast with reading a book?

EXERCISES

2-1: INTERVIEW A TOP-LEVEL FEMALE MANAGER

Schedule an appointment to interview a top-level female manager of your choice. The purpose of this interview is to get her thoughts and advice on women in business and to allow you an opportunity to network. Design your questions.

Background Data

Name_____

Employer_____ Present title _____

Years with present organization_____ Years in management _____

Education_____ Number of subordinates _____

Phone number (office) _____

---

1. How did you get into management? How long were you employed by your organization before you were promoted?

2. What is the most difficult part of being a manager?

3. What is the most rewarding part of being a manager?

4. Of the basic management functions—planning, organizing, staffing, directing, and controlling (POSDC)—which do you feel is the most important in your present position? Why?

5. Did you have a mentor? Are you a mentor?

6. How did you gain recognition/visibility?

7. Did you set goals or have a plan?

8. Do you currently set goals?

9. What position will you seek next?

10. What professional clubs/organizations do you recommend or belong to?

11. How do you cope with stress?

12. What advice can you give me?

13. Obstacles?

14. Do you feel being a woman in management has any special challenges, obstacles, problems? Can you share some you have faced and discuss how you overcame them?

15. How many top-level women does your company have?

16. What is the attitude of women in top-level positions in your company?

17. How many hours do you work a week now?

18. What success strategies for top-level management positions can you suggest?

19. Do you have an updated resumé that you can share?

20. What skills, specific abilities, or factors do you feel are the most important in determining success on the job and in receiving promotions?

2-2: INTERVIEWING THE SMALL BUSINESS OWNER/MANAGER

A. General Questions Concerning the Business—Its History, Growth, Problems

1. When was the business started?

2. Are you incorporated? Partnership? Other?

3. How long have you owned the firm?

4. How did you happen to get into this business?

5. Did you have experience in it?

6. Were you trained for it? In school?

7. Did you have any difficulties in getting financial backing?

8. Did you have difficulties in getting a building in the desired location?

9. Did you have any difficulties in getting equipment or fixtures?

10. Did you have any difficulties in getting materials or merchandise?

11. What would you say were your biggest problems during the first year? Or even the first months?

12. How did you solve each of your problems?

13. Who has been of particular help? Bank? Suppliers? SBA? Others?

14. What do you consider to be your greatest strength as a business?

15. How do your policies differ from those of other businesses of this type?

16. Who are your major competitors?

B. The Typical Customer

1. Do you appeal to any particular type of customer in terms of age, income, etc.?

2. What area do you try to serve?

C. Sales and Advertising

1. What media do you use if you advertise?

2. What advantages do the ones you use have?

3. How often or how much do you advertise?

D. Records and Controls

1. Does your business call for a complete accounting system?

2. Do you do this yourself, or have an outsider do it?

E. Plans for Expansion

1. Are you content with the size of your firm as it is?

2. Would you care to tell me (us) of your hopes or plans for the future?

F. General Advice to Prospective Small Business Owners

1. What advice would you give to someone who wants to start out as you did?

2. Have you any particular business philosophy or rules that you have come to depend on?

2-3: WHAT EFFECTIVE MANAGERS DO

To become a more effective, efficient, and productive manager, answer and achieve solutions to the following questions.

1. List three primary goals of the organization

    a.

    b.

    c.

    Department

    a.

    b.

    c.

    Boss

    a.

    b.

    c.

    Your professional long-term goals

    a.

    b.

    c.

    Your professional immediate (4-6 month) goals

    a.

    b.

    c.

2. What two decisions must be reached within 2 weeks? Weigh cost benefits of each.

    a.

    b.

3. What two problems must be solved within 2 weeks? Weigh cost benefits of each.

    a.

    b.

4. What costs can be cut?

Area	Amount or %	Target date
a.		
b.		
c.		

5. What waste can be reduced or eliminated?

Area	Amount or %	Target date
a.		
b.		
c.		

6. Rank/prioritize your

   a. To-do list

   b. Objectives

   c. Goals

   Concentrate on the "bottom line."

7. What needs must be met within the next 2 months?

   a. Client's/customer's needs

   b. Boss's needs

   c. Your professional needs

8. How can you improve your communication?

   a. To your boss

   b. To your peers

   c. To your subordinates

9. How can you improve provision of information to subordinates or your boss?

10. What are two procedures, methods, or policies that you can simplify within the next 2 months? Explain.

11. List changes/trends that you can predict that will affect your profession, organization, and job between now and 1990.

SUGGESTED READINGS

Asman, D., and Meyerson, A. "The Best of the Manager's Journal." *The Wall Street Journal on Management.* Dow Jones & Co., New York, 1985.

Augustine, N. R. "The Complexities and Conundrums of Today's Business Management." *Augustine's Laws.* Viking Penguin, New York, 1983.

Blotnick, S. *Ambitious Men.* Viking Press, New York, 1987.

Culligan, M. J., Deakins, C. S., and Young, A. H. *Back to Basics Management.* Facts on File, New York, 1983.

Fritz, R. *Rate Yourself as a Manager.* Prentice-Hall, Inc., Englewood Cliffs, NJ, 1985.

Geneen, H., with Moscow, A. *Managing.* Doubleday, New York, 1986.

Grove, A. S. *High Output Management.* Random House, New York, 1983.

Harrison, P. *America's New Women Entrepreneurs.* Acropolis, Washington, DC, 1986.

Heller, R. *The Super Managers.* E. P. Dutton, New York, 1984.

Hennig, M., and Jardin, A. *Managerial Woman.* Pocket Books, New York, 1979.

Heyel, C. *The Encyclopedia of Management* (3rd ed.). Van Nostrand Reinhold Company, New York, 1982.

Kelly, F. J., and Kelly, H. M. *What They Really Teach You at the Harvard Business School.* Warner Books, New York, 1986.

LeBoeuf, M. *GMP—Greatest Management Principle in the World.* Berkley Books, New York, 1985.

McGregor, D. *The Human Side of Enterprise.* McGraw-Hill, New York, 1960.

Naisbitt, J. *Megatrends.* Warner Books, New York, 1982.

Naisbitt, J., and Aburdene, P. *Re-inventing the Corporation.* Warner Books, New York, 1985.

Ouchi, W. G. *Theory Z.* Avon Books, New York, 1981.

Pascale, R. T., and Athos, A. *The Art of Japanese Management.* Warner Books, New York, 1981.

Posner, M. J. *Executive Essentials.* Avon Books, New York, 1982.

Quick, T. L. *The Manager's Motivation Desk Book.* John Wiley & Sons, New York, 1985.

Scollard, J. R. *No-Nonsense Management Tips for Women.* Simon & Schuster, New York, 1983.

Sloma, R. S. *The Turnaround Manager's Handbook.* The Free Press, New York, 1985.

Uris, A. *101 of the Greatest Ideas in Management.* John Wiley & Sons, New York, 1986.

Yeomans, W. N. *1000 Things You Never Learned in Business School.* McGraw-Hill, New York, 1985.

3

MANAGEMENT STYLE AND LEADERSHIP

OBJECTIVES

- Define management-related terms
- Explain concepts, techniques, and guidelines of good management
- Identify qualities of effective managers
- Identify traits that lead to success
- Understand reasons for failure among executives
- Provide "how-to" guidelines for managers
- Identify three major areas of management
- Enhance your ability to manage yourself
- Provide techniques to motivate people
- Address problems of inept managers
- Differentiate between management and leadership
- Identify two main approaches of leadership
- Define situational leadership style
- List benefits of quality control circles
- List abilities of successful managers

The functions of management may be universal, but the styles of individual managers are as different as the personalities of the managers themselves. Most activities of management fall into one of five functions: *plan, organize, staff, direct,* and *control.* The way in which a manager approaches these five basic functions provides indications of that manager's style and leadership qualities.

Managers bring different backgrounds to each of these five functions. Education, both formal and informal, may vary along with experience, abilities, personality, and motivation. Intangible qualities such as selecting the best organization to work for and surrounding yourself with people who can help you move ahead also contribute to a manager's success. No single factor predicts success in management. In looking at top executives who run large corporations, Sorcher (1982) writes, "We are forced to conclude that perhaps one-third of them would not be selected again."

Management is a living science that must be seen as a lifelong learning process rather than a static creation that has a point of final resolution. Throughout a manager's career, different needs and situations will demand a variety of styles for effective leadership and decision making, all under the general title of managing.

MANAGERIAL QUALITIES

To be a successful manager, you must possess certain attitudes, motivations, and abilities. Quite likely, these are the qualities that initially identified you as a candidate for a management job. Once you have the job, the following nine qualities help you strengthen your positions, refine your skills, and eventually take the next career step. Effective managers are

Decisive. Strong managers have definite goals and plans for achieving them. By contrast, the ineffective manager may hedge opinions until the opinion of the group has been expressed. Effective managers may wait for the facts, but they know that they must make a decision and proceed if work is to be accomplished.

Perceptive. These people can see the entire company and its mission instead of just viewing their own tasks and responsibilities. Weak managers concentrate on their departmental objectives and jobs to the exclusion of everything else.

Self-actualized. According to Maslow's hierarchy, human beings have needs beyond basic food, shelter, and clothing. These higher needs lead to self-actualization and include the desire to learn, try new experiences, evaluate values, assimilate culture, and choose new directions in personal or professional life.

Self-confident. Whether the job calls for human, technical, or conceptual skills, an effective manager has the self-confidence to move ahead. At times a manager has to make a hurried decision or resolve a crisis without benefit of input from top management. Without self-confidence the manager cannot summon resources quickly, much less inspire subordinates to follow through on the plan of action.

Inquisitive. Effective managers are life-long learners. They want to read the latest technical literature and stay current on business trends. They seek training opportunities when possible and may take business courses on their own to update or refine their skills. Regardless of the level of schooling managers complete, they realize the need to continue the learning process.

Ambitious. Few people move ahead in corporate circles without the desire to achieve. Reluctance to advance to the next level stonewalls a managerial career. A willingness to accept additional responsibility and to be accountable for decisions will help demonstrate the desire for upward mobility.

Sensible. Common sense is a valued commodity in any business endeavor. The ability to analyze a situation objectively or examine a problem with well-thought-out logic can be valuable when a company begins a new project or wants to introduce a new item.

Personable. Managers do not have to be universally loved or even liked. Indeed, some decisions will undoubtedly be unpopular with employees or superiors. However, an effective manager must be a solid judge of people and be able to build teams, resolve conflicts, and channel talents in such a way as to get the job done.

Mature. Emotionally stable people will function more effectively under the stresses of management. An open mind, self-reliant character, and positive outlook help a manager stay balanced when employees are moody, selfish, or unrealistic in their demands.

Managerial Traits

Managers and entrepreneurs share many of the same traits that lead to success. Lecker (1986) defines the *success factor* as the collection of traits enabling you to use your intelligence and personality. How you feel about being successful as well as how others react to you are both involved.

Lecker identifies the following eight traits for success:

Rigidity. Rigidity includes many strengths managers need. A rigid personality can ignore the possibility of failure under stress and therefore can succeed more often. With no tolerance for distractions, a rigid person is more likely to persevere toward the final goal. Being deliberate can be an asset in business situations in which you need to analyze a number of facts before making important decisions.

Organization. Organization includes the ability to control yourself and your environment to the greatest possible extent. Time management, internal accountability, and a tendency to act rather than react all reflect strong organizational skills. Successful managers are willing to hold themselves responsible for failures as well as successes without blaming others. They consider themselves responsible for attaining the success they seek and look inside themselves for ways to achieve it.

Self-esteem. Self-esteem goes beyond pride, which sometimes carries a negative or egotistical connotation. Self-esteem is the value we place on ourselves rooted deep within our personality. Parents and teachers who practice a system of rewarding positive behavior rather than always punishing antisocial behavior contribute to high self-esteem in adults. Self-esteem gives a manager the courage to go on in turbulent times. A person with high self-esteem expects to win and is highly resilient to the ups and downs of the business cycles.

Tough mindedness. Tough mindedness should not be confused with stubbornness. A tough-minded person can conceptualize a problem in a novel way and persist until the problem is solved. Instead of relying on the fight-or-flight mechanism that naturally occurs under stress, a person who has developed a tough mind can get the job done without an unnecessary show of strength.

Introversion/extroversion. Successful managers need a balance of introversion and extroversion. Introverts generally excel in individual pursuits while extroverts excel in group endeavors. The solo player can be more dominant and exhibit less need to be popular when it comes time to make hard decisions. On the other hand, the team player can tune into other people's needs and feelings when making a decision. Either style can succeed, but successful managers know which of the two complements their personality and try to adapt to that style.

Health. There is no substitute for good health. Staying in shape helps you handle stress, fight off illness, and keep your personality on a more even level as you meet the demands of work. Health is vital to successful managers who generally hold more stressful jobs the higher they move in the corporate structure.

Intelligence. Not every manager possesses a high IQ. However, by constantly reading, researching, and educating yourself, you can increase your potential. A solid educational background is important not so much for what is learned but for the fact that studying, taking tests and writing reports develop skills you will use throughout life.

Creativity. Managers should never be satisfied with old solutions to new problems. They must adapt case studies, financial statements, and company resources to meet changing needs. Creativity in the form of an imagination, a good memory, and the ability to verbalize new ideas can help bridge old to new ways as a manager takes command.

A Manager's Job

Within the overall function of managing, managers must take responsibilities in six areas:

- *Achieve objectives.* Managers must know where they need to be and how they intend to get there. Whether their results are measured on a profit and loss report or in terms of corporate growth, they must achieve objectives if they are truly managers.
- *Make decisions and solve problems.* Managers are paid to make decisions. Although one person can make all the business decisions necessary in a day's work, a manager is given certain parameters for decision making and the authority to make those decisions.
- *Reduce waste and cut costs.* Managers must conserve company resources. Indeed, they will be judged as stewards of the people and budgets under their control. They must concentrate on bottom-line results at all times as the primary indicator of their performance.
- *Set standards.* Managers provide an example to subordinates of how the company expects executives to act and perform. Management by example is an important function of the corporate structure.
- *Direct employees.* Without direction, work cannot proceed in an orderly way toward meeting objectives. Deciding methods

of delegating work, prioritizing tasks, and controlling schedules are all part of managing employees.

❑ *Communicate.* The manager forms a link between the entry-level employees and the upper management. In addition the manager may serve as a direct link with clients and customers outside the company. Communication—whether giving instructions or outlining plans—is a skill that determines the success of a manager.

Fatal Flaws

Just as there are techniques for effective management, there are pitfalls that can sabotage your managerial career. In a study by the Center for Creative Leadership in Greensboro, NC, published in 1983, 10 reasons for failure among executives were identified:

1. *Insensitivity to others and the loss of the ability to relate to others.* As some managers moved up the corporate chart, they forgot the human element of work. Managers need a balance between conceptual skills and human skills to survive.

2. *Arrogance and intimidation.* If others view a manager as untouchable or unreachable, communication will be stifled both with superiors and subordinates.

3. *Betrayal of trust.* For staying power, managers must be true to their word. Keeping promises and confidences increases credibility.

4. *Excessive ambition or politics.* Ambition must be a driving force behind a manager, but when it overrides technical or human skills, the manager may never move ahead.

5. *Failure to maintain performance level.* Managers can never rest on past success. They must maintain a continuum of quality as they master one job and move on to the next challenge.

6. *Overmanagement or the inability to delegate.* Every manager has to give up enjoyable tasks in order to perform managerial duties. Delegation is imperative in seeing that tasks are completed by people on appropriate levels.

7. *Poor selection of staff.* Building a team starts with an employment interview. By the time a candidate is trained and on the job, the company has a sizable investment. Hiring someone for convenience or out of desperation to meet a pressing deadline can be a costly mistake.

8. *Unclear strategy outlines.* Goals or objectives are meaningless without adequate communication to staff members. Workers cannot accomplish goals without a clear understanding of where they are, where they are going, and where they need to be.

9. *Inability to adapt to different management styles.* Just as you do not expect to be in one job forever, people on other levels of management expect to move up. Getting used to one style of management may be a hindrance; if the company undergoes a merger, takeover, or restructuring, employees need to adapt.

10. *Dependence on a mentor to the loss of self-reliance.* Mentors can help a new manager learn from shared experience. The drawback comes when a manager outgrows a mentor or the mentor refuses to let go. Avoid packaging you and your mentor as an unbreakable team since management may have plans that include only one of you.

ESTABLISHING YOUR STYLE

Becoming an executive is part of the American dream. Advertising messages, television programs, and movies all portray the executive as the standard of success. We think of an executive as someone who makes decisions, takes pride in appearance, cares about health and education, earns a top salary, and enjoys a life of high energy and ambition. Executives work not only for money but also for the challenge of trying to use their creativity, power, and identity to affect their environment.

Executives have a desire to succeed. They are aggressive, confident, articulate, persuasive, responsible, decisive, honest, dependable, disciplined, and creative. Effective executives do not have to be superhuman, they just need to have a realistic sense of their strengths and weaknesses. They can then work on improving weak points through learning and training and building on strong points as they achieve new goals.

A new manager enjoys the opportunity to develop a personal style. In the 1980s and 1990s managers can learn not only from experience but also from current literature, the experiences of others, and classroom discussions, all of which can contribute qualities that effective managers can use.

In *The Effective Woman Manager*, Stewart (1978) discusses several "how-to" guidelines for managers. First and foremost is to *know your job well.* You must understand your assigned functions and how they relate to the work of the company. As with any employee, you should have a job description and be familiar with its contents. This enables you to know what the company expects from your performance.

However, a manager must extend this knowledge. Managers must know the extent of their responsibility and authority along with their standards of performance and future expectations. Are you responsible for the performance of a certain number of employees or just those employees involved on a certain project? Can you hire and fire employees? Are you consulted before promotions or raises are given? Are company policies structured as they relate to your department or will you be asked to set standards for performance?

These questions can help you determine your unwritten job description. For example, many firms have regular evaluations for employees. Your job description might include a provision for an annual review. For managers, the review will likely cover not only the individual's performance but also the performance of the employees under the manager's supervision. A manager needs to be aware that her performance will be rated on the performance of others as well as her own.

A manager manages many things besides people. Three other major areas of management include time, risk, and bureaucracy of the business.

1. *Manage time.* In the *Effective Executive*, Drucker (1967) writes: "Effective executives do not start with their tasks. They start with their time—finding out where it actually goes. They know time is the limiting factor because it is the scarcest resource. One cannot rent, hire, or buy time, and it is totally irreplaceable."

2. *Manage risk.* In business, the best surprise is no surprise, to paraphrase a popular advertising slogan. Managers cannot control every variable within the complex role of staffing, directing, planning, controlling, and supervising. However, with practice, managers can reduce risks by looking at previous performance and learning from mistakes. Some common sense risks may be as simple as buying an extra light bulb for a slide projector so that the success of a $1000 presentation does not depend on a $2.75 bulb. Complex risks such as corporate spying, information leaks, security threats, or theft may require assistance from trained consultants to solve the problem.

3. *Manage bureaucracy.* Bureaucracy or red tape can be de-

fined as the number of steps or people you must go through in order to get something done. The larger the organization, the larger the bureaucracy. Bureaucracy has a negative connotation based on what people perceive as the inefficiency of a bulky machine. In some offices the bureaucracy dictates filling out certain forms in order to receive office supplies, completing reports in triplicate and routing them to certain company officers, or gaining authorization from a certain number of people in order to proceed with a plan of action.

These bureaucratic steps are probably necessary for central control, although they may be frustrating to people trying to get things done. As a manager, you can make the bureaucracy function smoothly for you; for example, by scheduling meetings around report deadlines and distributing copies in that way or by putting an often-used form on a computer to avoid routine typing.

As you become more adept at managing the bureaucracy, you may gain the opportunity to streamline procedures. Remember that people are resistant to change and in order to gain acceptance you will not only have to prove that your way of doing things is easier but also that it meets the same performance goals as the old method.

MANAGING YOURSELF

Managing yourself is the toughest challenge a manager faces. As a manager, you have to relate effectively to those above you and below you in the corporation. This balance requires a special blend of skills in order to be viewed as effective by both groups. Seven guidelines for managing yourself include the following

1. *Be neither dominated nor dominant.* Try to maintain a continuum of responsiveness and responsibility. This behavior encourages superiors and subordinates to view you in a positive way as an individual instead of a superhuman trying to be the ideal manager.

2. *Keep communication open to those you work for and those who work for you.* Although the groups will need to know different things, appropriate communication keeps them involved with your work. On a given project, you might tell your boss your plans and then share the same plans as priorities to employees as you delegate the work. Fostering an atmosphere of accessibility:

helps both groups know they can talk to you before a small problem becomes a larger one.

3. *Use authority commensurate with the situation.* Pulling rank or making a decision simply because you are the boss can be effective but should be reserved for situations in which other methods have failed. Otherwise employees may get the idea that you have no reason for your actions except for your stated authority. If a situation calls for an informal discussion, save more formal procedures for a more serious infraction.

4. *Simplify work whenever possible.* Productivity and quality should be high on the list of priorities for every manager. Evaluate the work of employees regularly and discuss how work can be simplified. Work simplification results in higher morale as employees find they gain more time to work on other matters once they are freed from routine jobs. Be innovative when you apply new solutions to old problems.

5. *Avoid becoming complacent.* When you have mastered one job, take on additional responsibility to stay challenged. New challenges force you to think and grow instead of remaining satisfied with the current level of performance. Even if you have given notice that you will be leaving to take on a new job, remember that others are still taking note of your performance until the minute you walk out the door.

6. *Keep your perspective when dealing with others.* Learn to take and give criticism. If you are giving criticism, try to make it constructive or at least sandwich the corrective message between points of praise for prior good performance. If you are receiving criticism, concentrate on taking the advice without taking the message personally. As a supervisor, you can make the criticism objective by setting standards of performance. Then the employee will know in advance if the standards have been met or not. If you are the employee, you can ask for standards to better gauge your performance before starting the job. Perspective also means saving emotional energy for large problems. Reacting with a temper tantrum to small annoyances of little problems is counterproductive to being a good manager.

7. *Be patient and learn how to motivate.* Whenever you are tempted to be impatient, remember your first days on a new job. Think about how you felt and what the supervisor finally said to make you do a better job. Empathizing with employees can be helpful as you seek to motivate them for the good of the company.

MOTIVATING PEOPLE

SOME TIPS ON MOTIVATING PEOPLE

- *Start with the right person for the right job.* Whenever possible, match interests and aptitudes to the task in order to have a satisfied employee.

- *Introduce new employees.* They may not remember everyone's name from the first day of work, but they will have your help in breaking the ice as they form new relationships at work.

- *Stimulate enthusiasm.* The supervisor often functions as the barometer of office attitude. If the boss is happy, workers are more likely to be happy. Enthusiasm can enhance productivity and maintain attention to quality control as employees see the end results of their work.

- *Be fair in dealing with employees.* Making exceptions can turn a manager's role into a nightmare. If one employee occasionally gets to take a different lunch hour or rearrange a vacation schedule, be sure the same privileges are offered to other employees when they have special needs.

- *Show how each person contributes to the company.* People can do a better job if they have an idea of how they fit into the overall picture. A telephone operator might seem far removed from the business of banking, yet the operator's voice is often the first contact with a potential customer for the bank. Helping employees see how they form a team builds self-esteem for their work.

- *In addition to detailing employee contributions, take opportunities to keep employees informed.* A company newsletter or meeting may help squelch rumors of takeovers, mergers, or transfers. Employees do not want to hear about a plant closing on the 6 o'clock news any more than you do. They may not need to know all the particular details of a transaction, but if they are informed they can work in an atmosphere of security about their jobs.

- *If the company has stated rules and policies, enforce them impartially.* Failure to enforce a rule once shows employees the rule is not administered to every situation and leads to abuse of the agreed-upon standards. Most company personnel directors understand the importance of documenting performance in regard to company policies. This way if you must fire an employee, you will have solid evidence to back up your decision. If, however, the rules were not enforced uniformly, you may risk accusations of having favorites or letting personal feelings impede your work.

❏ *Maintain discipline within the workplace.* Encourage people to make suggestions or streamline work within guidelines you develop. Discipline is vital as an organization or department grows larger so that every person knows the responsibilities of the job. If discipline is administered by habit you can avoid reprimanding people for coming in late, taking too much sick leave, or missing deadlines when an important project is in the works.

❏ *Be specific.* You cannot read your boss's mind or your employee's mind. They need signals from you when you have questions or comments. Tell them what you need and expect in specific terms to avoid misunderstanding or bobbled communication.

THE PROBLEM OF INEPT MANAGERS

A good manager must have training, knowledge, sensitivity, and the desire to be a manager. Sometimes an organization will promote an employee to the rank of manager and find out too late that the promotion was a mistake. Once a manager is in a position, the company may face several obstacles in trying to solve the problem. An inept manager may stay hidden behind company politics, advancing retirement age, or years of seniority.

Ways in which managers can hide their lack of managerial skills include

Seniority. Most companies prize seniority as a mark of experience. However, seniority alone may not indicate effective performance.

Blaming others. Poor performance may be blamed on weak employees or other departments when in reality the manager is at fault. If many projects seem to go wrong for one manager, this may be an indication that changes need to take place.

Shuffling papers or other busywork. Arranging tours for company personnel or always attending social functions may indicate that work is not getting attention. As more offices streamline to cut personnel costs, few can afford to pay a manager who does not get the work done.

Isolating the department. Some managers keep their employees in fear of going above their heads. Upper management may not have any idea that a manager is actually unproductive. A system of checks and balances that includes other managers can help avoid this problem without jeopardizing the jobs of subordinates with their direct supervisor.

LEADERSHIP

"Effective leaders first create visions of potential opportunities for their organizations, and then direct and empower their employees to translate that vision into reality," according to Bennis and Nanus (1985). They use the analogy of orchestra conductors who elicit the best performance from the musicians they lead. To be a leader you must

Have a voluntary following. Companies can assign titles, but they cannot create leaders. People must want to follow you before you can be considered a leader.

Accept responsibility. As a leader, you are no longer a unit of one. Your decisions must reflect the impact of the decision on the followers as well as on yourself.

Understand your weaknesses and strengths as well as those of your following. Take into account your resources and your limitations when making a decision or arriving at a solution.

Delegate successfully. No general ever won a war alone. Any well-defined plan requires the commitment of many people on a variety of levels of responsibility.

Achieve your goals and demonstrate that you can help others achieve their goals as well. People are drawn to winners who can get results.

Continue learning. Leaders never stop trying to motivate themselves and others as they learn from experience. Any new piece of information immediately becomes part of their overall viewpoint to be used in solving the next challenge.

Understand power without abusing it. Power follows leadership, but requires a balance between reluctance and zeal to maintain a perspective. Power for power's sake can become obsessive, leading to a lack of tangible results.

Encourage two-way communication. Take suggestions from subordinates. Allow people to participate in decisions that affect them when possible. Keep an open mind to new solutions. Often creative approaches thrive within a team.

Sustain leadership qualities in times of crisis. Stress is the true test of leadership. Many leaders falter when the pressure mounts. True leadership often emerges in a crisis situation.

Table 3-1 Leadership Styles

INEFFECTIVE	EFFECTIVE
Theory X	Theory Y
Task oriented	People oriented
Concern for production	Concern for employee
Autocratic	Democratic
Directive	Participative
Authoritative	Team work
Centralized	Decentralized

Leadership Styles

Two contrasting approaches of leadership are *work oriented* and *person oriented* (Table 3-1). The work-oriented style is character-ized by an authoritative approach in which a supervisor directs employees to complete designated tasks. The person-oriented approach encourages participation and consensus in making de-cisions. This style is more democratic in contrast to the dictato-rial style of the work-oriented style.

Between these two approaches is the structured approach. This style lets people know what is expected of them and relates the task to the employee. The style is oriented to the work that needs to be done but not to the restrictive level of an autocracy.

Situational Leadership

Fiedler and Chemers (1974) describe a leadership style they call *situational leadership*, in which effective leadership depends upon the situation. As the situation varies, leadership requirements also vary. Variables for leadership effectiveness include the em-ployees or the followers, the task, and the organization.

Situational leadership maintains that any style can be effec-tive in specific situations. Situational leadership as described by Hersey and Blanchard (1982) covers four distinct styles.

1. *Telling style.* This style is directive in that it defines roles, sets goals, gives instructions, and tells people how, when, and what to do. An analogy to this style might be the classroom teacher who hands out a test defining the role of student and teacher and proceeds to give instructions on completing the as-signment.

2. *Consulting style.* As its name implies, in the consulting style the leader consults, supports, directs, and gives information without direct hands-on supervision. The consulting-style leader retains final authority over decisions, but allows latitude in the way in which things are accomplished by the followers. An example might be the head of a marketing department who turns over the task of writing an annual report to employees. The department head might furnish a list of contents that must be included such as the financial statement and a letter from the CEO plus a deadline for the rough draft. The writing team enjoys creative leeway in drafting the report, but the department head retains final editorial control over it.

3. *Participating style.* The participating style reduces the directiveness of telling style even further, although it retains the support of the consulting style. However, it allows subordinates to participate in the decisions that affect them or their work. Communication and facilitation become primary tasks for leaders who use this style. The participatory style comes into play when a production manager asks employees how to improve safety conditions at a plant or when a sales manager asks the sales staff what clients are asking for in the way of new products. With this participatory input, managers can refine the information and implement workable suggestions with high expectations that the staff will follow through, since they have a part in making the decisions.

4. *Delegating style.* This style recognizes that some people require little active leadership. Highly skilled or motivated people may function more effectively when the leader steps back and lets them work on their own. This approach uses less direction and support than any of the other four styles. The success of this style depends largely on correctly analyzing the self-motivation of the followers or employees. Examples of this might occur in a data processing operation in which a manager delegates programming responsibilities to a group of programmers and asks to be updated on the group's progress at certain intervals. The programmers are then free to proceed as they choose, knowing the end result of their assignment.

QUALITY CIRCLES

The success of the participatory style of management has led to implementation of *quality circles* in many firms. Participation improves satisfaction and morale, lowers resistance, and improves interaction with formal authority. Quality circles are groups of employees who meet to solve problems with the goal of enhancing the quality and productivity of their work. The benefits of quality circles include

- ❑ Increased worker cooperation
- ❑ Increased organizational productivity and morale
- ❑ Increased product or service quality

Quality circle participation is usually voluntary and is characterized by short meetings that enjoy the approval of management without direct intervention. In the quality circle process, management must first be committed to the concept, retaining an open mind to any ideas that arise from the meetings as well as a good-faith effort toward implementation of workable ideas. Without this commitment, employees may resent time given to meetings that produce no results.

Quality circle members and leaders must be trained. The leader of a quality circle can best be described as a facilitator who draws out ideas from fellow workers. Members must be trained to concentrate on current problems in meetings rather than turning the meetings into sessions dominated by peripheral problems or personal feelings.

Once in place, the quality circle identifies problems and starts to develop solutions. Members may ask the leader for more technical information to find out what is available as a solution or for more information on why a company uses certain policies. Once the solution is developed, it is presented to upper management for review. Management has a responsibility to weigh the solution against cost and time effectiveness. Often the idea will be presented from a different perspective as employees involved in direct production or customer service give their ideas of what customers want and need.

If management decides to implement the solution, quality circle members can be involved in training other workers or explaining the reasoning behind the new concept. The quality circle team should be recognized as the source for the idea: the credit encourages future quality circle involvement and lets other workers know that the idea stemmed from fellow employees rather than from upper management.

After the plan is implemented, management and the quality circle members should evaluate the results independently. These results may help refine the original idea or if the idea is considered a success, the team is open to identify the next problem in the ongoing cycle.

Managers versus Leaders

A manager needs exceptional administrative, technical, and verbal skills. A leader needs these but must also have exceptional interpersonal, advocacy, and coaching skills. In addition, a leader needs the intuitive skills of bridging, negotiating, and translating to employees or followers what must be done and why. The terms manager and leader need not be mutually exclusive.

Fritz (1985) provides a measuring device for managers, stating that managers fail because they

1. Do not know what is expected
2. Do not know how they are doing
3. Cannot or will not do the work
4. Lack organizational support or have a poor relationship with their superiors

Each situation can be corrected once it is discovered.

Successful managers have these abilities:

1. *Impact.* To create a good first impression and to command attention and respect
2. *Communication skills.* To be persuasive, to make a clear presentation of the facts, and to be effective in written communications
3. *Judgment.* To reach a logical conclusion and sensibly handle day-to-day affairs of a department.
4. *Planning and organization.* To organize and control a function
5. *Initiative.* To originate action on their own or delegate responsibility to do so
6. *Creativity and problem solving.* To come up with imaginative, productive solutions to work-related problems
7. *Sensitivity.* To recognize and respond to the needs of others
8. *Leadership.* To get ideas accepted, to guide a group, and to create a team atmosphere

Very successful managers have two more qualities:

9. *Compelling vision.* An ever-present "consciousness" about the outcome they desire
10. *Concentration.* To focus their attention on reaching the desired outcome

SUMMARY

Although managers have many of the same qualities, their management styles will be as different as the individuals involved. Managers need qualities of intelligence, creativity, good health, and maturity to meet the challenges they will face. More and more techniques of management focus on supporting the workers and giving positive reinforcement or constructive criticism instead of using negative techniques.

Inept managers exist in some firms because they use different methods to hide their incompetence or ineffectiveness. Effective managers must not be content to manage, instead they must demonstrate leadership in a variety of styles adapted to particular situations.

TERMS AND CONCEPTS

communication skills
compelling vision
concentration
consulting style
creativity
delegating style
health
impact
initiative
intelligence
introversion/extroversion
judgment
leadership
management
organization
planning

participating style
person-oriented leadership
  approach
quality circles
rigidity
self-esteem
sensitivity
situational leadership
  approach
style
success factor
telling style
tough mindedness
work-oriented leadership
  approach

REVIEW QUESTIONS

1. Out of the nine qualities for managers discussed in this chapter, name three and describe how they relate to a manager's success.

2. How can a manager give constructive criticism to an employee?

3. A major pitfall of managers is unclear strategy. What part does communications play in solving this problem?

4. What are three major areas of management?

5. What distinguishes the consulting style from the delegating style of management?

6. What is a quality circle and how does it work?

7. What traits build leadership in managers?

8. What is the toughest challenge a manager faces?

9. List the two basic ways some inept managers hide their lack of managerial skill.

10. Review the four situational leadership styles. Which style best describes your approach? Your boss's style?

11. Are you more introverted or extroverted? Is your boss more introverted or extroverted?

SUGGESTED READINGS

Albrecht, K. *Executive Tune-Up*. Prentice-Hall, Inc., Englewood Cliffs, NJ, 1981.

Ash, M. K. *Mary Kay on People Management*. Warner Books, New York, 1984.

Bennis, W., and Nanus, B. *Leaders*. Harper & Row, New York, 1985.

Center for Creative Leadership. *Best of Business* 5(2) (1983).

Crosby, P., and Gallwey, T. *Personal Management Strategies*. Success Guide, Success Unlimited, Inc., Chicago, IL (no date).

DeVille, J. *The Psychology of Leadership*. Mentor Books, New York, 1984.

Drucker, P. *Effective Executive*. Harper & Row, New York, 1967.

Drucker, P. *Innovation and Entrepreneurship*. Harper & Row, New York, 1985.

Editors. *Success* Magazine. *A Personal Achievement Guide to Motivation*. Success Guides, Success Unlimited, Inc., Chicago, IL (no date).

Editors. *Working Woman* Magazine with Bryant, G. *The Working Woman Report*. Simon & Schuster, New York, 1984.

Fielder, F., and Chemers, M. *Leadership and Effective Management*. Scott, Foresman, Glenview, IL, 1974.

Fritz, R. *Rate Yourself as a Manager.* Prentice-Hall, Inc., Englewood Cliffs, NJ, 1985.

Hamermesh, R. G. "How Senior Managers Produce Results." *Making Strategy Work.* John Wiley & Sons, New York, 1986.

Hart, L. B. *Moving Up! Women and Leadership.* AMACOM, New York, 1980.

Hersey, P., and Blanchard, K. *Management of Organizational Behavior.* Prentice-Hall, Inc., Englewood Cliffs, NJ, 1982.

Hickman, C. R., and Silva, M. A. *Creating Excellence.* Plume Books, New York, 1984.

Josefowitz, N. *You're the Boss!* Warner Books, New York, 1985.

Kleinfield, S. *Staying at the Top: The Life of a CEO.* New American Library, New York, 1986.

Lecker, S. *Success Factors.* Facts on File, New York, 1986.

Mitton. D. G., and Lilligren-Mitton, B. *Managerial Clout.* Prentice-Hall, Inc., Englewood Cliffs, NJ, 1980.

Pascale, R. T., and Athos, A. G. *The Art of Japanese Management.* Warner Books, New York, 1981.

Peters, T. J., and Waterman, R. H., Jr. *In Search of Excellence.* Warner Books, New York, 1982.

Rodgers, F. G., and Shook, R. L. *The IBM Way.* Harper & Row, New York, 1986.

Sorcher, M. *Predicting Executive Success.* John Wiley & Sons, New York, 1982.

Staff of Rohrer, Hibler & Replogle, Inc. *The Managerial Challenge: A Psychological Approach to the Changing World of Management.* Mentor Books, New York, 1981.

Stewart, N. *The Effective Woman Manager.* Ballantine Books, New York, 1978.

Werther, W. B., Ruch, W. A., and McClure, L. *Productivity Through People.* West Publishing Co., St. Paul, MN, 1986.

4

SUPERVISION AND TEAM BUILDING

OBJECTIVES

- Define supervision and the role of a supervisor
- Understand supervisory responsibilities
- Contrast supervisory and nonsupervisory activities
- List characteristics of effective work teams
- Understand how to build and facilitate an effective team
- Compare how to increase or decrease group cohesiveness

Supervision is achieving desired results by means of the intelligent utilization of human talents and facilitating resources in a manner that provides the greatest challenge and interest to the human talents. It is a subfunction of control, which refers to the overseeing of subordinates' work activity.

Supervisors must mentally evaluate the various aspects of a particular task in deciding the best way to achieve results. Supervisors must develop the three basic managerial skills—*technical, human,* and *conceptual*—discussed in Chapter 3.

- ❑ *Technical.* A supervisor must have a complete understanding of the work, its difficulty, and its unique characteristics.
- ❑ *Human.* A supervisor must take individuals and mold them into a team that can achieve results.
- ❑ *Conceptual.* A supervisor must analyze, plan, integrate, and coordinate the practices, ideas, and concepts of workers.

All three areas are interrelated, although they vary with the level of managerial responsibility. Supervisors cannot rely on technical skill or former work knowledge to help solve problems. They must constantly acquire and develop new skills. However skilled you were at a particular job, you will not automatically be able to supervise people until you develop the necessary skills in all three areas. Supervisory qualities are not innate; most people become effective supervisors after someone sees their potential and helps them use their own initiative to develop the characteristics needed by a supervisor.

SUPERVISORY CHARACTERISTICS

Legally a *supervisor* is someone who meets the requirements of the federal wage and hour law for exempt status. Supervisors must have at least two people reporting to them and must do work that is significantly different from their employees. A supervisor cannot simply be a senior member of a team of equals. A supervisor must be in a supervisory capacity over the employees.

Beyond the legal definition, a supervisor is one to whom workers report. A supervisor has moved away from the entry-level position of a doer who carries out the plans of a superior. A supervisor is a thinker as well as a doer. A supervisor, now on the first managerial level in a company, has downward authority to delegate. A supervisor is responsible for her own time management as well as the time management of others, but does not manage other managers or supervisors.

SUPERVISORY RESPONSIBILITIES

Supervisory responsibilities include

Ensuring that others accomplish daily work in a timely manner according to the standards of quality and production. In an ideal situation a supervisor does very little of the actual hands-on work once the staff is trained and operating at full capacity.

Controlling and administering resources. A supervisor assigns funds, equipment, training, supplies, time, and staff members in a constant cycle of scheduling, evaluating, controlling, communicating, and administering policies.

Making recommendations. A supervisor must be a thinker contributing ideas on personnel, procedure, planning, and policies appropriate to the assigned level of authority. (Exercise 4-1.)

Supervisory versus Nonsupervisory Responsibilities (Table 4-1)

The *supervisor* sets priorities and communicates them to the work team. The *nonsupervisory* worker carries out work according to priorities set by the supervisor.

The *supervisor* develops plans, communicates them to the work team, and then controls their progress. The *nonsupervisory*

Table 4-1 Supervisory versus Nonsupervisory Jobs

SUPERVISORY	NONSUPERVISORY
1. Sets and communicates priorities	1. Carries out work priorities
2. Develops and communicates plans	2. Implements plans
3. Analyzes and reviews work	3. Performs with limited point of view
4. Gathers information and advises	4. Receives information and advice
5. Makes decisions	5. Carries out decisions
6. Outlines work to meet objectives	6. Functions with work outlines
7. Designs controls for completion	7. Works to best of ability
8. Delegates utilizing human and social skills	8. Completes technical work in specific skill area
9. Evaluated on effectiveness of team	9. Evaluated individually

worker carries out the work necessary to implement a plan or a work schedule.

The *supervisor* analyzes work to be done and reviews it in terms of the overall picture. The *nonsupervisory* worker performs work within a more limited point of view, focusing on the immediate task to be performed.

The *supervisor* gathers information and communicates advice to the team. The *nonsupervisory* worker receives information and requests advice.

The *supervisor* makes decisions that the *nonsupervisory* worker carries out.

The *supervisor* helps employees outline their individual work in order to meet objectives and priorities while *nonsupervisory* workers function under those directives.

The *supervisor* designs controls to ensure satisfactory completion of work. *Nonsupervisory* workers complete work to the best of their ability.

The *supervisor* accomplishes work through other people. Nonsupervisory people do technical work in a specific skill area.

The *supervisor* will be evaluated on the effectiveness of the team. The *nonsupervisory* worker is evaluated on the quality of individual work.

Supervisors as Coordinators

Supervisors have day-to-day contact with several distinct groups. With each group, the effective supervisor must use a different blend of skills to form coalitions and teams to get the job done. These groups include

Employees. Supervisors interact with employees both individually and as a group.

Unions. In many situations, supervisors deal directly with labor representatives; cooperation and negotiation skills are vital.

Staff specialists and consultants. Supervisors work with specialized personnel such as accountants, engineers, or personnel managers who may have information that will aid supervisors in performing their duties.

Other supervisors. Supervisory peers require communication and coordination to obtain productivity.

Superiors. Higher levels of management need updates and information on the progress of work since they will eventually evaluate the supervisor's effectiveness.

SUPERVISORY ROLES

Although a supervisor's job description might include many duties and the day-to-day details might number in the hundreds, most of the supervisory roles can be divided into five general categories:

1. *Leading and training employees.* Supervisors have a primary responsibility to develop employee skills and motivate employees to use these skills effectively. A supervisor must provide adequate instruction both in training staff members and in delegating assignments. Along with instructions, the supervisor must encourage initiative among workers to follow through on the job. (Exercise 4-1).

2. *Implementing ideas.* A supervisor enjoys a unique perspective as the person between the first-line workers and the upper levels of management. A supervisor can balance the needs of management with the day-to-day observation of the actual work being done in order to suggest new methods, techniques, or improvements. At times the supervisor's department can function as a hands-on laboratory to try new ideas on a small scale before implementing them throughout the organization.

3. *Cooperating with other supervisors.* Communication with peers can be as important an indicator of success as communication with workers and upper levels of management. A supervisor must accept a place in a peer group and work to influence peers with the same attention given to upper management and entry-level people in the company.

4. *Following policies set by superiors.* Supervisors truly lead lives in the middle, functioning both as employees and employers at different times and in different situations. In addition to being able to lead and train, supervisors must be able to follow and take direction from their own bosses. (Exercise 4-2.)

5. *Mediating employee needs.* The unique position of supervisors, who are between employees and top management, emphasizes the need for negotiating skills. The supervisor forms a link communicating both positive feedback and grievances to the next levels of the corporate organization. The supervisor must also be able to translate the company's point of view in appropriate ways to employees who may not be able to understand the role cost- or time-effectiveness plays in company decisions.

BUILDING A TEAM

Many aspects of business relate to the analogy of a team with different yet interrelating parts functioning as a unit toward a common purpose. Any organization with more than one employee must build a team or group spirit in order to get things accomplished. From the first telephone operator who answers calls to the shipping department, every person must perform a certain task in order to maintain the flow of commerce.

Some teams may seem to function effortlessly as each staff member goes about an assigned job like a well-ordered cog in a machine. With most offices, however, a combination of personalities, agendas, and demands of the work creates friction that can hamper teamwork.

Some characteristics of effective work teams, adapted from *The Human Side of Enterprise* by McGregor (1960), include being

1. *Involved.* Effective teams are interested in the overall success of the group and stay involved to achieve that success. Individuals must subordinate their needs to the needs of the group as they share in the work.

2. *Relaxed.* Group members must feel comfortable with each other. An informal atmosphere of mutual trust allows workers to function without feeling threatened by individual team members.

3. *Expressive.* Team members recognize the need to express ideas and attitudes freely among themselves. Without this open communication, small problems quickly grow large enough to impede success.

4. *Communicative.* Just as team members need to be able to speak their minds, they must also engage in effective listening. They must be willing to listen to instructions from superiors, to ideas from other team members, and to ongoing evaluations of the project's outcome as the work progresses.

5. *Constructive.* Criticism or conflict occurs in teams, but effective groups use principles of constructive criticism and positive resolution to strengthen the team. Effective teams cannot take criticism personally or allow conflict to block success.

6. *Decisive.* Effective teams rarely take decisions to a vote. Instead they rely on decisions by consensus with the group reaching a conclusion together. Consensus gives each team member a voice in a decision rather than a vote that may put some team members on opposing sides of an issue.

7. *Trained.* Team members must have clear assignments and the training to accomplish the desired results. The task must be accepted and understood before work can begin.

Team members must have a solid idea of the roles they will play. They must be qualified to carry out those assignments in an atmosphere of cooperation, trust, and compatibility. They must share common goals to the extent that the success of the project unifies their work. They have shared responsibility in the beginning and shared credit when they complete the work.

Teams can function only in an atmosphere of support with authority from upper management.

The golden rule of team building is "What is good for the individual is good for the organization." The team concept accepts the theory that workers will perform at high levels of quality and productivity when they feel valued and challenged in an environment of mutual respect.

Women and Teams

Before the advent of Title IX, which mandated equal expenditures in athletics for men's and women's teams, many women were unfamiliar with the concept of teamwork. Men, on the other hand, came to the business world with first-hand experience in baseball, football, basketball, or other sporting teams. Women athletes were often concentrated in areas of individual achievement such as swimming, tennis, and gymnastics.

Men understand figures of speech widely used in business such as "playing the game" or "doing their part for the team." Even concepts such as strategy and coaching all relate to the sports metaphor.

Women without a sports background need not be handicapped in business as long as they are willing to learn the terminology and implement basic elements of team participation. The spirit of teamwork is highly rewarded in the corporate world. Instead of trying to do a job alone, enlisting the help of others even to the point of sharing the credit can be a starting place in building team experience.

Making a Group Work

Just calling a group of people a team is not enough to ensure a positive outcome. To build an effective team you should

1. *Always hire people who are smarter than you.* Even though you may feel threatened at first, realize that you need to hire

people with certain skills to ensure the team's success; this will reflect positively on your performance.

2. *Concentrate on building a team of generalists rather than specialists.* Cross-train employees so that they can perform a variety of functions and lend varied perspectives to any given problem. Generalists can interact more effectively with one another because they will have a grasp of the overall work even though their talents may be greater in a certain area.

3. *Model yourself after what you expect from your subordinates.* The best team leader is an example to team members in terms of commitment, involvement, discipline, and motivation. Team members can learn by following the leader's behavior.

4. *Earn the trust of staff members.* Methods of enhancing trust include developing listening skills, exhibiting traits that show you are approachable, and keeping confidences when team members share information.

5. *Involve everyone in a decision who will be affected by it.* Even though a decision might seem routine, you can expect greater staff support for any new idea if people have a part in reaching the decision. By allowing staff members to voice opinions, they can "buy into" the final plan and realize their investment in its success.

6. *Keep your sense of humor.* Good advice for supervisors is to lighten up on themselves. Employees might as well learn that you are not perfect. The ability to laugh at one's shortcomings or habits can go a long way toward humanizing the supervisor in the eyes of employees.

7. *Avoid an us-against-them approach to team building.* Just as individuals feel more positive in a win-win situation than in a win-lose situation, groups also function more creatively when the challenge is positive rather than negative. Mobilizing the team against an attack may be appropriate in certain crisis situations, but should not be used for long-range projects as a general rule.

8. *Demonstrate your faith in the team.* You must be willing to defend the team to your superiors and convey your loyalty. If a team decision seems faulty, try to redirect it rather than abandoning the entire concept. If upper management questions a team decision, try asking for more time to solve specific problems rather than turning your back on the team.

9. *Give a team room to function.* Supervisors are leaders, examples, and role models, but if they assimilate themselves into

the team, they cannot accomplish their supervisory tasks. Some teams require more direct supervision than others, but giving them space to make decisions and implement plans can help develop new pools of leadership for the company.

10. *Foster mutual respect from team members, upper management, and supervisory peers.* Each level has a certain job to do. Remembering the part each level plays in the larger corporate team can bring appreciation of the importance of the individual to the overall goal.

In *Making Groups Work* Napier and Gershenfeld (1983) offer this advice to group facilitators:

1. *Be sure of yourself.* Act as if you are sure of yourself and you will soon believe that you are.
2. *Assess the group needs before planning a design for the group.* Does the group need more training? Should you add a team member with certain skills to achieve more successful results? These questions can alleviate problems within the team concept as the project continues.
3. *Tell the group why they are there and what will be accomplished.* Clear direction can prevent future confusion over roles or assignments.
4. *Listen to both verbal and nonverbal clues in responding to a group exchange.* Silence can communicate as much as the most vocal group member when a discussion is underway.
5. *Show enthusiasm for the group and allow your high energy level to permeate the group members.* This will enable the group to leave meetings motivated to succeed.

Several specific actions can increase or decrease the cohesive factors in a group (Table 4-2).

To strengthen cohesion, facilitators may

☐ Gain agreement on group goals
☐ Make the group more homogeneous in nature
☐ Encourage more group interaction
☐ Decrease the size of the group
☐ Introduce competition from other or outside groups
☐ Reward the group as a whole rather than individually
☐ Remove a dominant member from the group
☐ Isolate the group physically from other groups

Table 4-2 Actions That Can Increase or Decrease Cohesive Factors in a Group

INCREASE	DECREASE
1. Agreement on group goals	1. Disagreement
2. Group more homogeneous in nature	2. Heterogeneous
3. More group interaction	3. Restricted interaction
4. Decrease size of group	4. Increase size
5. Competition from other or outside group	5. Disband group
6. Reward group as a whole	6. Allocate rewards to an individual
7. Remove dominant member	7. Introduce dominant member
8. Isolate physically from other groups	8. Remove barriers that isolate group

To decrease cohesion when a group is becoming ineffective, supervisors may

- ❑ Induce disagreement on group goals
- ❑ Make the group heterogeneous in nature
- ❑ Restrict interaction between group members
- ❑ Increase group size
- ❑ Allocate rewards to individuals instead of the whole group
- ❑ Remove barriers that physically isolate a group
- ❑ Introduce a dominating member to the group
- ❑ Disband the group

HANDLING PEOPLE

Managing people is a major part of a supervisor's work. Because of the in-between niche that supervisors hold, they must manage their subordinates as well as manage interaction with their peers, their relationship with their superiors, and, of course, themselves.

MANAGING UP

Usually we are trained to manage only those over whom we have authority. *Managing across* or *up* requires more subtle skills than managing down. Successful supervisors have the ability to size up their boss and to adapt their behavior to earn rewards that result in a positive boss-employee relationship.

To size up your boss, ask yourself these questions from *Winning at Office Politics* (DuBrin, 1978):

1. What is your boss trying to accomplish?
2. What practices by subordinates usually irritate your boss?
3. Does your boss accept compliments graciously?
4. Who are your boss's enemies?
5. What is the number one problem facing your boss?
6. What are important personal facts about your boss?
7. What does your boss regard as good performance?
8. What forms of office politics does your boss practice?
9. Does your boss welcome conferring with subordinates?
10. What are your boss's mood cycles?

The answers to these questions should give you an outline profile of your boss. For example, if you know the boss is usually in a bad mood around deadlines for important reports, try to save new ideas or concepts for times when the mood is lighter and the boss is more open to change. Knowing what makes a boss happy or unhappy can help you modify your own behavior to achieve a more positive relationship. In addition, knowing problems your boss faces along with personal facts can help you define the value system your boss uses in business decisions and deals.

In dealing with a boss, try to develop a cordial yet professional relationship. Too close a friendship may make a boss feel uncomfortable when discussing performance evaluations or money matters. Even a mentor-mentee relationship that grows too close can do more harm than good if the two people become viewed as an inseparable pair that cannot function individually. Keep conversations to topics that relate directly to the job. A few personal questions about family or home can help break the ice, but do not dwell on matters that show your mind is not on your work.

Use common sense in treating a boss as you want to be treated. Using positive instead of negative language helps create higher office morale. Respecting your boss's time is a way to show efficiency as well as consideration for the demands of upper-level executive jobs. Prepare for discussions or follow through on requests to demonstrate traits of effective time management on your part. Try to prevent problems whenever possible. Prevention is always more effective than trying to solve a problem. Thinking situations through to avoid problems will earn you high marks as a competent supervisor.

As with any human relationship, do not expect your boss to read your mind. In a work situation, we sometimes think that because we have spent 8 hours a day, 5 days a week with someone, they must know what we want and what we expect. Not receiving what we want builds resentment; we might even imagine a boss is trying to punish us by withholding a raise or an extra day off. In business, if you want something, ask for it. Be as specific as possible whether you want to attend a training session or earn $100 more a month. Do not assume that just because you have hinted that you need a raise or would like to be considered for a promotion that you have conveyed your message. Choose an appropriate, private time to talk to your boss about your goals or needs. Then your boss has a fair chance of assessing those needs in relation to the company and can come to a decision.

If your boss succeeds, you have a better chance of succeeding. Often, bosses on their way up the ladder bring along competent people they have worked with along the way. Some activities you can practice to increase your chances of effectively managing your boss include the following:

❑ *Pick a promotable boss.* Look for someone who wants to move ahead. If you select someone who is stuck in a dead-end job, you will be stuck too, at the next lower level. If you discover too late that your boss is unpromotable, ask for a transfer as soon as possible.

❑ *Help your boss reach stated objectives.* If your boss wants to achieve something, join the team effort to see that the goal is reached. This demonstrates not only loyalty but also effectiveness in completing the job. Cutting costs, simplifying methods, generating revenue, and handling customers can help any department look better.

❑ *Report only to your boss except in an emergency.* Bypassing the chain of command may earn top management's attention on a single issue, but you will sacrifice important trust between you and your boss. Few bosses ever forget an employee who goes over their heads to top management because the boss inevitably loses face.

❑ *Make your boss look good.* To use a political analogy, your boss is your candidate. By helping your boss win higher office, you may carve out a better niche for yourself.

❑ *Focus on the positive.* Concentrate on what is good about the department or the business. Change anything you can to make it better. If you must criticize, do so in private to avoid any chance of being perceived as disloyal.

❑ *Document your achievements as well as your boss's achievements.* Keep your boss informed of your accomplishments so that superiors can see that you are growing and developing in your current level of responsibility. Keeping up with your boss's achievements shows your interest in future success. When you have a success, share the credit with others including your boss so that the positive outcome reflects on the entire department.

❑ *Keep confidential information private but volunteer information that can help your boss when appropriate.* Alert employees can hear things among co-workers that may not be available to top management. The company grapevine is still an important source of advance knowledge that can be helpful in decision making.

❑ *Resist the urge to gossip.* People cannot trust someone who leaks information or carelessly talks about other people in an office. Discretion is a vital quality for upper management and should be practiced at every level of corporate involvement.

❑ *Know the unwritten rules of the company.* Even if your company has no dress code, modify your wardrobe to match your boss's. Dress for the job you want, not the job you have. If the boss constantly arrives at work 10 minutes early, adapt your schedule to that time frame. Unwritten rules reveal the values of upper management and can be clues to succeeding in their world.

❑ *Choose your fights carefully.* Do not let your boss bully you but do not make a war out of every battle. Some conflicts must be set aside to save your power for a really important point later on. Expressing displeasure with every decision only characterizes you as a whiner; you therefore lose credibility even when you are right.

MANAGING DOWN

Managing subordinates calls for two foundational skills: *motivating them to do what you want* and *disciplining them when they fail to do what you want.* Take a piece of string. Pull it along a desktop. Now try to push it back. The string stays limp. You can start pulling it in another direction but you cannot push it back.

People are like that piece of string. They can be led more easily than they can be pushed. For this reason, management has begun emphasizing techniques of positive reinforcement such as *The One Minute Manager* rather than negative reinforcement such as reprimands or firing. By the time an employee is brought in for an interview, interviewed, hired, and trained, the company has a sizable investment in an unknown quantity. For cost-effective use of human resources, it is almost always better to salvage an employee by learning how to motivate her than to terminate an employee and have to start making the investment all over again.

The One Minute Manager stresses ideas such as catching employees doing something right. Public praise and private criticism are axioms of the philosophy. In cases in which criticism is deemed necessary, the authors Blanchard and Johnson (1982) stress sandwiching the negative statements between two positive statements to reinforce the idea that the boss is criticizing the work rather than the worker. Their motto is "The best minute I spend is the one I invest in people."

MASLOW'S HIERARCHY OF NEEDS

Abraham Maslow has postulated that all people share needs that can be arranged in a hierarchy of levels:

1. *Physical*-the needs for food, air, water, shelter, and other survival needs
2. *Security or safety*-the needs to safeguard against danger, threat, or deprivation
3. *Social*-the needs of being loved and belonging to a group of friends or associates
4. *Self-esteem*-the needs of self-confidence, achievement, competence, status, recognition, and respect
5. *Self-actualization*-the need to be able to develop one's own potential for growth and self-development
6. *Wisdom*-the need to achieve understanding, intellectual growth, and the ability to analyze concepts
7. *Transcendental*-the need to relate to a being or universe beyond one's own self

Maslow theorized that the lowest need is the strongest motivator. A person who is hungry will concentrate on finding food before moving beyond that basic need. A satisfied need is not a motivator. For example, once people have food and shelter, they are no longer motivated by fulfilling these survival needs. Instead they move up the hierarchy seeking job security and status or self-esteem.

Maslow's pyramid can be applied to the workplace. Self-esteem needs and self-actualization levels can serve as direct sources of motivation; but lower level needs are more a source of dissatisfaction when they are not met than a source of motivation to work more effectively. In other words, lower level needs, such as a safe place to work or fringe benefits, are maintenance factors that must be present to keep workers satisfied, but they do not facilitate motivation.

MOTIVATORS

Applying a common sense approach to the hierarchy of needs, many supervisors can motivate employees to do a better job without spending money on maintenance factors such as wages, fringe benefits, office remodeling, or other comforts. Many motivational messages require only attention to details such as finding out the satisfiable needs of employees and meeting them.

Supervisors can motivate employees by

Showing confidence in employees. If employees are assigned a task, give them the authority they need to complete the job. Allow enough room for them to try their ideas and methods without supervising every detail.

Giving credit for an employee's good work or ideas. Write a memo of commendation with a copy going to the personnel file or create a system that rewards employees with a certificate or plaque for extra effort.

Promising only what can be delivered. If you do not know the answer or cannot grant their request, do not be afraid to explain the situation in terms they can understand. If you promise to research a fact and get back to an employee, follow through on the request to retain credibility.

Creating a sense of security in the office. Give fair ratings and recommendations. Build a sense of teamwork among employees to promote harmonious working relationships.

Making discipline fair and firm. Administer criticism fairly but always in private. Try to avoid making exceptions so that company policies remain intact without promoting favoritism.

Enriching the employee's job. Grant more responsibility when an employee is ready. Make training opportunities available. Delegate work with an eye to developing leadership. If an employee seems bored, try cross-training employees so they can rotate jobs occasionally.

Giving employees full attention when listening. Listening shows you respect their ideas and their right to express them. Listening can also give you clues about what motivates that employee.

Whenever possible, explaining why. Giving reasons allows employees to relate their suggestions or problems to the overall goals of the company or department. The reasons need not be detailed, but should be appropriate for the employees' level of knowledge about a project or a goal.

Using vehicles for public recognition where appropriate. Public recognition conveys a dual message. It shows the employee involved that the work is appreciated and it also tells other workers that the company appreciates quality work on an individual level. In other words, when they perform well, they can expect recognition, too.

Methods of recognition may include

- A handshake from the CEO in front of the entire group
- A certificate or plaque marking the achievement
- An article in the company publication or newsletter
- A press release to the local newspaper
- A pin or pen and pencil set with the corporate logo
- A bonus check or savings bond

Note that not all of the motivators cost money. Even the ones that represent an investment may be worthwhile if employees begin working harder to receive the reward.

Opportunities for recognition might include

- Achieving a production goal
- Reaching a sales quota or a breakthrough with a new client
- Submitting a cost-cutting suggestion
- A year of perfect attendance with no sick leave or late arrivals
- Participating in community service work or a civic project
- Suggesting a new product or a new use for an existing product
- Receiving a commendation from a customer for good service
- Completing a training program or some other business-related course

DISCIPLINE AND FIRING

The reverse of motivating employees is discipline and firing. Ideally the majority of a manager's time should be spent on motivating and directing employees in a positive way. Eventually, every manager will be in a situation that requires disciplining an employee with a reprimand, negative reinforcement, or even firing an employee.

Although many employees fantasize that they would enjoy the power to punish or fire other workers, most managers dread this sort of negative confrontation. The responsibility of adding negative information to an employee's job history or ending an employee's career with the company is not one managers take lightly. Even though firing and disciplining employees may be distasteful, it is a responsibility that comes along with the privileges of management.

When positive motivation fails, the supervisor can follow these guidelines in deciding the next course of action.

1. *Do you need to cool-off before making the decision?* Some infractions must be dealt with immediately, particularly if they relate to the safety or welfare of other employees or customers. Other mistakes can be discussed within a reasonable amount of time. Allowing both parties to calm down after a frustrating incident may give the manager time to choose an appropriate course of action and may allow the employee to weigh the seriousness of the mistake.

2. *Do you have all the pertinent information and facts?* One side of the story–either the customer's, the employees', or another supervisor's–is not sufficient grounds to reprimand the employee. A supervisor must function as a news reporter seeking answers to who, what, why, and where before sufficient information exists to seek disciplinary action.

3. *What is the employee's record of similar previous offenses?* Documentation is a key part of discipline. Whenever an incident occurs, the manager should write down all the pertinent facts in memo form with one copy for the employee, one copy for the personnel files, and one copy for the manager's files. The memo should contain the job objectives and the reason for finding the person unsatisfactory in completing the objectives. The memo should also indicate the consequences of failure to correct the problem. The employees should sign the file copies to show that they are aware of their actions and the seriousness with which the company views them. These memos also can be helpful if the problem

is not corrected. Even if a former supervisor has moved on, the present supervisor will have the benefit of knowing the employee was warned earlier about consequences of a similar mistake happening again. Written documentation can also help back up a supervisor when an incident necessitates firing an employee. With written evidence, supervisors protect themselves from charges that a termination was arbitrary or based on criteria other than job performance.

4. *What is the employee's work record in terms of productivity, attendance, and seniority?* Once again, if a company emphasizes documentation, these records will be available to the supervisor in the form of sick leave reports, yearly evaluations, and other memos in the personnel files. If an employee's record shows no past infractions, that can be a clue to the supervisor to try to find the cause for such inconsistent behavior. Perhaps personal problems or problems with co-workers are keeping employees from achieving their potential. If the records show a trend toward habitual tardiness or absences, then the supervisor can assess the effectiveness of future warnings toward eventual termination.

5. *In the past, what type of disciplinary action has been taken for similar offenses?* Just as employees expect consistency in other aspects of management, they also need consistent disciplinary techniques. Company policy may demand that an employee who is late more than a certain number of times be subject to firing. If a manager overlooks that policy or makes an exception, employees will get the message that company policies can be ignored as unenforceable rules. Managers need to acquaint themselves with written company policies for specific rules on reasons for termination. They must also research unwritten policies administered in similar circumstances to let employees know that management is trying to treat employees fairly and equally.

6. *What are the alternate forms that discipline may take?* Discipline may mean suspension from work without pay, a poor evaluation that goes into the personnel file, or a demotion in authority or cut in pay. Try to match the discipline to the company norms for similar situations, taking into account the employee's work record. Sending an employee home early may lead to low morale among fellow workers when a more private memo in an employee's personnel file may be enough to modify future behavior.

7. *Will your own management support the disciplinary action?* Reviewing past company history can give you clues about

management support for administering discipline. When you discipline an employee, you need the backing of upper management in all areas. If employees think they can negate your disciplinary decisions by going over your head, you will lose your supervisory authority in future matters. Some companies have a supervisor's manual or ongoing training that lets supervisors know the limits of their authority in given situations. If you have a question, ask the personnel department or your immediate supervisor before proceeding. Most companies would rather be safe than sorry in an era in which employees have been known to take companies to court to solve grievances.

8. *If you have a union shop, have union officials been notified to limit the possibilities of future misunderstandings?* Labor relations can be sensitive in the area of discipline and firing. Be sure that you know procedures for filing reports and notifying union officials to protect the company's interests at all times. If you are considering an action, inform only the parties involved on a management level to prevent leaking information or premature speculation that could damage the relationship between labor and management.

9. *If your decision is questioned, could you make a solid case before an arbitrator in a grievance process if necessary?* Managers must look at the worst case scenario in disciplinary actions. If the matter were to go to a court or to an arbitrator, who would be the winner? Of course, the manager's goal is to proceed in such a way as to resolve the matter with the least inconvenience and expense to the company.

10. *Will the disciplinary action result in improving the behavior of the employee?* The process of interviewing, hiring, and training employees is expensive. A manager's goal must be to hire the best employees and motivate them to do the best possible work. When that fails, the supervisor must decide if the employee can be salvaged and thus save time in hiring and training another new employee or if the situation has progressed to the point that the employee should be terminated to reduce future losses.

SUMMARY

Supervisors hold a unique place in business as they relate both to entry-level employees and to upper management. They direct, coordinate, and design controls to achieve results within their work. An important part of their job is to build teams of employees that work together to achieve a common goal. Teams need the cohesion of a unifying purpose and motivation in order to succeed. Effective supervisors analyze their employees' needs and try to motivate them by satisfying those needs. Supervisors not only manage employees, but they must also manage their relationship with their boss. Helping your boss achieve goals will indirectly help you achieve your goals as well.

TERMS AND CONCEPTS

cohesiveness
managing down
managing up
nonsupervisory
supervision
supervisor

REVIEW QUESTIONS

1. From a legal standpoint, who is a supervisor?
2. What groups do supervisors work directly with on a regular basis?
3. What characteristics lead to an effective team?
4. Name three techniques you can use to increase the agreement on group goals.
5. If your boss is in a dead-end job, what course of action is recommended?
6. Where does the need for friends fit into Maslow's hierarchy of needs?
7. What is documentation as it relates to the disciplinary process?

EXERCISES

4-1: ARE YOU AN IDEAL SUPERVISOR?

Instructions: Evaluate your supervisory potential by answering each question—insert a check mark in the appropriate column to indicate rarely (R), sometimes (S), or consistently (C).

	R	S	C
1. Able to do or understand jobs of the employees?			
2. Set up reasonable, clear-cut goals with employees?			
3. Recognize the difference between good work and anything less, pointing out the distinction frankly but tactfully?			
4. Stay aware of the needs of the group and anticipate them at least half the time?			
5. Reward effort and achievement?			
6. Provide incentives and opportunity for employees to advance within the organization?			
7. Make constructive suggestions and establish methods for helping workers improve their skills?			
8. Recognize that individual differences exist in people, and create working conditions best suited to these differences rather than dealing with people according to a fixed set of rules?			
9. Communicate effectively so that each person in the group knows exactly how they stand?			
10. Act as an effective spokesperson to management on the worker's behalf?			
11. Never pass the buck?			

	R	S	C
12. Treat people with dignity and respect?			
13. Make it easy for workers to discuss their problems and be a good listener?			
14. Administer fair but firm discipline?			
15. Convey leadership—which means inspire team effort that is greater than the sum total of worker's individual effort?			
16. Get results and never miss a deadline?			
17. Give employees credit for work well done?			
18. Direct employees and equipment in the most efficient way possible, with the objective of providing maximum profit for the organization and job security for employees?			

Reread each item marked rarely (R) and sometimes (S). Prepare a list of those items that need improvement to become the ideal supervisor. Based upon the text's information, how can you improve each item? Brainstorm.

4-2: ARE YOU AN IDEAL EMPLOYEE?

Instructions: Evaluate your employee potential by answering each question—insert a check mark in the appropriate column to indicate rarely (R), sometimes (S), or consistently (C).

	R	S	C
1. Work well alone and without calling attention to yourself?			
2. Seek a better way of doing the job?			

	R	S	C
3. Work at a steady pace, without apparent effort or strain?			
4. Possess neat work habits?			
5. Look for ways to save time, cut costs, avoid waste, generate profits, and improve customer service?			
6. Understand how the job fits into the overall picture, and cooperate with other employees on every level in contributing to a group effort?			
7. Work as though you owned the business, as though you had to sell the product and produce a profit?			
8. Clarify instructions and ask questions before working?			
9. Possess an open mind to new ideas, new processes, new equipment, new people; understand that constructive change is progress and that the company's progress is directly beneficial?			
10. Listen effectively?			
11. Confront problems?			
12. Admit, correct, and forget mistakes?			
13. Treat employment as an opportunity, rather than a privilege that is guaranteed by a supervisor, company, or union?			
14. Separate personal relationships from work?			

Reread each item marked rarely (R) and sometimes (S). Prepare a list of those items that need improvement to become the ideal employee. Based upon the text's information, how can you improve each item? Brainstorm.

SUGGESTED READINGS

Allison, M. A., and Allison, E. *Managing Up, Managing Down.* Simon & Schuster, New York, 1984.

Bittel, L. R. *What Every Supervisor Should Know.* McGraw-Hill, New York, 1985.

Blanchard, K., and Johnson, S. *The One Minute Manager.* Berkley Books, New York, 1982.

Bramson, R. M. *Coping with Difficult People.* Doubleday, Garden City, NY, 1981.

DuBrin, A. J. *The Practice of Supervision.* Business Publications, Dallas, TX, 1980.

DuBrin, A. *Winning at Office Politics.* Ballantine Books, New York, 1978.

Gould, R. *Sacked! Why Good People Get Fired and How to Avoid It.* John Wiley & Sons, New York, 1986.

Kossen, S. *Supervision, Practical Guide to First-Line Management.* Harper & Row, New York, 1981.

McGregor, D. *The Human Side of Enterprise.* McGraw-Hill, New York, 1960.

Mosley, D. C., Megginson, L. C., and Pietri, P. H. *Supervisory Management, The Art of Working with and through People.* South-Western, Cincinnati, OH, 1985.

Muzyk, J. P., Schwartz, E. B., and Smith, E. *Principles of Supervision, First- and Second-Level Management.* Charles E. Merrill, Columbus, Ohio, 1984.

Napier, R., and Gershenfeld, M. *Making Groups Work.* Houghton Mifflin, Boston, MA, 1983.

Plumez, J. H., with Dougherty, K. *Divorcing a Corporation.* Villard Books, New York, 1986.

Rue, L. W., and Byars, L. L. *Supervision, Key Link to Productivity* (2nd ed.). Irwin Publishers, Homewood, IL, 1982.

Warrick, D. D., and Zawacki, R. A. *Supervisory Management.* Harper & Row, New York, 1984.

5

TRANSITION

OBJECTIVES

- Ease the transition process
- Identify transition mistakes to avoid
- Enhance risk-taking abilities
- Understand the concepts of bypassing, networking, positioning, role modeling
- Recognize impact of image and of dressing professionally
- Provide travel tips

Change is the only thing we can truly count on. One day you are sitting in a classroom as part of a group of students. The next day you graduate and suddenly you are part of a different group as you report to your first job. At the job you grow accustomed to reporting to management. One day your boss says the words, "You've been promoted," and suddenly you have moved from being one who is managed to one who manages.

Each stage involves the idea of transition. In each case, you are still the same person, but your relationship with those around you has changed. From the time you assumed your new role, you began to act and react to people differently as you became oriented to the newest stage of your life.

For women managers, transition can be a challenge. Some women never mentally prepare for a career as a manager, settling instead for an entry-level position. Until recently, few women had the opportunity to read or study problems unique to women managers. Women also lack female role models who can show by example how women can perform effectively in the business world.

CHANGING FOCUS

Life provides many lessons in transition. People grow up, go to school, leave home to establish independence, take a job, marry, divorce, have children, or move to other cities in a constant cycle outlined by a mobile society. In spite of these ordinary transition periods in our lives, many women remain unprepared for the transition that comes from a job change.

People generally resist change, particularly if their needs are closely linked with security. Eventually, women who seek a career will be forced to make decisions that threaten that security. Faced with a dead-end job that has lost its challenge or appeal, employees may decide to push for a promotion to a new position or to venture forth on their own as an entrepreneur instead of working for someone else.

Either of these decisions will entail a changing focus as you move from a subordinate to a superior role.

To ease the transition, you can retrain your mind to think along these new lines:

Realize your role is changing from doing to managing. A common stereotype of women in business is that they are too easily caught up in details to be effective. One major reason for this is that many women began their careers in jobs that involved organizing details for others as secretaries, administrative assistants, or management trainees. When a women moves into management, she must let go of the details associated with the day-to-day work and see herself as the person responsible for managing the work of others rather than the person responsible for accomplishing the task itself.

Develop human and conceptual skills. Skillful managers move from being task oriented to being people oriented. They manage work, but, in the larger sense, they manage people. They have to take the experience gained by successfully completing assignments as a subordinate and apply those skills to understanding how every person's job fits into the overall goals of the group or company and to analyzing and planning the future.

Solve and prevent problems. In the hierarchy of corporate structure, almost every job has people on the next level who have the final authority to make decisions on everything ranging from company policy to hirings and firings. As a manager, you move up the corporate chart and suddenly you have employees on the level below your position seeking your help. Effective managers develop techniques that allow them not only to solve problems when they arise but also to predict and prevent future problems.

Recognize differences between working relationships and friendships. Jean came to work in a department of six employees soon after graduating from college. Some of the first people she met in her new city were her co-workers. She went to lunch with them often and spent time with them on the weekends. When she was promoted, she faced a transition in her new role. Now she had to evaluate their performance, decide who would receive future promotions and raises, and administer company standards for productivity. As long as Jean works with colleagues who first knew her as their equal, she will have to develop new rules for the relationships. Professional, cordial behavior is the key to maintaining a line between employer and employee relationships. Otherwise, emotional distinctions can blur the effectiveness of a manager.

Form peer alliances. Since you can no longer be friends with people who were formerly your equals, the place to look for new contacts at work is on your own level. Although professionalism is still the key to making new friends at work, the people who have similar responsibilities can be important in making a transition to a new job. They may have knowledge about company policies or unwritten rules that they will be willing to share. They may also provide insight into your chances for promotion or transfer based on their experience.

Give credit and support. As you are in transition, realize the people you now supervise are also adjusting to a new boss and new procedures for their work. As you train them in your way of doing things, recognize good performance and reward it verbally or financially. By helping subordinates through transition, you can build loyalty that will increase your confidence as you make your own adjustment to management.

A new manager moves from being

- A doer to a delegator
- A specialist to a generalist
- A reactor to a planner
- A follower to a leader

TRANSITION MISTAKES

Almost all managers can recount a number of things they would do differently if they had the chance to start over in their position. One of the most important things for a new manager to realize is that you are not going to be perfect. Admitting that mistakes are going to happen is a big step not only in accepting the reality that you are human but also in protecting your self-confidence before disaster strikes. The only way to avoid making mistakes is to sidestep every decision and responsibility and to do nothing. Obviously managers have to be able to take some risks in order to move up the corporate ladder.

Every day managers are called upon to make decisions ranging from which telephone call to return first to how to organize a department. The only true mistake occurs when you learn nothing from your actions.

As you pursue a management career, there are some skills you can develop to learn from mistakes:

Trade being liked for being respected. When you are on equal footing with other employees, it may be easy to be friendly and cooperative to build friendships on the job. However, once you are a supervisor you must realize that your employee's respect is more important than their personal feelings for you. For many women, this is a difficult transition because most women are conditioned to believe that being popular and well liked are measures of status. Pam was promoted to head a research and development laboratory after working in the division for 3 years. Her co-workers thought she would be sympathetic to their demands because only a few months ago she had been one of them. Her first test came when a colleague asked her to change the work schedule to give her an extra 3-day weekend. Pam realized that any exception to the scheduling policy would create long-term problems in the lab since other employees would ask for special privileges, and therefore she denied the request although she knew her decision would probably lose the friendship of the employee.

Learn to listen.   No matter how competent you are, you can still learn from others. Emerging technology brings new information to most fields more quickly than colleges can produce graduates. Failure to listen can be a fatal pitfall to managers in transition. Most people enjoy talking about themselves and their work. A new manager should make it a point to schedule time to listen to employees. Often the person who has worked in a department for years holds the key to improved productivity, but has been waiting for an opportunity to share it. New managers may be tempted to let their minds wander to the next task they face in the first hectic days of a new job, but this temptation can mean losing information vital to future success.

Build coalitions.   Whatever their field, managers are basically in the people business. When you take a new job, mentally survey the situation. Who confides in whom? Who seems to know the most about the department? When the CEO issues a memo, who is on the routing list? Whose opinions do others respect? And perhaps, most importantly, who can you trust? Remember that it is easier to lead people than to push them in directions they resist. One way to build the support you will need in a new position is to plan time with each employee to find out what they perceive as the strengths and weaknesses of the department. You may find out that you can raise morale by simply rearranging the furniture or implementing regular staff meetings to keep workers informed.

Gain support before you make changes.   The worst thing a new manager can do is to arrive at work the first day and begin making extensive changes in the way business is done. Even if you were hired to restructure a division or company, you may sabotage your chances to succeed unless you proceed at a less threatening rate. People need to trust you before they can trust your ideas. If you are contemplating changes, try inviting a few key employees into your office as a testing ground. Although you will want to retain control of the overall goal, you can ask them for ideas on implementation or setting a realistic deadline for the change. Then when the plan is finalized, be sure to give credit to employees who provided concepts that you incorporated into the final outline. This gives the employees an investment in the plan's outcome as they share responsibility for developing the changes.

Practice saying, "I don't know, but I'll find out." If you were not faced with charting unknown territory, it would not be a challenge. If you honestly do not know the answer to a question, it is far better to admit ignorance and then quickly follow up on your promise to find out than to act as if you know and then make a worse mistake later. No one ever claimed that education or work experience provides all the answers. What these factors do in reality is to help you develop skills with which you can discover answers or teach you the tools to use when you need extra resources. While it may be temporarily embarrassing to admit that you are missing a budget number or the name of a contact person, you can minimize the damage to your image of competency by admitting you do not have the information at that time and then getting the facts as quickly as possible.

If you make a mistake, admit it and report it to your supervisor as soon as possible. Some experts call this *"damage control."* They mean that once you have made an error, you cannot take it back, but you can work to lessen its repercussions. Companies attach a high value to honesty among all employees but particularly among managers. If you admit a mistake, you can retain the respect of others while trying to rectify a bad decision or careless incident. Blame someone else and you lose credibility. Cover up a mistake and what may have started out as an innocent action takes on worse implications through deliberate deceit.

TAKING RISKS

Unless you already hold the position of CEO in your firm, chances are you see yourself moving up in the corporation or moving out to start a business of your own. Either way, you will be taking the risks that come from leaving a routine but secure job that promises little more than a paycheck every week.

People who are ready to take a job risk generally fall into two categories. Either they are bored with a job that means repetitive tasks and little responsibility or they have reached a point in their careers at which they are too busy or overworked with projects and details to feel they are making a worthwhile contribution. In both cases, the employees are likely candidates to develop attitude problems if a change is not forthcoming. Rather than blame others for the lack of a challenge or become irritable over circumstances you cannot control, use the symptoms to assess your chances to get out of a dead-end job.

In *Strategies for Women at Work*, LaRouce and Ryan (1984) raise several questions for employees wondering about their next job move.

1. Does your present job level provide opportunities for growth and learning or would you have to look outside the job or company to acquire them?
2. What is the "boredom quotient" of your job, that is, are you likely to become bored with what you are doing in 5, 10, or even 15 years?
3. Does your present job allow you to interact with people you like?
4. Does your present job provide you with access to and participation in the circles to which you aspire whether social or intellectual?
5. Are your day-to-day activities more or less interesting to you than those involved with higher level jobs in your company?
6. Taking into account expected raises, can your job provide you with sufficient financial rewards? (Try to analyze your finances independently of any dependence on shared income from a marriage or relationship.)
7. How much independence do you want or need and how does your present job fulfill that need?
8. Is your present work meaningful to you?

The authors warn that employees sometimes have to accept a less-than-perfect job in order to reach a higher goal. In taking a job, always weigh the pros and cons of the decision. Try to find the job that best fits your needs as you now know them.

Once you decide to move up, you have to convince your superiors that you are the right person for the job. People rarely get promoted on the basis of hard work alone. Jill was an accounting major out of college when she took her first job. She hoped to spend 5 years gaining experience and eventually become assistant controller for a manufacturing firm. She hoped her long hours and attention to accuracy would make her a prime candidate for a job. When the opening finally was available, her boss promoted someone else. When she finally worked up the courage to ask why, she was told that while the company had appreciated her work, no one had any idea that she wanted to be considered for the job.

Jill made several tactical errors in planning her career, but her major omission was that she failed to let her supervisors know she viewed her work as a career with a future rather than simply as a job. If you set your sights on a better job, be sure to communicate that desire to people who may someday be in a position to help you obtain it.

Once you decide on your next career step, you will have to begin to sell yourself to people empowered to make decisions on hiring and promoting. If you lack the training or education for the job, take steps to complete courses so that you have your diploma or certification before the job becomes open. Once the job is available, it may be too late to enroll in a training program.

Even before you make a job move, do your corporate homework. Find a policy manual and annual report and read them to learn everything you can about the internal structure of the company. Study a corporate chart to find out how departments interrelate and who reports to different supervisors. Look at the people who are moving ahead in the company. Study their image, how they dress, and even their work habits to find out what the company values. Adapt their strong points to your own personality and style within the company norms.

If a job change seems years away for economic or personal reasons, you can still benefit from taking risks by making attitude changes. Concentrate on being the best you can be both personally and as part of the boss's team. Document your performance and make sure it becomes part of your personnel file just in case you want to use the company for later references.

Use creativity to increase productivity or efficiency and share your accomplishments with your superiors. At appropriate times, discuss your future plans with your employer. Use evaluation meetings to spotlight past successes and how they fit into your overall career outline.

MOVING UP

Successful people often identify techniques that helped them gain a job or promotion when other candidates were equally experienced or qualified. Although some may dismiss any factor other than being in the right place at the right time, four methods can help you improve your chances.

BYPASSING

Bypassing means (1) overcoming career barriers that keep you from moving ahead, by selecting alternate career path choices, (2) seeing obstacles as challenges that can be overcome rather than blocks to advancement, and (3) identifying the persons who can provide the resources and information to assist you in your objectives and going directly to them, regardless of title and position.

Suppose you let your supervisor know that you would like to be considered for a leadership training seminar. The supervisor may counter that the company has already selected the delegate. Some employees would accept this answer and hope for another chance at a later time.

With bypassing, you could graciously accept your supervisor's answer and then take concrete steps to ensure that you get another opportunity. You could write a memo to your boss asking that you be considered next year with a carbon copy to the company's personnel director or training coordinator. You could reinforce your interest by asking to be included on the routing memo of any reports the delegate brings back to share with the company. You could attend similar seminars or workshops on your own time at local colleges or training sessions and send copies of completion certificates to your supervisor.

Some business situations seem totally negative, but by bypassing the event as a temporary setback, you can minimize any damage to your career.

FIVE COMMON BARRIERS TO ADVANCEMENT

1. Taking criticism personally instead of trying to learn from mistakes
2. Adopting an all-or-nothing attitude that excludes any chance for a face-saving compromise
3. Focusing on self-development more than being part of a winning team which makes everyone look good
4. Capitulating to others' wishes without making your own thoughts known
5. Failing to take risks that could ultimately benefit your career

POSITIONING

Positioning means developing strategies that put you in favorable situations, preferably close to people who have the authority to make decisions. If the boss does not know your name or what you do, how can you be on the list of potential candidates for a promotion? Some experts estimate that 80 percent of promotions can be attributed to positioning and only 20 percent to performance. That is a shocking figure when you consider that most people spend 80 percent of their time working diligently when only a small percentage of that time makes a difference.

One way to develop positioning skills is to increase corporate visibility. People are less likely to forget someone they see. Attend community and corporate functions such as Chamber of Commerce events or company picnics. Realize that these activities are for business rather than social purposes and maintain the same kind of behavior you would at work. Join professional organizations and take leadership positions whenever possible. Being elected president of an organization for certified public accountants or professional business women reflects a positive image for both you and your company.

SOME OTHER IDEAS FOR POSITIONING

1. Volunteer for high-visibility projects that allow you to showcase your skills.
2. Accept any opportunity for public speaking, whether it is to summarize your group's findings for a company meeting or address a community group about your business, so people get to know you and how you think.
3. Use the company newsletter to report your promotions or achievements. If company policy allows, send an extra copy of the news release to the local newspaper.
4. Document your performance with memos to your supervisor and to the personnel files. You may photocopy a complimentary letter and attach a short note, forward a copy of a certificate earned in completion of a training class, or compile a brief report on the progress of a project to convey positive messages about your work.

NETWORKING

Before networking was a word in the business vocabulary, it was a way of life. *Networking* means using personal contacts to achieve a goal or objective. Networking occurs when you ask people where they shop or who is a good dentist. In a professional sense, networking takes the power derived from positioning and links it with mutually beneficial referrals. Hopeful job applicants have always used job references to back up an interview and resumé. The U.S. Bureau of Labor estimates that 48 percent of all jobs come from personal contact, reinforcing the idea that is not what you know in business but who you know.

Networking may be as informal as telling a friend about a job opening in your company and encouraging her to apply. Networking may also be more formal in clubs and organizations that promote the sharing of information, job leads, and business acquaintances. For many years, women tried to get along in business without the benefit of networks. Now professional women in many major cities have banded together to form network groups. These organizations stress getting to know business executives in the community and using their services and referrals whenever possible. "The good old boy's network" is a term used for the informal business relationships enjoyed by men. Now women have adopted the strategy to help themselves and other women succeed in business.

You can use several of the techniques for positioning in a networking context. Although positioning builds visibility within a company, networking builds on the in-house strategies and expands them to include your community, state, or entire business field. Some additional networking tips follow:

1. *Carry business cards and exchange them readily.* If your company does not provide them, have some printed so that you can give them to other business people to help them remember your name and what you do.

2. *Take time to send notes of congratulations to people when you read about their promotions or new business ventures.* Send them clippings you think they can use or offer to help them when they are getting started.

3. *When you meet people for the first time, extend a self-confident handshake and repeat their name as you try to memorize it.* Nothing flatters people more than realizing that you remember their names.

4. *Realize networking is a system of trade-offs.* If you ask someone for a letter of recommendation, for example, offer to return the favor and follow through if asked for something in return.

MENTORING AND ROLE MODELS

Human learning is a complicated process. Although we learn many things by reading and studying books, some ideas are best communicated by observing the behavior of others. *Mentoring* and *role models* are two closely linked concepts that can be beneficial when applied to a corporate setting. A *mentor* is simply someone who either knows more than you do or has more experience than you do and is willing to share that wisdom. A mentor can be a teacher, a supervisor, a co-worker, or a friend. Many successful people can point to one person who adopted them early in their careers and helped them learn the complexities of business. A mentor can help you chart a path up the corporate ladder or provide a consultation on a specific problem.

Mentors generally share several characteristics. They do not feel threatened by younger or newer managers, and are willing to see others achieve results. They feel pride in their work and are willing to help others who share their ideals. They know that they could not have reached their present position without assistance from others and they are willing to give that effort back by helping another person's career.

In some cases, the relationship of a mentor/mentee is formalized. A professional women's networking organization in Amarillo, Texas, worked with high school, area college, and university counselors to match women in various professions with students who showed an interest in that career field. In a survey of participants, 70 percent of the students said participation would influence their career direction, 80 percent said they made new contacts, and 90 percent said they would recommend the program to others. The results were equally favorable among the professional women who served as mentors. Their responses showed that 90 percent would follow up contacts made through the program and 81 percent would participate again if the program were offeered.

Sometimes a mentor can serve as an inspiration without ever knowing it. These people are our role models. A *role model* is someone whose behavior, attitude, image, or performance sets an example that we want to emulate. From early childhood, parents serve as role models to teach you how to relate to other people, how to behave in public, and even how to learn. Teachers, public figures, and friends may also be role models for different aspects of behavior. One of the long-standing rules of etiquette is to wait and see what others do and then adapt your behavior along those lines. This advice holds true in business just as in other situations that call for interaction.

Although some people may be able to readily name their role models or mentors, most people are constantly compiling small bits of information from a large resource of friends, acquaintances, and even from the media to learn more about success. If you are seeking a mentor, look for someone in the company that you trust. Start cautiously by asking questions as you learn your job. Eventually you will determine if your chosen mentor is comfortable in that role. If the match is compatible, you may be able to enhance your partnership by asking for advice, using the mentor as a reference or resource, and working with the mentor in areas of positioning and networking.

Role models are more easily found. Read biographies of corporate and political leaders to learn from their strengths and weaknesses. Follow the careers of leaders in your community to study regional differences in values and success. Think back over your early years to realize whose behavior you followed as you were developing your personality—were you more interested in what your friends thought or how teachers and other adults evaluated your behavior? The group that influenced your behavior served as your role model and probably determined much of the value system that has become part of your adult life.

IMAGE

In business, people are constantly sizing each other up for different qualities. How do they look? Do they exude a self-confident manner? Are they well groomed? How well do they express their ideas?

The way people see you is your image. *Image* is a major factor in achieving business success. By the time you have talked to someone for 30 seconds, they have already formed an opinion about you. This first impression will stay with them throughout your relationship. They may learn more about you later, but chances are they will always remember that first encounter, whether it was positive or negative.

For women managers, a professional image means the difference between being treated like someone's daughter and someone's colleague. From the first day you start a new job, your behavior will be under a microscope. The more effort you invest in making a strong first impression, the more your co-workers will be apt to treat you as you want to be treated at work. Some nine image builders to consider follow:

Study how company leaders behave and follow their example. If they always wear a suit, assume that they will look favorably on employees who follow their unstated dress code. If they always arrive 5 minutes early and stay 5 minutes past the official quitting time, adjust your schedule so they see that you have adopted their values for punctuality and giving the company the extra effort.

Separate business and personal life. Casual talk about personal problems or ailments blurs the lines between professional and social relationships. You can be friendly without telling coworkers too many personal details. Otherwise, you may wish you had kept silent when you are passed over for a promotion or transfer because you shared a potential weakness.

Office romances have happy endings only in the movies. Office dating generally backfires because it can have only two logical outcomes. Either the parties break up and make co-workers uncomfortable or they marry and face on-the-job problems associated with married couples in the same company. If the breakup is particularly devastating, the parties may leave or lose a job because of an uncomfortable personal situation. If the couple marries, many firms have nepotism policies that prohibit relatives from working for the same supervisor or corporation. Either outcome can be a disastrous career setback by ruining your credibility at work.

Keep complaints to yourself and concentrate on positive comments. You do not have to be a walking public relations department for the company, but you owe it your loyalty as long as you earn a paycheck. Negative comments are often overheard and taken out of context. A positive statement may still be misquoted, but at least you will have a better chance of portraying the company in a favorable light.

Die before you cry. Crying at work is the number one image killer for women. Although women understand that crying is an expression of anger as well as hurt, most men interpret crying as a weakness because they were taught that boys don't cry. If you feel tears coming on, excuse yourself to the restroom or make up an acceptable excuse, such as a pending telephone call, to diffuse the stress and regain your emotional hold. One person has suggested bypassing the situation by saying, "I'm afraid if we continue this discussion, we will both say things we don't mean. Let's take a break and reconvene in 5 minutes." In this way, no one admits weakness, but both parties can cool off and reorganize their thoughts.

Watch for speech patterns that betray indecisiveness or ineffectiveness. Always starting a statement with "Don't you think? or "Can I?" shows a lack of forcefulness on the part of the speaker. Use declarative sentences and monitor your tone of voice so that statements do not end in an upward inflection that may be interpreted as asking for permission or approval. Managers are in the business of making decisions and sticking with them. Even if you question a decision, your speech should not betray your doubts.

Use principles of group dynamics to maintain your image. If you allow a person to interrupt you, you are robbing yourself of control. Likewise, always sitting at the back of a meeting room and never raising your hand to ask a question can demonstrate that you see yourself in a role of low importance. Exude confidence so that people will realize you are a force to be dealt with rather than a pushover.

Control your temper at all times. Righteous indignation has no place at work. Staying cool helps you keep a situation manageable. Impatient or rough language may be overheard and interpreted as the inability to avoid stress. If someone makes you angry, try to look at the situation objectively and solve the business problem at hand rather than letting personal feelings interfere.

Pay attention to social obligations within a business context. If you ask a colleague to lunch, pick up the bill without regard to your guest's gender. If you accept an invitation to dine or play golf with an associate, try to reciprocate with an appropriate invitation. If you cannot afford to buy dinner or join a country club, look for less expensive alternatives such as a meeting for brunch or attending an art exhibit.

Dressing the Part

Looking businesslike heightens a professional image for women. As women began entering the work force in large numbers, they had few role models to study on effective ways to dress on the job. Soon whole books were being written to advise women on effective workplace wardrobes. John Molloy's *Dress for Success* (1975) and *Women's Dress for Success* (1977) pioneered the research in the way we relate power and image to a person's dress.

Although experts may differ on whether a woman needs to wear a navy blue skirted suit to the office each day, they agree on a few basic concepts:

Dress appropriately for a business situation. Sheer blouses, deep necklines, short hems, or any style that seems provocative is better left for weekend parties. At work, study how other women dress and adapt your wardrobe to those styles. If you work in a fashion industry, your needs will differ from the woman who works in a manufacturing plant or hospital. As you buy new items of clothing, keep in mind acceptable standards for your own job.

Dress for the job you want, not for the job you have. Most job applicants know they must dress appropriately to make a good first impression in an interview, but they may forget that they have to maintain a professional image on the job to be considered for a promotion. If you dress beneath you, chances are you will be overlooked when it comes time for a promotion because you do not look the part. Buy the best clothes you can afford. A single well-tailored suit will make a better impression than several inexpensive items that look worn after a few months. Budget your purchases so that you have built a professional wardrobe after several seasons.

If you have wardrobe questions, err on the side of conservatism. Flashy styles do not give the same message of stability and security in business. Accessories should be simple and emphasize quality. Costume jewelry is acceptable as long as it is of good quality and does not detract. The goal is to have people remember you rather than what you wore.

Pay close attention to fit. Tight clothes may make you look overweight. Choose styles that flatter without being overly sexy. If you think you have a less than perfect figure, dress to emphasize strong points and minimize weak areas.

If you have specific questions, ask for advice before you experiment. The personnel director or a trusted veteran co-worker may be able to save you the embarrassment of being asked to change clothes. Almost every office situation has an unwritten dress code barring overly casual clothes for employees who have contact with the public and upper management.

Many stores in larger cities offer the services of professional shoppers or wardrobe consultants to their customers. Consultants may receive an hourly fee or be paid a commission on the garments they sell. The advice of a professional may be a smart investment if you are building a career wardrobe on a limited budget.

If no consultant is available, you can analyze your own wardrobe by taking everything out of your closet and making an inventory. In one section, put clothes which can only be worn after business hours or on weekends. This includes both formal wear and leisure-type outfits. Sort the remaining clothes for items that are out of style or no longer fit. Make a list of all items that comprise your working wardrobe—skirts, blouses, slacks, and suits. Note the color next to the item as well as any repairs, such as torn hems or missing buttons, which are needed. Use the list to help you see which basic items you need to buy, such as a black skirt, to go with existing garments. The list can also help you mentally mix and match outfits to extend your wardrobe until you add the pieces you need.

Business Etiquette

Entertaining clients, attending business-related functions, or organizing a welcoming party for a new colleague are all examples of situations that require adherence to business etiquette outside the office. Some women avoid these situations rather than risk feeling awkward about entertaining a male client or attending a reception alone. However, professionals realize that important deals are sometimes made in these quasi-business environments. Some things to remember in business entertaining are

Use common sense and logic to think through every situation. Good manners are basically an extension of common sense and consideration. These traits can help smooth even a potentially awkward situation. Try to think of ways to put the client at ease by realizing what makes you most comfortable.

Pay attention to details. To avoid being embarrassed, call ahead for reservations or make arrangements to pay for the bill privately. An important business luncheon is not the time to try a new restaurant or explore unfamiliar territory.

Appearance is important, particularly if the client is of the opposite sex. In this case, appearance not only includes dressing for success but also how others might perceive the situation. Meeting for breakfast or lunch is less threatening than meeting for dinner or drinks, which may give a less businesslike impression. As a professional, you do not want an important business meeting to become the topic of gossip at the office.

Stay in control of the situation. Set yourself a limit of one drink if you must drink at all and then switch to a nonalcoholic beverage. Plan to meet the client at a designated place so you can leave separately when the meeting is over. Unless you are acting as the host, you do not have to stay past an hour you feel comfortable. Politely excusing yourself early makes a more favorable impression than being the last one to leave.

TRAVEL

Nowhere is business etiquette more vital than in corporate travel. For years, travel was an uncharted experience for women. Now hotels, airlines, and travel agencies have begun to realize that women professionals have formed a new market for their services.

The basic rule of business travel for women is that from the time you check in at the airport until you return, you are representing the company. Dress as you would for any business day. Ask meeting planners about the kinds of clothes you will need in case formal receptions or informal outings are part of the agenda. Even in informal sessions or receptions at out-of-town meetings, the standards of business behavior must prevail. A professional cannot afford to return home with rumors of inappropriate behavior.

If you entertain clients out of town, try to arrange a meeting outside of your hotel room. Unless you are fortunate enough to have a suite, your client may feel awkward in a bedroom setting. Some hotels have sitting areas or small meeting rooms which can be reserved ahead of time.

To alleviate problems, clarify arrangements in advance. Be sure you know the details of your accommodations so that you are not surprised when you arrive at the hotel. Confirm reservations so that you can have fewer details to worry about when you arrive. If you feel uncomfortable in a strange city, ask the hotel clerk or concierge to refer you to good restaurants or points of interest. Tip appropriately as a reward for good service to ensure professional treatment. Do not be intimidated into spending every spare moment in your room eating off room service trays. Even if you are alone, you are entitled to try regional food specialties or investigate tourism spots after meetings.

Ask about special services when you travel. Most large hotels have photocopiers, secretarial services, and translators to help business people. They may also supply specialized equipment such as slide projectors or videotape recorders for meetings for a small fee. Renting equipment from the hotel saves time in locating services in an unfamiliar city or shipping company equipment to the site.

Keep accurate receipts on trip expenditures. Many women prefer to use credit cards when traveling to avoid the risk of carrying cash and to have itemized receipts later to document tax returns. Follow company policy in regard to expense accounts for meals, entertaining, and transportation. If the company does not reimburse you for some expenses, you may still be able to deduct certain costs if you can prove they were directly related to business. If you are on a per diem, you may want to have light breakfasts and lunches in order to have a more relaxing evening meal.

Regular travelers know to pack lightly since they often have to carry their own bags. Veteran travelers often bypass cumbersome baggage check routines and opt to take only what they can carry on the plane so they know their luggage will stay with them through the entire trip. Purchase sample sizes of products you use to save space in your luggage. Plan your traveling clothes around a general color scheme, such as blue or black, so that you can pack fewer accessories and shoes. Select comfortable clothes which resist wrinkling since you may not have time to send clothes out for pressing before your first meeting. With practice, you will become a seasoned traveler ready to take off with only a few hours notice.

Plan ahead to make the best use of your travel time. If you can sleep on planes, you may use the time to catch up on your rest. You may use the time on the plane to catch up on reading professional journals. Some executives travel with portable computers or dictating equipment to draft correspondence. Most business travelers can count on extended layovers and delays in traveling. Instead of being frustrated and bored in the airport, take advantage of the time to make telephone calls or study notes for upcoming meetings.

Think of business travel as an opportunity rather than an assignment. The company thinks enough of you to ask you to be its out-of-town representative. Concentrate on business first, but allow yourself some time to see a different part of the world and learn about a new city. If you are traveling to a meeting on Monday or Friday, see if you can make travel plans so that you have some free time on the weekend at your own expense. Since the company will be paying for the plane ticket, you may be able to afford an extra night in a hotel for sightseeing. Take advantage of what distant cities offer when you have the opportunity once the business day has ended. Call the Chamber of Commerce or ask hotel staff members about places you can see on a limited schedule. The concierge may be able to arrange for tickets or transportation to popular destinations. Keep a file on each city for future reference.

CONCLUSION

Getting a job is not enough for a person who wants a career with a future. Whether that future is in the corporate structure or as an entrepreneur, women face a complex series of transitions as they move into traditional male domains.

Just as the risks are great, so are the rewards. Rather than seeing business behavior and etiquette as a group of limiting rules, women need to use the codes of business as a guide for their own success. Knowing your image and the image you want to project will go a long way toward making a favorable first impression. After that, you can use techniques such as networking or positioning to make the most of opportunities for advancement.

As long as we believe that we can influence the odds of luck in our favor, we have the potential to achieve our goals.

SUMMARY

With every stage of life—from high school to college, from college to work, from first job to management—we face transition. Coping with these changes effectively can make the difference between success and failure. New managers have an opportunity to advance in their careers if they can learn to listen, to build coalitions, to admit mistakes, and to gain support before they make changes. Taking risks is a part of the transition process.

To ease transition, managers can use a variety of techniques such as networking and positioning to gain more visibility for their skills. Along with skills, the manager needs a professional image that includes dressing and acting like a manager in all situations in which you are representing the company.

TERMS AND CONCEPTS

bypassing   networking
damage control   positioning
image   role model
mentor   transition
mentoring

REVIEW QUESTIONS

1. What skills must be mastered in moving from doing to managing?
2. What are some factors involved in taking a risk to leave a present job or start a new one?
3. What homework can you do to find out about a company before you make a job move?
4. What is bypassing and how can it help a new manager?
5. What percentage of promotions can be attributed to positioning?

6. List three techniques of networking with other professionals.

7. What guidelines govern business travel for women?

SUGGESTED READINGS

Audette, V. *Dress Better for Less.*   Meadowbrook Press, Minneapolis, MN, 1981.

Baldridge, L. *Letitia Baldridge's Complete Guide to Executive Manners.* Rawson Associates, New York, 1985.

Gabriel, J., and Baldwin, B. *Having It All.* Warner Books, New York, 1980.

Hart, L. B. *Moving Up! Women and Leadership.* AMACOM, New York, 1980.

Jacobson, A. *Women in Charge, Dilemmas of Women in Authority.* Van Nostrand Reinhold, New York, 1985.

Kassorla, I. C. *Go For It!* Dell Books, New York, 1984.

Kleiman, C. *Women's Networks.* Ballantine Books, New York, 1980.

Kram, K. E. *Mentoring at Work.* Scott, Foresman, Glenview, IL, 1985.

LaRouche, J., and Ryan, R. *Strategies for Women at Work.* Avon Books, New York, 1984.

Malloy, J. *Dress for Success.* Wyden, New York, 1975.

Malloy, J. *Women's Dress for Success.* Follet, Chicago, IL, 1970.

Sitterly, C., and Duke, B. "Networking." *The Secretary* (May, 1986).

Sitterly C., and Duke, B. "Breaking Out of a Career Rut." *The Secretary* (January, 1987).

Staff of *Catalyst* Magazine. *Upward Mobility.* Holt, Reinhart & Winston, New York, 1981.

Welch, M. S. *Networking—The Great New Way for Women to Get Ahead.* Warner Books, New York, 1980.

6

GOAL SETTING

OBJECTIVES

- Understand the process, importance, and advantages of goal setting
- Learn guidelines for expressing goals
- State four basic steps to collecting the information you need
- Prepare meaningful, well-written, and clear goals
- Understand the systematic way to organize goals
- Learn the strategies to convert failures into successes
- Relate characteristics of an effective management by objective system
- Compare benefits and drawbacks of MBO

If you do not believe in yourself, you can hardly expect anyone else to. To succeed, we must think in terms of results. Emerson said, "It's not enough to be busy . . . so are the ants." What are we busy about? Most of the achievements that highlight our lives can be reduced to a one-and-a-half page resumé. This may tell us where we have been, but without goals, it won't tell us where we are going.

Try to think of where you would like to be a year from now. Do you imagine a relaxing vacation on a beach or a seat of corporate power in a board room? You may dismiss the vision as simply a dream. But dreams can come true if we use them as a starting point to set achievable goals.

Dreams are a healthy outgrowth of our unlimited imagination. They are not just for children. As adults we may prefer to label our dreams as goals. A *goal* is a desired outcome or planned result. The process of achieving our goals or dreams stretches our potential. Many people never find those dreams because they do not know what they want. Humorist Will Rogers said, "Even if you're on the right track, you'll get run over if you just sit there."

GETTING STARTED

Deciding what you want is a lifelong process. Before you can set effective goals, you have to learn. For example, if your goal is to buy a seat on the New York Stock Exchange, you should start by learning how to become a stockbroker.

Four basic steps to collecting the information you need are

1. *Read.* Public libraries are an economical source of information in books, magazines, journals, and newspapers. Research assistants are usually available to help you get started.

2. *Experience.* Accept an internship in a field you want to explore. In earlier decades, ambitious young people apprenticed themselves to master craftsmen to learn a trade. Apply this method by asking a working professional to spend some time answering your questions.

3. *Consult.* Talk to anyone who may be able to give you information. College counselors, employment agencies, or members of a professional group may all have different perspectives on a job or situation.

4. *Listen.* Take time in your exploration to absorb the wisdom others have to offer. Listen to television and radio pro-

grams, attend speeches by prominent lecturers, or review conversations with people you respect to discover more about your options.

As you start to set goals, do not limit yourself to one area. Although your parents may have their hearts set on a certain career for you, realize that you are ultimately responsible for setting your own goals. Explore several different possibilities until you are comfortable with your choices. Life is a do-it-yourself project and goals are the rules.

Keep options open as you learn about yourself. Be sure you are the one in charge of that change. Change does not come quickly; it is a continual process. Using goals to direct change can give an added dimension of success to life. Achieving goals will keep life meaningful and worthwhile.

If you fail to plan, you are planning to fail. You must decide on a strategy. Your bridge to success is goal setting. Condition your mind to the never-ending activity of setting goals .

Goals and Life

Goals affect all areas of your life—social, physical, intellectual, educational, professional, and financial.

To achieve a goal, you must keep your priorities clear and well defined. Try to avoid the secondary gain trap that keeps you going to work, getting your paycheck, and going out once a week. You get so caught up, you forget your main goals.

Make an inventory of your skills. Each of us is an individual with special needs and differences. Use your unique combination of talents to establish the confidence needed to achieve your goals. Assess and learn to value your skills. Throughout the goal-setting process, develop a passion for winning and generate enthusiasm. Your attitude will give you the underlying strength to achieve your goals.

Achievers expect more of themselves and develop a sense of urgency as they imagine the rewards and the benefits that come with attaining their goals.

ANALYZING VALUES

Our value system consists largely of the values passed on to us by our parents. Did they grow up in the Great Depression of the 1930s when job security was an overriding goal? Did they serve in World War II and gain a new appreciation of loyalty to their country? Did they go to college in the 1960s when individualism was prized?

Whatever their values, we learned by watching them. By discovering the values that are important to us, we can develop a context within which to frame our goals. The values we rank most highly will be our strongest motivators.

Listed below are major values in our society and examples of how these values are expressed by people. As an exercise, rank the values from 1 to 10 with 1 being the value that you rank highest.

VALUE INDEX

❑ *Achievement.* A person who wants to have a resumè full of awards and honors to her credit

❑ *Security.* A person who stays with a known quantity rather than take a risk

❑ *Location.* A person who takes a less important job to stay in a town they like or to stay near friends or relatives

❑ *Loyalty.* A person becomes attached to a company or person and follows that dedication throughout her career

❑ *Self-realization.* A person who needs to grow and learn as much as possible about herself

❑ *Challenge.* A person who always wants to top records and better previous performances. Athletes would be easily recognizable in this group

❑ *Enjoyment.* A person who seeks a high quality of life with personal pleasure

❑ *Prestige.* A person who values a corner office, an impressive title, or recognition among respected groups

❑ *Power.* A person who needs to control her own life and influence the lives of others

❑ *Friendship.* A person who recognizes a strong need to be liked as well as a need to interact with other people

REALIZING NEEDS

Some people express their values in terms of needs. A need analysis offers insight into what makes you function or what drives you toward a goal. Our unique combination of needs may be a powerful force in pushing us toward or pulling us away from our objective. Some common needs that people express include the need

❑ To please— or live up to others' expectations

❑   To be independent—or to follow your own mind

❑   To accomplish—or to reach a personal milestone

❑   To avoid risk—or to maintain the status quo

❑   To have fun—or to maximize personal pleasure

❑   To avoid embarrassment—or to show vulnerability

❑   To gain status—or to accumulate outward trappings of success

❑   To be recognized—or to have others acknowledge your accomplishments

You may be able to pinpoint other needs such as practicality or thriftiness that are overriding factors when you make life decisions. Needs are neither good nor bad in themselves. In the workplace, however, our needs may be the cause of certain behavior. For example, if you are a risk taker, you may be willing to occasionally be embarrassed; if you are not, you may not have what it takes to incur the loss of security.

Try to match the job to you and your needs rather than vice versa. If you need accomplishment and recognition, you will likely be happier in a field in which you will not always have to work behind the scenes. On the other hand, if you are in a job that does not fit your needs—such as an entrepreneur who constantly longs for the security of a weekly paycheck—you may have to decide if you still value being your own boss.

Susan grew up in a military family. In 12 years, she attended 14 different schools. When she graduated from college, she vowed that she would take a job that would offer little chance of being transferred so that she could put down the roots she had always wanted. After 2 years of a management training program, she received her assignment in the same office in which she had trained. Suddenly, she had feelings of being stifled. She almost felt jealous of her classmates in the program who were leaving for other plants.

Susan had a deeply ingrained need for change and challenge. Fortunately she realized early in her career that she thrived on new people and locations and was able to develop goals with her needs in mind.

AN ONGOING PROCESS

Ralph Waldo Emerson said, "A person's wisdom is to know that all ends are momentary. That the best end must be superceded by a better." In other words, the entire process of life is one of rethinking experiences, analyzing current needs, and moving to the next step even as you are reaching a nearer goal. As you complete one goal or project, you must be thinking of the next one.

The person who has low goals or expectations is never disappointed. If a bright student sets a goal of simply passing a course, she never has to push or compete with herself. For a poorer student, the goal of passing might involve a semester-long struggle.

Take a few moments to think of a goal you hope to achieve within the next 3 months. Will it take a great amount of effort or will it happen almost by itself? Now imagine that you have achieved that goal. What's next for you? Successful goal setters never totally complete their list. They realize that goal setting is a lifelong process.

Fortunately, Americans live in a country with a long history of people who have achieved their goals. Whether we realize it or not, they serve as role models to remind us that we can do whatever we dream, regardless of our race, religion, or economic status. A few factors may stand in our way such as timing or being in the right place at the right time. These are factors over which we have no control. The main factor we can control is our ability to set goals and work toward achieving them.

Why Set Goals?

Ask a group to write their life stories with any ending they want, and they will likely see the exercise as creative writing. Ask the same group to write down their goals and you may hear protests.

Why are people reluctant to set goals? Often they have set goals in the past and failed. Or they may see goal setting as a futile exercise if they feel they lack the power to change their future. In the day-to-day challenge of the business world, we do not take much time to set goals. We must have a plan or a strategy. A plan is a blueprint for action. How are you going to achieve what you want without a plan? No business executive ever reached the top of a Fortune 500 company without a plan. Likewise, a top salesperson cannot sit behind her desk and decide to let the customers come to her. She must have a plan and a sales goal not only to motivate herself but also to measure her performance at the end of the quarter. Working hard is not enough.

SETTING GOALS

As you start to set goals, you must distinguish between real goals and imagined goals. Many people would like to be a rock star, but unless they are musicians to begin with, they may only be articulating a dream rather than setting a goal. Although each of us needs to have some special long-term goals in our life, we need to be realistic in setting short-term goals.

Goals can be divided in three areas:

- ❏ *Things you must have.* Your needs and values dictate that you see these things as essential.
- ❏ *Things you would like to have.* These goals represent the next level because your needs and values tell you that you would like to have them, but you are willing to work toward them if you cannot have them immediately.
- ❏ *Things that would be nice to have but are not necessarily crucial.* These extras or luxuries give you incentive to stretch your dreams, but you can be content if you never gain them.

Write down five goals you want to accomplish. Then go back and prioritize them according to these three categories. Distinguish between them, realizing that you may have to work toward your goals one step at a time.

WRITING GOALS

For goals to be meaningful, they must be written. Writing clarifies thinking and helps you edit out unnecessary or distracting concepts. Writing also symbolizes a commitment to a goal or objective. The process of putting an idea on paper means that you are one step closer to accomplishing it.

Several goal-setting aids have been developed to make the initial goal writing easier. After you become comfortable with the goal-setting process, the only goal-setting aids you will require are a pencil and a piece of paper.

To begin writing goals, decide on a plan to organize your goals. You may want to organize them chronologically or in the order you hope to achieve them. An example of this might be listing short-term goals first and then long-term goals. Another organizational plan might involve dividing goals into personal and professional categories. Goals may also be grouped into the three broad categories discussed in the preceding paragraphs according to things that you must have, things you would like to have, and things that are luxuries but would be nice to have.

Using the plan that best fits your needs, take a sheet of paper and divide it into three vertical columns. (See Exercise 6-1.) In the first column, write down your goal. At this point, think of the paper as a worksheet or a rough draft rather than a final copy, realizing that whatever you write you can refine later.

As you write, consider these general guidelines for expressing goals:

❑ *Goals should be personal,* that is, written for you and no one else.

❑ *Goals should be comprehensive* or should cover your intent in a complete way.

❑ *Goals should be specific* to your present or future situation, so that you can relate to your progress.

❑ *Goals should be realistic,* so that you do not build in frustration and failure.

❑ Some *goals should be visionary,* looking past what seems possible at the moment, but without using realism you will soon be discouraged.

❑ *State your goals in a positive way.* Even if a goal involves something negative such as a weak point in your skills, state the goal in positive terms.

❑ Finally, *goals should be worded in the present tense* rather than the future tense, so that you can begin working on them today.

Use the second column to write down possible solutions to help you obtain your goal as well as barriers or hurdles you perceive are keeping you from your goal. Try to be more specific than simply putting down lack of time or money. For example, if the goal in the first column is to obtain a promotion within the company, the second column might include areas that you know need work. Instead of writing down, "work harder," be specific. If you know that a promotion will go only to someone with an accounting background, write down "complete a course in accounting," and if you know your superiors will consider only top sales people for the job, write down "achieve consistently high sales quotas."

The third column gives you space to mark a time frame for each goal. If you have decided to get specific training, write down a deadline of the month or year you expect to reach the goal. If your personal goal involves weight loss, write down a date by which you hope to reach your ideal size. This column can be used later when you review and update your goals to see how you are progressing. Goals that have been completed can be checked off and goals that are nearing your self-determined deadline can be monitored more closely. If situations have changed from the time you first wrote your goal, such as a corporate transfer or takeover, reassess your original deadlines to make sure they still represent a realistic picture of where you hope to be.

Positive Mental Attitude

Some people can write down well-worded goals with ease, but the goals remain only words on paper. The action inherent in achieving the goals never becomes assimilated into their lives.

For goals to have a meaningful impact on life, you must develop a *Positive Mental Attitude* or *PMA*. A positive attitude enables you to believe that you can reach the goal you want; it is one of the few factors that allows you to exercise complete control. A positive attitude sets the achievers apart from the dreamers. Both groups have high expectations, but the achiever's PMA allows these expectations to be fulfilled. Corollary qualities that supplement PMA include self-discipline, concentration, commitment, and enthusiasm. All these traits blend to create a person who can achieve goals.

People who do not care do not get there. Goal setters must learn the art of self-motivation. At different times in our lives, parents, teachers, bosses, and even friends can motivate us, but the most important source of motivation is still yourself.

Goal setting is not an end in itself; setting goals can strengthen both the business and personal aspects of your life. Goal setting

- *Helps to clarify values.* Questions such as, What is it that I really want to do with my life? or What things are most important to my life? can be more easily answered.

- *Eases decision making.* Your goals provide a framework of items you consider critical to your success. Any decision can be assessed in terms of whether it helps you move closer toward achieving a goal.

- *Pinpoints where you are now.* Instead of wondering how a certain job or position fits into your total career plans, you can see what skills or experience you can gain from your current position even if your goals are pushing you higher up the career ladder.

❑ *Saves time.* Instead of investing energy in a variety of tasks, you can focus your efforts on work that helps you achieve your goals.

❑ *Builds self-confidence.* Just as checking an errand off a things-to-do list makes you feel as if you have accomplished something, achieving a goal you have set for yourself creates the high self-esteem necessary to carry you to your next goal.

Remember, if there were no obstacles to achieving a goal, it would not be a goal and if there were no obstacles, the thing you want would already be within your grasp. Use goals to overcome obstacles to that success or to make a commitment to pursue a secret project or ambition that might never be accomplished without a personal, written goal.

WRITING OBJECTIVES

A goal is a long-term objective. If you can think of a goal as the completed project, *objectives* are those activities that lead to the goal. Objectives are the blocks from which final goals are built. For example, your goal might be to supervise an accounting department for a major manufacturing company within 5 years. Below the goal, you list objectives such as transferring to the head corporate office, passing the Certified Public Accountant examination, and qualifying for management training within your organization. The objectives are the way in which you arrive at the overall goal.

Developing objectives becomes easier with practice. Effectively written objectives must be

❑ *Reasonable.* If they are not reasonable, you can sabotage your future with built-in failure. Use past experience as a guide or ask the opinions of others if you are unsure; for example, ask how long it will take you to complete a project of a certain magnitude.

❑ *Require improvement for growth.* If you write down something you have already accomplished or something you know you will accomplish with ease, you cannot truly consider that statement to be an objective. Objectives must be more than a things-to-do list if they are going to advance you toward your goal.

❑ *Change from year to year.* Last year's objectives may be used as a guide to measure progress, but if reused they become a habit rather than a statement of future progress.

❑ *Measurable.* Well-written objectives need to include statements of quantity, such as time, sales quotas, or numerical ratings. An objective might state that as a producer at a local television station, you want to be number one in the viewer ratings within 12 months. By including these numerical goals, you will be able to gauge the success of your objective at the end of a year. Without these measurements, it is impossible to determine accurately if an objective has been met.

Here are some suggestions for writing objectives:

1. *Start with an action verb.* Good examples are save, expand, achieve, and gain. These words express the forward momentum necessary to reach a goal.

2. *Identify a simple or key result for each objective.* Since objectives are stepping stones to goals, decide how each objective will advance you toward the final outcome. Summarize that step within the written objective.

3. *Give yourself a deadline or completion date to measure each objective.* Set realistic time limits so you can monitor your progress.

4. *Seek opinions of co-workers, professors, or other experts who can help you more clearly define objectives.* One manager of a marketing firm saw a project dismantled because she estimated a 75 percent return from a direct mail solicitation of clients. Later a consultant told her that a 15 percent return would have been considered successful. Had she researched the objective before setting an unrealistic measurement she might have saved her campaign.

5. *Avoid business jargon and use clear, concise language.* After you write your objective, try to read it again from the perspective of an outsider who knows nothing about your job. Some specialized businesses such as the transportation or medical industries may require more technical terms, but try not to clutter objectives with too many words.

A Step-By-Step Approach

Now that you have written goals and objectives, it may be helpful to look at a step-by-step plan for setting and organizing a specific goal.

Step 1. *Think of something you want to accomplish in the next month.* Do you want to change yourself or do you want to have something? Write it down in clear terms and decide to achieve it within 30 days.

Step 2. *What personal and specific benefits will be yours when you have attained your goal?* What will you do with the money or with your new self-confidence? What will the results mean to you?

Step 3. *Begin to see yourself as already possessing these benefits.* Picture yourself as having achieved the goal. Does it feel comfortable? Do you really want that goal?

Step 4. *List obstacles in your way.* Why don't you already have the benefits? What are the reasons you have not already attained your goal?

Step 5. *How will you overcome the obstacles that are in your path?* It can be done and you will do it, but you must have a plan.

Step 6. *What is the first move that will now make toward attaining your goal?* Is there any reason not to begin now?

Step 7. *Review your progress every day or as often as possible.* Use your progress to motivate yourself to continue.

SUCCESS FROM FAILURE

Failure to meet a goal need not bring only disappointment and frustration. Sometimes success evolves out of failure as we analyze shortcomings in our original plans and strive to correct past mistakes. Some ideas to redirect failures toward future success are:

❑ Study written goals to determine which ones you still want to achieve.

❑ Make it a habit to review your goals daily and write down ideas that come to mind as you review.

❑ Concentrate on what you want and ignore peripheral issues.

❑ Research new ideas and methods as they relate to your goals.

❑ Use a mental exercise to picture yourself attaining your goal. Think through the steps that helped you reach the objective.

❑ Surround yourself with positive people who are also working toward their goals.

❏ Use self-suggestion in the form of motivational quotations or slogans when you feel discouraged about your goals.

❏ Seek knowledge from others and be willing to reciprocate by sharing your experiences.

❏ Determine daily what one activity will propel you toward your goal and assign it a high priority.

❏ Never postpone fulfilling objectives to reach a goal. Whenever possible, take action now, not later.

MANAGEMENT BY OBJECTIVE

When goal setting reaches the corporate level, it becomes a systematized management technique. Most companies use some form of management by objective or MBO because it has proved to be a valuable resource for companies, just as goal setting is valuable on a personal level.

Management by objective is simultaneous goal setting between supervisor and subordinate. By agreeing on a set of objectives for the employee, department, or division, the company has a built-in guide to measure performance. For example, if a sales manager decides on an objective that states that her group will exceed the previous year's quotas for the last quarter with no additional sales force, the company will be able to measure performance by that standard once the final figures become available.

MBO makes certain assumptions about people:

People possess higher needs. People are not content to go to work every morning, earn a paycheck, and go home. Most people want to feel that they are working at a job that has worth and are making a significant contribution to the overall success of the venture.

People want to satisfy these higher needs through work. They will work harder when they know they are working toward a goal. They will accept responsibility for productivity and quality if they understand how their job fits into the larger picture of the corporation.

People have the ability to increase knowledge about a job and correct their behavior to achieve a goal when they know what is expected of them. MBO fosters a sense of teamwork and cooperation between supervisors and subordinates.

MBO is a cycle. The supervisor first helps subordinates develop and write objectives. The subordinate sets goals based on the direction from the supervisor. The supervisor then modifies the written goals and the two reach an agreement on the objectives. As the subordinate works toward the objective, the supervisor periodically checks on the progress using informal methods. At the agreed-upon time, the subordinate reports on the accomplished work and the cycle begins again.

Benefits of MBO

Effective MBO includes eight characteristics that make it an effective tool for supervisors.

1. *Specific measures.* Because objectives incorporate measurable quantities of time or performance, MBO allows managers to evaluate results based on agreed-upon standards. If an objective states that Division A will exceed sales quotas for the same quarters last year by 10 percent, then MBO allows the sales staff and the sales manager to gauge performance on that basis.

2. *Results orientation.* MBO concerns itself with the bottom line. Each objective states a task or a step toward an overall goal in a way that allows comparison as steps are completed.

3. *Role clarity.* MBO allows all parties to distinguish assignments within a group. The objective defines not only what you are responsible for but also what others must achieve to complete the objective as it is written.

4. *Adaptability.* MBO defines the work that must be accomplished to reach a goal. If at some time during the course of completing an objective, an employee or a supervisor realizes that the objective is unrealistic in light of new developments, the objective may be redefined. In some cases, an economic boom may make last year's quotas artificially low. By monitoring an objective, the plan can be modified to fit the latest data available.

5. *Feedback and communication.* One of the greatest advantages of MBO is that it serves as a built-in forum for managers and employees. At specified times, the two parties will come together to evaluate objectives: Did we accomplish what we set out to do? Why or why not? Did the objective fulfill the need of advancing us toward the overall goal? Why or why not? At these formal sessions and even during less formal sessions between evaluations, both parties have an opportunity to grade themselves and each other on performance and effectiveness.

6. *Participation.* From the time objectives are written to the final evaluation, MBO is a participatory process. Arriving at the objective requires a consensus from those involved; meeting the

objective requires a commitment from the group, and analyzing the objective's effectiveness demands that participants confer with each other. MBO integrates the wide variety of human resources available in a company and reassures supervisors that they do not have to reach the firm's goals by themselves.

7. *Upward perspective.* With participation comes an understanding of how each unit or employee fits into the overall picture of the company's work. Employees can find greater meaning in routine tasks if they realize that their job is vital to achieving an improved safety record for the plant or higher visibility and more growth for their installation.

8. *Top management support.* The upward perspective has a reciprocal side. When top management perceives a team effort on the part of employees, the result is a system of positive rewards due to higher productivity.

Drawbacks of MBO

Before embarking on an MBO system, supervisors should realize that every management tool has a negative side. People are *resistant to change* and instituting a new system of setting goals, writing objectives, and monitoring progress may threaten employees who are accustomed to a different way of doing business. Some of the obstacles employees may raise include

Distrust of the system. Just as setting personal goals for the first time may seem uncomfortable, employees may have doubts about determining objectives. The process may seem time consuming until they realize that planning actually saves time later.

Resentment. Employees may think that management is using MBO for other purposes, such as cutting back jobs or streamlining operations. Anything that may expose lack of productivity may carry the threat of job elimination. Employees need reassurance that MBO is a good-faith effort toward higher productivity which could lead to increased rewards.

Ego problems. Some mid-managers and white collar workers may think that their jobs defy measurement. They may see objectives as an attempt to decrease the importance of a job by giving it quantitative measurements. Although a supervisor may be sensitive to people who rebel at anything that compartmentalizes them, effective MBO stresses the need to involve the entire firm.

Limitations. Putting objectives into concise, written form may seem to limit performance by overly defining the work to be done. This objection can be overcome by stressing that although management has a high commitment to achieving the objectives, MBO involves adaptability and flexibility.

Writing Objectives for MBO

As with the personal and professional objectives outlined earlier in the chapter, MBO brings a checklist for effective implementation. To begin writing objectives, start with a goal and then decide what has to be achieved and when it must be done to accomplish the goal.

Objectives help define areas of responsibility. Review job descriptions to determine where the objective will best be assigned. The objective may involve a number of people or only one employee. While you may have distinct ideas about the necessary objectives, effective MBO involves participation. Establish objectives and discuss and agree on them. Determine accomplishments and times for performance review.

Focus on both types of statements: quantitative and qualitative (Table 6-1). *Quantitative* statements reveal how much improvement is expected, how much sales will increase, or how large a firm will grow. Quantities are generally expressed as statements of a number or percentage that can be readily calculated. *Qualitative* statements define how well an activity will be completed, how aspects of production can improve, or how workers can improve knowledge of the job. Qualitative statements may include a target date (for example, when certain employees will have completed a training sequence), but the ideas are more difficult to measure in terms of quantity (see Exercises 6-2 and 6-3).

MBO emphasizes visibility for both manager and employee; commitment to MBO provides a way to measure success. Accomplishment, in turn, builds confidence.

Table 6-1   The Differences between Quantitative and Qualitative Goals

QUANTITATIVE GOALS	QUALITATIVE GOALS
1. How much improvement is expected	1. How an activity will be completed
2. How much sales will increase	2. How aspects of production can improve
3. How large a firm will grow	3. How workers can improve their knowledge of the job
4. Expressed in number or percentage	4. More difficult to measure in terms of quantity

CHECKLIST FOR EFFECTIVE OBJECTIVES
WITHIN MBO

- ❑ Is it concise and well written?
- ❑ Does it include a target date for completion?
- ❑ Can it be defined in terms of results?
- ❑ Does it take current resources into consideration?
- ❑ Can it be reviewed?
- ❑ Does it provide milestones of achievement?
- ❑ Does the statement have accountability assignment to management?

CONCLUSION

Goals can mean success personally, professionally, or for an entire corporation through MBO. Goals help achieve power and, with practice, will expand the range of possibilities for you and your company. Experienced goal setters set better goals. Goals can be induced from overall performance, and weak points from past objectives can be reviewed. Goals may be a trade-off in which a short-term idea is sacrificed for long-term success.

As you become more comfortable in setting goals, you can determine what makes you happy, what motivates you, and what pushes you beyond your current situation. Every time you review goals, use the results as a starting place for new goals. Concentrate on what is really important so that you can visualize your goals. If you can see it, you can achieve it.

SUMMARY

Knowing where you want to go is the starting point for setting goals. Without goals, you neither know what direction to take nor know how to measure your progress along the way. Experience, interviews, and articles can all help you narrow your goals. Most people are motivated by either achievement, power, or competency. By understanding these needs, you can focus on the things that will give you satisfaction in life. Goals should be written, specific, and measurable in order to be effective. Under each goal, you can include objectives or action plans to describe how you plan to meet the goal. On a corporate level, this is called management by objective (MBO). This can be an effective way of directing a group's work and evaluating its effectiveness.

TERMS AND CONCEPTS

goal	qualitative goals
management by objective (MBO)	quantitative goals
objective	values

REVIEW QUESTIONS

1. What values influence a person's goals?
2. What are the three basic areas when dividing personal goals?
3. What are some qualities of a well-written objective?
4. How often should you reevaluate objectives?
5. Who must agree on goals for effective MBO?
6. What are some benefits of effective MBO?
7. How can management overcome obstacles to MBO?

EXERCISES

6-1: GOAL SETTING

GOAL	SOLUTIONS	TIME FRAME
1.		
2.		
3.		
4.		
5.		

6-2: TARGETING QUANTITATIVE AND QUALITATIVE PROFESSIONAL GOALS

Instructions: Write five specific, comprehensive quantitative and qualitative professional goals with target dates for each.

QUANTITATIVE GOALS—HOW MUCH IMPROVEMENT

examples: increase_____% by_____% by_____

decrease_____% by_____% by_____

SPECIFIC GOAL   TARGET DATE

1.

2.

3.

4.

5.

QUALITATIVE GOALS—HOW WELL THE EMPLOYEE HAS DONE

example: write procedures manual, complete report on_____

SPECIFIC GOAL   .   TARGET DATE

1.

2.

3.

4.

5.

Integrate your professional goals with those of your boss, department, and organization.

6-3: INTEGRATING PERSONAL AND PROFESSIONAL GOALS

Instructions: Write at least three specific, comprehensive, and measurable goals for each area with target dates. Be specific, e.g., 3 months, 6 months, 1 year, 2 years, 5 years.

PROFESSIONAL	TARGET DATE
1.	
2.	
3.	

PERSONAL	TARGET DATE
Financial (salary, earnings, investments, assets)	
1.	
2.	
3.	
Residential (buy, sell, expand, move)	
1.	
2.	
3.	
Physical	
1.	
2.	
3.	
Educational	
1.	
2.	
3.	
Recreational (trip, hobby)	
1.	
2.	
3.	

SUGGESTED READINGS

Blanchard, K., and Johnson, S. *The One Minute Manager.* Berkley Books, New York, 1981.

Donnelly, J. H., Jr., Gibson, J. L., and Ivancevich, J. M. *Fundamentals of Management* (5th ed.). Business Publications, Dallas, TX, 1984.

Fink, S. *Crisis Management.* AMACOM, New York, 1986.

Garfield, C. A., with Bennett, H. Z. *Peak Performance.* Warner Books, New York, 1984.

Gup, B. E. *Guide to Strategic Planning.* McGraw-Hill, New York, 1980.

Hopkins, T. *The Official Guide to Success.* Warner Books, New York, 1982.

Kassorla, I. C. *Go For It!* Dell Books, New York, 1984.

Kossen, S. *Human Side of Organizations* (4th ed.). Harper & Row, New York, 1987.

Lee, N. *Targeting the Top.* Ballantine Books, New York, 1980.

Noe, J. R. *Peak Performance Principles for High Achievers.* Berkley Books, New York, 1985.

Sitterly, C. *Learning Guide for Kossen's Human Side of Organizations* (4th ed.). Harper & Row, New York, 1987.

Suters, E. T. *Succeed in Spite of Yourself.* Hawthorn Books, New York (no date).

Tregoe, B. B., and Zimmerman, J. W. *Top Management Strategy.* Simon & Schuster, New York, 1980.

7

SUCCESS THROUGH ASSERTION

OBJECTIVES

- Understand basic assumptions about assertiveness
- Contrast assertiveness, nonassertiveness, and aggressiveness
- List women's assertive rights and responsibilities
- Deal with male chauvinism
- Contrast assertive, nonassertive, and aggressive body language
- Apply assertive techniques

ASSERTIVENESS

Assertiveness is standing up for your rights in honest, direct, appropriate ways that do not violate another person's rights. Assertiveness contrasts with behavior we describe as *aggressive* in that aggressive behavior rarely takes the other person's rights into account. Aggressive behavior steamrolls over the other person, forcing a certain outcome without asking anyone else's opinion or permission. Assertive behavior also contrasts with nonassertive behavior.

Nonassertiveness is allowing your rights to be violated by failing to express your feelings. In this reactive type of behavior, you submit to another person's needs or wants at the expense of your own.

During the late 1960s and early 1970s, assertiveness became trendy, as women sought to stand up for themselves in positive, confident ways. Books such as *When I Say No, I Feel Guilty* (Smith, 1975) topped the bestseller lists as women tried to learn how to develop an assertive personality.

Assertiveness is more desirable than either aggressiveness or nonassertiveness. In aggressive behavior, one person is the aggressor and one person is the victim. In nonassertive behavior, one person dominates and the other person is left in a no-win situation. In assertive behavior, both people can retain a win-win attitude because even if they do not agree, they can both emerge from the exchange with their rights intact.

The issue of assertiveness has now come full circle from consciousness-raising groups to management training for women. To function effectively in the business world, women managers need to identify assertive and nonassertive behaviors and responses and learn to implement assertive behavior when appropriate to gain the desired results.

Fundamentals of Assertiveness

Assertiveness is based on two fundamental assumptions:

1. You will more likely obtain what you desire by letting others know clearly what you think, feel, or want.
2. You will more likely establish climates of cooperation rather than confrontation by respecting the rights, needs, and priorities of others.

Although the first assumption may seem too basic for inclusion in a text for aspiring managers, women must realize that no one is capable of reading their minds. From our personal to our professional lives, many disappointments stem the false expectation that someone we love or have known a long time will intuitively know our desires.

For example, a common complaint from women in entry-level jobs is that they were not considered for a promotion. Before passing judgment on archaic promotional or hiring policies, ask the employee if she ever told anyone that she wanted to be considered for the job.

Although few women expect an employer to make them an unsolicited job offer, many women think nothing of expecting a supervisor to read their minds on the matter of promotions within the company.

The second assumption follows as a corollary. Building a climate of effective management often means stemming confrontation by building alliances and teams to foster cooperation. Assertive techniques have sometimes been grouped with aggressive behavior. Aggressive behavior is expressing feelings or stating wants in a manner that is often dishonest, inappropriate, domineering, overbearing, or belittling. Assertive behavior, on the other hand, works to establish the rights not only of the speaker but of the audience as well, whether the audience is one person or a group of people.

At its best, assertiveness training will enhance your professional and personal relationships by teaching you how to express ideas, feelings, and needs in a manner that is both personally satisfying and socially effective in preventing or solving problems.

A WOMAN'S BILL OF RIGHTS

Too often women have been conditioned to defer to the feelings of others at their own expense. The different responses to a report with several mistakes in accuracy clearly reveal the differences between an assertive and a nonassertive manager.

Assertive response: This will have to be retyped.

Nonassertive response: "Oh, that's all right" (even though it clearly is not), or "I should have made my directions clearer" (the speaker wrongly assumes blame), or even worse, "Let me give it a try" (taking back responsibility once it has been delegated).

First and foremost among assertive rights are:

1. *The right to your own feelings and emotions.* Other people may dispute the facts of or the causes behind a situation, but not how you feel. If you resent the way a co-worker handled one of your clients in your absence, admit your true feelings even if you cannot pinpoint what was wrong. All other assertive rights reinforce this basic rule. Having grown up in the context of someone's daughter, someone's wife, or someone's mother, women often do not develop their own identities. If you are intelligent enough to seek a career as a manager, you are intelligent enough to assimilate information and form your own opinions about issues and decisions. Your ideas are worthwhile, too.

2. *The right to express your feelings.* This may mean agreeing, disagreeing, or admitting that you do not know. All of these responses are perfectly acceptable within the bounds of assertive behavior as long as the response reflects your feelings. In the context of a board meeting, your superior would rather have an honest "I don't know" than a rubber-stamp "Yes" which is unsupported by research or thought. To express your feelings, you must first be in touch with yourself; you can then communicate your feelings to others. Expand your vocabulary so that you can express your feelings precisely rather than speaking in vague generalities.

3. *The right to change your mind.* A common stereotype is that of the woman who changes her mind several times over a trivial issue. Changing your mind has a negative connotation; however, flexibility can be turned into a management strength. Most colleagues have greater respect for the manager who can change her mind and even admit to making a mistake rather than stubbornly clinging to incorrect plans or data only to see a project fail. If you change your mind, avoid the temptation to overexplain your reasons or overelaborate on your position. Listeners may misinterpret your explanation and think you are still trying to convince yourself instead of your audience.

4. *The right to be heard.* Learning to accept and express your feelings may be a moot point if no one hears you. The right to be heard carries assertive training into the arena of the speaker as well as the audience, since communication must involve both. Remember the frustration you felt in school when you knew the answer and held up your hand only to have the teacher call on someone else whose hand caught her attention?

Your goal as a manager must be to make your point

well heard as well as soundly grounded in your research. Do not get caught up in put-downs from managers who possess chauvinistic opinions. *Chauvinism* is a form of prejudice that unfairly stereotypes certain groups of people because of their sex. It is closely linked to sexism, that is, treating people differently because of their sex. Sexism leads to a double standard in communication. For example, some men talk down to women, treating them as if they were children or somehow less intelligent. "Don't worry your pretty little head about this" and "I'll take care of this for you" are statements that patronize female colleagues.

One way to describe these phrases is the *little lady syndrome*. This is a reaction that discounts or discredits the contribution or potential worth of a woman based on the belief that women are inferior because of their sex. If you feel you are being patronized, summon up a firm tone of voice and interject, "My research shows" or "This is a good time to add" to let the speaker know you mean business and are equally serious about your work. If you feel you are being consciously cut out of a conversation, gently but firmly interrupt and make your point.

5. *The right to choose nonassertive behavior when you feel it is more appropriate.* After leaving a seminar on assertive training, many students think they must apply the techniques they learned to every situation. Not every business situation calls for a 100 percent assertive solution. Sometimes you will want to bide your time and wait for a more opportune moment. For example, if you are not given the opportunity to respond in a meeting, you may decide that a nonassertive response serves your purpose better than an assertive reaction. Rather than interrupting the flow of the meeting or distracting superiors and causing them to lose face, you may decide to follow up with a memo outlining an omitted point or you may privately ask to be placed first on the agenda for the next meeting to ensure that you can speak. If you always make your points in public, you will get your message across, but an embarrassed superior may never forgive you.

6. *The right to say, "No." Saying "No" is an art because most people want approval from their listeners.* They may want you to agree with their point of view or agree to do a job. Whatever their motive, you must remember that you always have the right to disagree or turn down an offer. There is an art to saying "no" so that the listener knows you mean it. If

the listener thinks a "no" answer means maybe, the listener will try that much harder to change your mind. If you plan to say "no," use a steady, unwavering tone of voice. Maintain eye contact instead of looking down or away. Be polite, yet firm. Repeat your negative reply if the listener begins to argue or debate. Explain your answer with a specific reason if you want to, but realize that you do not have to explain a negative answer any more than you have to explain a positive one. If you can think of a compromise, offer it as a possibility. Stay away from word traps such as "I'd like to but," which give the listener ammunition to change your decision. If you feel that you are wavering, ask the speaker for time to think over the proposal rather than changing your "no" to a "yes," a change you may later regret. Then you can privately weigh the pros and cons of the issue without the pressure of making an immediate decision.

7. *The right to be treated with respect.* The key to developing responsible assertive behavior is realizing and accepting the right to be treated with respect. If you treat subordinates and superiors with respect for their individuality, they will get the message that you intend to be treated in a similar way. You may not be able to change their behavior overnight, but your example will be reflected in the way people treat you.

Many people do not feel they have any rights or, if they do, they do not stand up for their rights. Whichever right you invoke, you will be building self-confidence and self-esteem, which translate into effective managerial performance.

RESPONSIBILITIES

No passage on rights is ever complete without a discussion of the accompanying responsibilities. Most of the responsibilities of assertive behavior draw their strength from common sense. The world of business etiquette is generally grounded in corporate logic.

As long as you think before you speak, your assertiveness will be effective. Many new managers rehearse a brilliant response before a meeting only to find that a more assertive co-worker jumps into the discussion and makes her point first. With practice, that assertive manager will be you.

All companies have codes of behavior. The best way to learn is by watching and listening to veteran co-workers. Take your cues from them. Do not be hampered by their nonassertive conventions, but rather build on their actions as role models to develop your own style.

To help develop your responses, here are a few guidelines:

Do your homework. For any issue that seems unfamiliar, gather all the information you can find. Ask questions of other workers, investigate books at the public library, and read newspapers and business publications to discover how other companies are approaching the problem. Research enables you to feel confident your conclusions are sound. If you have faith in your reasoning, you will be better equipped to speak assertively.

Know policies and procedures. Do not embarrass yourself or your boss by proposing an agenda item that is taboo for the company or one that has been tried and recently discarded for lack of results. Ask a trusted company veteran if you are unsure. Look before jumping into uncharted waters when the stakes are high.

Act in a manner worthy of respect. Your business image and mannerisms will be under fire when you begin to act assertively. By being prepared for some raised eyebrows, you can ward off unnecessary criticism by letting people know that you are a businesswoman and expect to be treated as such. Never confuse assertive behavior with rude behavior. Your superiors deserve your respect as long as you are working for them.

MALE CHAUVINISM

One of the greatest obstacles career women face is dealing with male chauvinists who constantly try to put women down or who use patronizing techniques that imply a condescending attitude. Calling adult women "girl," using nicknames for women such as sweetie, or honey, or shortening names such as Dorothy to Dot are all ways of keeping women on a subservient level.

The best way to deal with male chauvinism is to understand it. Many men feel threatened by changes in the traditional way of doing business. Men may have been brought up to think of families in which a man worked as the sole breadwinner and the woman functioned primarily as a homemaker and mother as the norm. Eventually women's on-the-job competence and performance will be the best argument against chauvinism.

Meanwhile, to overcome this obstacle, a businesswoman must

Avoid becoming bitter or defensive. Defensiveness indicates to the chauvinist that his behavior is affecting you and that you are vulnerable to his remarks. Strongly, but firmly, correct any misstatements of your feelings or the facts as you see them. Keep the tone of the conversation rational and cool to avoid digressing into an argument that will change no one's mind.

Keep an open mind. With practice, you can tell which remarks are openly chauvinistic and which are merely figures of speech. For example, people on the East Coast say "You guys" and people in the South say "y'all" as a way of expressing the plural you. Both expressions are genderless figures of speech and should not be taken as put-downs.

Use good judgment. In some cases you need to confront the chauvinist head-on, in other cases, you should wait for privacy, and in still others you should drop the matter completely. Many career choices are trade-offs. If you need to postpone a confrontation in order to achieve a career goal, realize that the overall goal is more important than a passing conversation.

Do not encourage chauvinistic behavior. Always conduct yourself professionally. Do not allow subordinates to use sexist language and do not tolerate sexism in written reports, company policies, or other portions of work over which you have control. If you can deal with the situation directly, try to do so in an appropriate manner before the conversation or remark is forgotten. Making a point of correcting a sexist remark weeks after it was said detracts from the corrective action.

IDENTIFYING ASSERTIVE BEHAVIOR

Assertiveness has a confusing reputation. Many people believe that if they assert themselves, they will hurt someone's feelings, show disrespect, anger someone, or damage a relationship. These are myths that more accurately describe aggressive behavior than assertive behavior, which respects the rights of others.

Assertiveness is a style of communication that is simple, honest, sincere, and direct. Assertive responses can lead to improved relationships because you can be seen as more effective and respected. Patricia Jakubowski and Arthur Lang (1976), assertive trainers, define three response styles that fit most situations: *assertive, nonassertive,* and *aggressive* (Table 7-1).

THE ASSERTIVE STYLE

Words alone do not create an assertive style. As with any response, volume, tone, posture, and eye contact are important.

Table 7-1   Comparison: Assertiveness, Nonassertiveness, Aggressiveness

ASSERTIVENESS	NONASSERTIVENESS	AGGRESSIVENESS
1. Open, honest, sincere	1. Submits, fails to express feelings	1. Invades, overbearing
2. Stands up to anxiety		2. Pushy, inappropriate
3. Share without blame or put-downs	2. Avoids confrontation, appeases	3. Blames
		4. Accuses
4. Expressing affection and appreciation	3. Sacrifices own desires	5. Threatens
	4. Pushovers	
5. Focusing on the real issue	5. Taken for granted	
6. Confident, frank, respected, visible, promotable	6. Passive, afraid to take risks	

Even your style of dress can contribute to assertiveness. If you are wearing a professional style of tailored clothing that is flattering, you are more likely to be assertive than if you are dressed too casually for the situation. However, most women first need to work on the spoken word; the other characteristics will follow with practice.

An assertive manager can be described by adjectives such as confident, respected, frank, visible, and, best of all, promotable. Achieving this style involves

1. Expressing yourself in an open, honest, and sincere manner
2. Standing up for your rights without anxiety and without violating the other person's rights
3. Letting others know how you feel without making them feel they are to blame
4. Sharing what you would like to have happen without voicing blame, put-downs, or guilt trips
5. Stating what you will give and what you expect to get
6. Expressing affection and appreciation
7. Focusing on the real issue without being sidetracked, even by insulting or annoying remarks

Situations in the Assertive Style

If you are making a presentation and someone interrupts with a statement that is unrelated to the business at hand, the assertive response would be, "Excuse me, but I would like to complete my presentation before moving to the next item for discussion."

Your boss comes to your desk at 4:50 PM with a project that must be completed today. The assertive response would be, "I have a commitment at 5:30 today that I must meet. We could have worked something out in advance if you needed me to stay late today."

NONASSERTIVENESS

Perhaps no other behavior in women managers causes as much frustration and resentment as nonassertive or passive behavior. In this response, the nonassertive person is likely to feel taken advantage of or taken for granted, largely because of the individual's inability to stand up for her rights. People who say, "How could I let them talk me into this?" or "If only I could have told them how I really felt about my project assignment" have fallen into the trap of nonassertive behavior. Nonassertive behavior takes the feelings expressed in assertive behavior and projects them internally instead of externally where they could be resolved.

Nonassertive people want to avoid confrontation at any price. They may fear that people will not like them or approve of them if they make their true emotions or feelings known. They willingly sacrifice their own desires in order to resolve potential conflict. They are generally seen as pushovers during negotiations and rarely stand a chance if they are communicating with an aggressive person.

One manifestation of nonassertive behavior is the *dancing-in-place syndrome*. In this syndrome, an employee is stuck—neither moving forward nor backward. No matter what the employee does, her career is on hold year after year. People with this syndrome wait to be recognized or assume someone will offer them a promotion or raise without their asking for it.

In an extreme case, Joan joined a firm shortly after finishing college. She wanted to move ahead, but she encountered an obstacle every time she tried to better herself. If she asked to be considered for a promotion, she was told she needed to go back to school. When she went back to school, she was told to wait for her next performance evaluation and so on. Finally Joan realized she had been on the job for 18 years without any hope of advancement. Alternatives to the dancing-in-place syndrome are to identify your career goal and decide if you can achieve it in your present situation. If you discover obstacles which are likely to remain in your way, you may have to seek a lateral transfer within the company or move to a different company. Remember, there is no such thing as a well-adjusted slave.

THE NONASSERTIVE STYLE

Once again these descriptions need to be considered in the total context of communication. Looking downward or hiding behind crossed arms will not do much to reinforce any assertive words. As a starting point, however, verbal responses point out weaknesses in the nonassertive style. Clues to this style include

1. Passively submitting to others' wants or needs at your own expense
2. Allowing your boundaries to be restricted or violated
3. Failing to express honest feelings, thoughts or beliefs at appropriate times
4. Being afraid to take risks and concealing desires and preferences

The nonassertive manager exudes an attitude of "My feelings don't count," or "You are more important than I am," or "I'm content to put myself and my feelings in last place."

Identifying the Nonassertive Style

Nonassertive individuals are usually shy and timid and either do what is expected of them or constantly ask permission. The *get-permission syndrome* involves always seeking permission to do something or even to have an opinion. Some people ask for permission, but others seek it in subtle ways such as inquiring by using eye contact or using words to evoke a positive response. Cue words for these responses are maybe, I guess, I can't, and I think. A common speech pattern among women is to always end a declarative sentence with an upward intonation that makes the statement seem like a question, somehow seeking the listener's approval.

Body language such as tapping feet and fingers, darting eyes, and slumped or stooped posture can also be clues.

Situations in a Nonassertive Style

You have earned a promotion with additional responsibilities and authority. Former peers, whom you now supervise, balk at taking your orders. You do nothing, and hope they will change.

You have been doing your job exceptionally well and you have been expecting a salary increase. When you discuss it with your boss, you hear, "The company cannot afford the raise right now. Wait 6 months and ask me again." You say, "Fine, I'll check with you then," and leave dissatisfied.

AGGRESSIVENESS

Few women managers want to be described as aggressive. While applying the adjective to a man is a compliment, a double standard still views aggressiveness as negative for women. Aggressive, when used to describe a woman's behavior, almost always seems threatening. Mental pictures of disagreeable or radical women somehow come to mind. The woman manager must meet this negative connotation head-on in order to perform her duties effectively without being relegated to a passive stance.

THE AGGRESSIVE STYLE

It is no coincidence that the thesaurus lists words such as fighter as synonymous with aggressive. Think of a boxer's stance and you will have a general idea of the nonverbal description of aggressive behavior.

The trademarks of aggressive communication are that

1. It invades other's boundaries in a threatening way.
2. It expresses feelings or beliefs in a way that is often dishonest, inappropriate, overbearing, or pushy.
3. It does not consider the ramifications and negative after-effects of communication.
4. It places blame or accuses others.

Situations in an Aggressive Style

You are coordinating a project with another person, but you find that you are doing all the work. You say, "You're not doing your share. If I don't get some cooperation, I'm going to the boss."

You make a call to another company and a secretary answers, "Who may I say is calling?" You become irritated and say, "It shouldn't make any difference who's calling. I need to talk to your superior."

BODY LANGUAGE

Body language for the three styles contrasts sharply. These qualities are signals of the nonverbal language expressed by each style listed in the following table:

NONASSERTIVE	ASSERTIVE	AGGRESSIVE
Darting eyes	Strong eye contact	Cold, icy stare
Slumped posture	Body erect	Hands on hips
Shifting weight	Feet firmly planted	Tense posture
Hands cover mouth	Natural gestures for emphasis	Finger pointing or clenched fists

You Have a Choice: Communication Response Styles

You have a choice in how you respond and how your responses influence the way you feel about yourself. Your feelings of self-esteem and self-worth all combine to make you a more effective communicator and therefore a more effective manager.

Assertive behavior is achieved by *behavior modeling,* that is, changing your actions through understanding and applying a set of skills. The overall goal of assertiveness is to enhance your self-image, self-confidence, and self-respect, and to increase your effectiveness in professional and social situations. Assertive behavior can also maximize an individual's contribution to an organization.

ASSERTIVE TECHNIQUES

To assert yourself, be straightforward and goal oriented. Know what you want and what you are willing to offer before you speak. Speak directly and clearly and maintain a clear sense of command. Try to keep to the subject and do not react to side issues that may divert your attention from your goal. Acknowledge any negative feelings that may arise and agree or disagree as you react.

Identify areas for possible negotiation in advance. If you are willing to concede a certain point in order to gain something else, state the alternative proposal. Do not accept exploitation, patronization, or put-downs. Repeat your request until you get a straight answer.

Management experts have identified some key techniques to help develop an assertive style.

Simple Assertion: State a simple need in a declarative or imperative sentence. In simple assertion, you are stating facts in a firm, matter-of-fact tone.

Example: "Please shut the door." "I need a copy of that report."

Empathetic Assertion: Acknowledge the listener's feelings and, at the same time, be assertive. Key points to remember here are that you do not want to assign blame or guilt. Using "I" statements that convey objectivity, rather than "you" statements that point an accusing finger, help get the point across. In this statement empathy is balanced with assertion so you achieve the desired results.
Example: "I know you have been busy, but the report must be finished by tomorrow."

Confrontative Assertion: Resolve a problem by pointing out an agreed upon set of circumstances; explain a specific discrepancy; and ask for a response that commits the listener to future action. In this exchange, the speaker confronts behavior and sets up a verbal contract to remedy the problem.
Example: "I thought we agreed that since we were both assigned to this project you would handle the data processing division. Now they are calling me and asking me for directions. What are we going to do about this?"

Soft Assertion: Express affection or sympathy using your own feelings as a basis for communication. As with all assertion, the speaker focuses on her own emotions rather than those of the listener. This kind of assertion may be helpful in facilitating a conversation with an employee or co-worker in a nonthreatening way.
Example: "As your supervisor, I want you to know that I am concerned about you."

Angry Assertion: Express anger without placing blame or being aggressive. This differs from the aggressive response because the speaker makes the complaint specific and clearly explains the situation that led to the anger rather than simply venting hostility and placing blame.
Example: "I feel angry when you miss a departmental deadline (specific cause) because it reflects poorly on the effectiveness of our section (explaining reasoning). Please meet these deadlines in the future."

Negative Assertion: Admit a mistake without becoming defensive or accepting guilt. Nonassertive behavior is always making apologies and saying "I'm sorry" without regard to where the blame really lies. Negative assertion admits that an error has occurred but does not automatically assume guilt or apologize for what may have been an unavoidable error.

Example: "I agree I made an error on the final report draft. I will double my proofreading efforts next time."

Assertive Disengagement: Postpone a discussion that would be more effectively held later. A new idea or a new problem may be too complex to discuss without further investigation. If you need time to devise a strategy or to develop an assertive approach, try to reschedule the discussion to give you time to prepare.

Example: "I have to return an important phone call right now. Could we talk about this tomorrow when I can give it my total attention?"

Fogging: Avoid taking unjust criticism while agreeing in part with the speaker. Fogging works because you diffuse potential arguments that develop when you disagree with everything the speaker says. By selecting which statements to agree with and which to disagree with, you retain control of the communication and allow yourself time to interject your own feelings and emotions.

Example: Speaker: "You must not really care about getting ahead if you do not want to volunteer for this committee chairmanship." You: "Yes, I can see how you might think that I do not want added responsibility, but the fact is that I am committed to serving on another committee that I feel will be more advantageous to my long-term career goals."

Negative Inquiry: Ask for a more specific criticism to clarify an objective. In confrontational situations, it is easier to generalize than to be specific. If you can encourage the speaker to be specific, even though you may not want to hear the criticism, you can use assertive techniques to address specific objections. Specific criticism helps put negative statements on the work where they belong instead of on the person who did the work.

Example: Someone says, "Your work lacks direction." You say, "What is it exactly about my finished product that gives you that idea?"

Broken Record: Repeat the statement to add emphasis. If you think that you are being ignored, try to restate your idea until you get a response.

Example: "I have to leave today promptly at 5:00 to catch a plane." A few moments later, "I must leave today at 5:00 to catch my plane at 6."

Ways to Become More Assertive

To the management student, the techniques may seem too pat and too scripted for real life on-the-job situations. However, practice can allow you to mesh the techniques with your own personal style, thereby comfortably blending assertive behavior and your personality.

Here are some tips you can use to help you become an assertive manager:

Take risks. When you are tempted to be nonassertive or passive, try to think of an assertive alternative and use the opportunity to practice your techniques.

Assume responsibility for your actions and add to your responsibilities when possible. Assertive behavior indicates that you want to be treated as an equal adult who bears responsibility for her decisions. Assertiveness can also help you add responsibility as you look toward future promotions.

Identify things that bother you. Once you identify areas in which you feel you have been taken advantage of, or taken for granted, you can develop strategies to determine how you feel about the situation and what you intend to do about it.

Set limits on what is expected from you. Do not try to be a superwoman through assertiveness. Part of asserting yourself is being realistic and not taking on more than you can do well. If you are getting more work, assert your right to have extra help or extra money commensurate with your duties.

Identify communication responses in others. Analyzing how others communicate can help you see which styles are effective and which are ineffective in different situations. By identifying techniques in others, you will be better able to adapt your own behavior to deal with their style.

Encourage subordinates to be assertive. Allowing subordinates to express feelings and opinions can overcome an underlying sense of resentment in them. Once you know how they feel, you may not always agree with them, but at least you will be able to understand their position.

Use the word "I" instead of "you" whenever you can to diffuse feelings of blame. If you say you feel a certain way because of another person's behavior, no one can deny you your emotions. If you cast blame or guilt, the other person immediately becomes defensive and erects barriers to communication.

Once we act rather than constantly reacting to a situation, we will gain a sense of control over our communication. If you feel you are being manipulated by others, ask yourself these questions:

- ❑ Have I handled this situation before?
- ❑ Was I pleased or displeased with the outcome?
- ❑ Do I really want to do this? Why or why not?
- ❑ What will happen if I say no? If I say yes?
- ❑ What are my options in this situation?

By answering some or all of these questions, you will soon discover your true feelings. Then act on these feelings, remembering that you have a right to them and no one can take them away from you.

CONCLUSION

While assertiveness is, overall, the most effective response style, it may not be the best style in every situation. Observe and identify the responses of others and develop the sensitivity to be aware of how your own behavior impacts on others. Observe yourself and try to judge your own communication style objectively.

Assertiveness will prove to be self-rewarding. It will help you improve communications and relationships and will satisfy needs. It is an ongoing process that will enable you to have more choices, more independence, more strength, and more control over your own life. It will lead to greater self-confidence and then, as the cycle continues, to greater self-assertion.

Both men and women prefer to work with assertive women because these women are willing to take risks, confront issues, and make decisions. Assertiveness gives you a choice in how you respond and the power to decide whether or not you will be influenced. Be firm, and remember people respect strength.

SUMMARY

Assertiveness, aggressiveness, and nonassertiveness are the three main communication styles. Assertiveness is more effective because it takes into account the rights of both the speaker and the listener. Assertive communication is a combination of body language, speech patterns, and words that convey your feelings and emotions as well as what you want and what you are willing to give.

Central to the idea of assertiveness is the right to have and express your own opinions. Techniques that can help you develop assertiveness include fogging, negative assertion, and empathetic assertion. Each has a place in the context of corporate communication.

TERMS AND CONCEPTS

aggressiveness	empathetic assertion
angry assertion	fogging
assertive disengagement	little lady syndrome
assertiveness	male chauvinism
behavior modeling	negative assertion
broken record	negative inquiry
confrontative assertion	nonassertiveness
dancing-in-place syndrome	soft assertion

REVIEW QUESTIONS

1. Compare the three response styles in terms of body language cues.
2. List three techniques of assertiveness and define them with examples.
3. What basic rights are inherent to assertiveness?
4. What is the get-permission syndrome?
5. In what way can changing your mind be a managerial strength?
6. How does aggressiveness differ from angry assertion?
7. What is fogging?
8. Give an actual example of the little lady syndrome and the dancing-in-place syndrome.

SUGGESTED READINGS

Allison, M. A. *Managing Up, Managing Down.* Simon & Schuster, New York, 1984.

Dyer, W. W. *The Sky's the Limit.* Pocket Books, New York, 1980.

Edwards, B. *Assertiveness for Success.* Training by Design, New York, 1983.

Jacobson, A. *Women in Charge.* Van Nostrand Reinhold, New York, 1985.

Lee, N *Targeting the Top.* Ballantine Books, New York, 1980.

MacNeilage, L. A., and Adams, K. A. *Assertiveness at Work. How to Increase Your Personal Power on the Job.* Prentice-Hall, Inc., Englewood Cliffs, NJ, 1982.

Sheehy, G. *Pathfinders.* William Morrow & Co., New York, 1981.

Smith, M. J. *When I Say No, I Feel Guilty.* Bantam Books, New York, 1975.

Viscott, D. *Taking Care of Business.* William Morrow, New York, 1985.

8

POWER
AND
POLITICS

OBJECTIVES

- List qualities that people want in a job
- Describe qualities that powerful people show
- Define power
- Define the types of power
- Develop your power potential
- Take risks
- Evaluate the power potential of your job
- Understand motives for power
- Contrast socially acquired needs
- Integrate competence to improve power

What motivates people to work their way to the top of a corporation? The first response usually given is money or financial reward. However, studies have shown that power is a stronger motivation to succeed than any amount of money.

A 1983 Public Agenda Foundation Study offered these top 10 qualities people want most in a job today:

1. Respect
2. Interesting work
3. Recognition
4. Skill development
5. Ability to have opinions heard
6. Chance for creativity
7. Seeing results of work
8. Efficient managers
9. Challenges
10. Opportunity to be well informed

Security, pay, and benefits were not even on the top 10 list. They ranked within the top 15, but when people responded to their most pressing needs, they put more emphasis on items that gave them a personal feeling of power than on any quality of work to which we regularly assign a dollar value.

Likewise many entrepreneurs when asked why they have risked starting their own business reply that they "wanted to provide a quality product outdistancing the competition" or "they wanted to be their own boss." No matter how they phrase it, the need to control one's own destiny and to make one's own decisions is often at the heart of the American dream.

Would you spend 2 years and millions of dollars trying to get a job that pays $89,500 a year knowing that every 2 years the process would begin again? Each year more than 335 people do; they are members of the United States House of Representatives. Obviously these professionals could command equal or better salaries in the private sector with far more job security. Their quest goes beyond simple job hunting. They invest their efforts to gain a job in the most powerful government in the world.

MANAGEMENT AND POWER

Power is not necessarily synonymous with management and leadership. For example, a person may hold an impressive title but wield no real power, such as a vice president of personnel who must gain approval from the CEO before firing an employee.

Power and management share some characteristics. Both terms connote strength. The test of power is in the results; that is, are orders forgotten or are they carried out as prescribed?

You can be a manager without having power or a leader without having authority. Effective leaders and managers are those who understand power and use it to achieve their goals.

Power is not a commodity that can be given. Rather it is there for the taking. Many smart supervisors have built their own kingdoms while others wait for someone else to give them approval.

CHARACTERISTICS OF POWER

Power is the desire to have impact, to have influence, to effect change, to make things happen, and to choose to change. In short, power is the ability to achieve objectives and get results.

People often do not understand *power;* they see it as a threat rather than as a skill to be acquired to enhance professional effectiveness.

Everyone knows someone they perceive as powerful. Take a minute to identify three powerful people you either know personally or have read about. Think of adjectives you would use to describe these people to a classmate. The description will furnish clues to the qualities powerful people share. Powerful people have

❑ *Visibility.* Are they noticed by others or do their efforts fade into the background?

❑ *Credibility.* Can they get the job done or do their co-workers constantly create alternate plans in case they cannot live up to their promises?

❑ *Influence.* Is cooperation obtained without argument or do they have to fight for every inch of ground they gain?

❑ *Enthusiasm.* Do they operate on a level of high energy or do they always need a pep talk to achieve results?

❑ *Autonomy.* If they get an idea, can they use their own authority to bypass red tape or do they face a bureaucracy while waiting for action?

❑ *Perspective.* Are they more interested in the overall picture or do small details and a need to dominate occupy their thoughts?

Think of the powerful people you identified at the beginning of this exercise. Which of these characteristics come to mind when you think of their lives and careers?

Adjusting to a New Way of Thinking

The lessons of power rarely find their way into formal education. Most business people learn them the hard way, through on-the-job training.

In school, they may have read the Horatio Alger stories in which a youngster worked hard and through luck and pluck became rich and powerful. As part of the "me-generation," young people were encouraged by world events to march for peace and to try, idealistically, to make a difference in the mythical military-industrial complex.

On the job, these same people are astonished when a less qualified applicant receives a promotion or when people say, "It's not what you know, it's who you know."

Today's job market stresses greater productivity with fewer people. In these competitive times, we have to garner the political savvy to make transitions when changes occur and adapt these to our life course.

TYPES OF POWER

Position Power

Position power, also called legitimate power, is the ability to exercise the assigned authority inherent in the job description, title, and specifications.

Position power derives from official job titles and descriptions. It is the legitimate power vested in the manager's position in the organizational hierarchy. The power already exists within the organization—managers may choose to use it or ignore it—but it nonetheless is as real a force in the workplace as any business cycle.

Position power is a logical starting point to discuss types of power because it is the type that is most readily apparent. Position power starts when you accept a job. The job description, whether written or oral, outlines the placement of your job in relation to the work of others in the business.

If you were given a written job description when you were hired, read over it carefully. Highlight those activities in which you are making a significant difference. If significant changes have occurred in your duties, volunteer to rewrite your job description to keep the information in the files current.

If you do not have a written job description, create one that lists your main activities, keeping in mind their relationship to the firm's main goals. If a business does not routinely file job descriptions, ask to see the corporate chart in order to get a broader view of how your work fits into the company.

Look at position power in terms of what you can do, not in terms of your limits. Power is not designed to keep you out; it is a tool that can be used to get results.

Once you have researched the job descriptions of your company, find significant things that will enhance your position. Do not start doing someone else's job, but volunteer for key assignments or ask to revise your own job description based on new duties you have begun to perform.

A sample job description of a division sales director might include the following:

- Provides a liaison between the home office and the district office
- Recruits, trains, and manages five district sales managers
- Updates monthly, quarterly, and annual reports at appropriate intervals
- Reviews and implements sales promotions on a timely basis
- Evaluates divisional progress based on management by objective

The job description above contains both specific and general information about the position. By analyzing the description, you can see that this job fits into the corporate structure between the home office and smaller district units. Although the description gives no clue as to the number of divisions within the company, you can assume that this job would be considered supervisory in nature.

Although the description spells out responsibility for a certain number of district offices, the role of liaison is open to interpretation in practice. For example, the division sales director could choose to bring in the district sales managers for divisional meetings or visit each office at regular intervals. Effective management might call for an approach that combines the two methods.

If the division director realizes that certain routine tasks are being performed regularly but are not included in the written summary, then steps should be taken to update the description.

Reward Power

Reward power is the ability to confer rewards or positive reinforcement on employees based on performance.

Effective managers have their own 3 R's: *reward, recognize* and *reinforce.* People often put off giving rewards because they think that money is the only thing people care about. As the study at the beginning of the chapter showed, money is only one of the rewards that can be used to motivate employees.

Discovering what employees want need not involve complicated research—only common sense. Employees want the same things that supervisors do. Phrases such as "Keep up the good work," or "I think you are really on the right track with this project" will go a long way toward giving employees the feedback they crave.

Nominate an employee for an award either within the company or the community. The nomination might be for a volunteer of the year award or the designation of outstanding young woman. The nomination is a vote of confidence in itself, and any accolades will reflect positively on the company as well.

Refer questions to specific employees. By taking advantage of their expertise, you not only show them your respect for their ability but also give them a chance to feel that their contributions play an important part in the project's outcome.

In business, the axiom used to be "things must be going okay, because I haven't heard any complaints." The most satisfied workers, however, are likely to be those who regularly hear both the good and bad news of the business day. Informed employees can be more productive because they do not have to worry that they will read about plant closings in the business section of the local newspaper.

Sometimes a letter of appreciation, a certificate, or a public acknowledgment of work well done will motivate employees to continue giving their best. Companies that continually emphasize the value of performance reap benefits in increased productivity and morale.

Peters and Waterman (1982), in *In Search of Excellence,* found reward power used well in many top companies. At North American Tool and Die Company, the authors document visits by the CEO to the plant to give the "freezer award" to an employee who has found a way to do something more safely or efficiently.

The cash prize is small in relation to the prestige of the public award ceremony with the boss presiding.

The advantage of reward power is that it can be the most cost-effective tool to build morale. A compliment that does not cost the giver anything may be the most treasured moment in the receiver's work week.

Coercive Power

Coercive power is the power to punish, fire, or demote. This is the reciprocal of reward power.

Positive reinforcement has proved to be the most effective tool for motivating employees, but occasionally the situation calls for the negative aspect of behavior modification. In cases in which a situation has become unproductive, it may be best to remove or replace an employee.

One of the strongest examples of coercive power stems from the threat of losing one's job. Exasperated supervisors might say, "If you can't meet this quota, we will find someone who will."

The importance of coercive power will always be inherent in the corporate structure. Each level maintains coercive power over all levels below it. Without the ability to fire an incompetent employee, the corporation would be reduced to a chaotic cluster of workers. Fortunately, most modern supervisors have learned that coercive power should be used only when other methods have failed. Threats should never be made without the intent of action. A threat that is not enforced not only makes the supervisor lose esteem in the sight of other workers but it also leaves the supervisor without any future options. For example, if a supervisor threatens to fire an employee the next time an employee is late for work, the supervisor must make good on the threat or any coercive power she possesses will be irreversibly eroded.

In the past, coercive power could be wielded with little thought of consequences from the disciplined employee. However, in this age of civil lawsuits and litigation, supervisors must ensure that any coercive power is administered fairly and equally to all employees.

In one case, a company fired an employee for habitual tardiness. The disgruntled worker took the case to the Unemployment Compensation Board. Co-workers testified that the employee was habitually late and had been threatened with termination should the situation happen again. The employee won the case because the board found that the supervisor threatened to fire the employee because of tardiness more than 20 times in the past. The board ruled that they could find no just cause for enforcing the twenty-first threat when earlier threats had been ignored.

Expert Power

Expert power is the power that comes from technical expertise or competence. Expert power can be the edge that allows you to take full advantage of career opportunities. This type of power will become increasingly important as businesses seek people capable of bridging the gap between standard operational practices and the highly technical demands of the future.

Sometimes expert power dramatically influences a career. Jan was a draftsperson for a growing regional oil business. One day the CEO walked through the drafting department in a panic; the company needed someone to take a photograph on short notice and no local photographers were available. Jan volunteered that she had amateur camera equipment at home and would be glad to attempt the shot. As the firm grew to national importance, the company began to rely on Jan's photographic expertise. Ultimately, she became the company's full-time photographer, shooting oil wells in the North Sea and other exotic locations. Jan would still have had a steady job with the company, but she would have missed a career opportunity if she had not been willing to use her expert power in a chance situation.

In the book, *Megatrends*, Naisbitt (1982) says that in the future, information will be power. Information is as vital to your cause as the budget, employees, office space, or transportation. The intelligent sharing of information will unlock keys to controlling other resources. If you want a larger office, find out who has the large suites and why. At budget time, you will be prepared to explain why your staff generates enough company dollars to have earned larger quarters.

Referent Power

Referent power is the least tangible of the various kinds of power. Referent power assigns authority to a person because of her personality or influence. Anyone who has watched a politician win votes or a preacher win converts knows that the elusive quality we call charisma can be powerful indeed.

A leader with referent power may hold no authority over a group of followers. Yet because of the leader's personal charm, the group remains loyal.

A United States senator, for example, may be very powerful in the legislature or wield little power at all. However, when the average person is introduced to a senator, that person soon realizes that powerful or not, the senator is one of only 100 people who have reached that level of influence.

The workplace is not the only arena for cultivating referent power. Trade associations, professional societies, or civic clubs may all be avenues to build referent power.

Consider the case of the president of the local homebuilders' association who was sought out for a quote by a reporter working on a story about the construction business in the area. By having your name associated with a quote in an authoritative manner, you can develop referent power not only with your co-workers and colleagues but also with the general public.

Referent power is the power at work behind the scenes in so-called "good old boy networks." In these informal structures, people who consider themselves to be equals socially or profes-sionally form a chain, linking information with others. These are the sources they seek when they want to make a business in-vestment or hire a new employee.

As a response to these networks, groups that may be new to the working world or groups that may have been excluded from the networks may form their own organizations to help them achieve similar goals. Minority chambers of commerce or profes-sional women's networks are examples of newly developing sources of referent power.

POWER ON THE JOB

The first commandment for supervisors is to assume that every company has a political realm because it probably does. Gener-ally larger companies have more complicated politics because of the greater number of personalities interacting. However, even a family business will have political aspects that can stump the most competent, aspiring manager.

In a survey conducted by Murray and Gandz (1980), the authors found that the 93 percent of the respondents thought of-fice politics was common in most organizations. In addition, 89 percent thought successful executives must be good politicians and 70 percent thought employees needed to be political to get ahead. On the negative side, they found that 70 percent of the people surveyed thought these politics were unfair. Although 74 percent thought powerful executives act politically, more than half of those surveyed thought office politics was unhealthy, bad, irrational, or inefficient, and 49 percent thought top management should try to get rid of politics.

This survey shows a striking paradox in the way we perceive political power. Although most workers know that office politics exist, most see it as a threat.

Building Power

❑ What is your pq or power quotient?

❑ Does power threaten you or intrigue you?

❑ Does it push you away or draw you toward it?

Use these examples to test your feelings about power:

The company CEO makes an appearance at a departmental function. When you see "the big boss," do you make an attempt to begin a conversation on the pretense of updating a report on a pet project or do you quietly try to fit in with a group for fear others will think you are too friendly with the boss?

You are assigned the task of building an itinerary for a visiting corporate vice president. Do you complain about being assigned work you consider clerical, or do you decide to use the work to your advantage by building in time that shows your department to its best advantage? Some people see their jobs as daily stints behind a desk. They can often be seen late at night working on reports or paperwork, whereas their colleagues are playing racquetball or spending an evening at home. Each, according to the standards used, may be successful.

Generally, the person who will seem most successful is the one who is perceived as efficient enough to do the required work in an average 40-hour week and the one who is more than a faceless person behind a desk.

Everyone in business can usually cite at least one example of a person who is lucky. They are the ones who are always in the right place to take advantage of a great business investment, or a job offer, or a personal contact.

Although power cannot change a person's perception of luck, positioning in the workplace can help a person maximize opportunities. Positioning means building a foundation of appropriate visibility within a given situation.

No responsible supervisor will knowingly waste time, yet avoiding all informal office conversations may have detrimental effects. Positioning in one firm may mean knowing a few basic personal facts about co-workers. Occasionally asking about someone's family can build a relationship of trust that can be helpful in later business situations. Using a moment after dictation to take a verbal pulse on employee morale may elicit the most honest feedback a supervisor will receive.

Some people disdain those with strong positioning skills. Indeed, many companies have their own slang terms for such practitioners. Positioning need not be insincere. Planning ahead to build an appropriate level of visibility while maintaining a high level of productivity can be achieved. Positioning requires strong time management skills in order to keep a balance of efficiency.

Visibility may be the key to why some employees immediately come to mind for a promotion while other equally experienced or qualified but less visible employees never make the list.

In business, there is no substitute for being in the right place at the right time. Consider the resumé of a news reporter who gained national prominence as a network anchor. The reporter was catapulted to the spotlight while working as a reporter for a local Dallas television station on the day that President Kennedy was assassinated. His ability to be cool under one of the century's most tragic and startling stories caught the attention of people in power. Sometimes being in the middle of the action can take precedence over any amount of technical knowledge.

STRATEGIES FOR BUILDING POWER

The "me-generation," which was more concerned with faded jeans and world peace, now finds itself having to function in a world that gravitates toward traditional values.

To cope with this alien structure, newcomers to the workplace must develop corporate styles that lead to enhanced power. The assigned authority may be inherent in the job description, but the ability to exercise that authority comes only with practice.

Some tips for power building include

Watch the behavior of others. Just as etiquette experts advise people to observe others at formal dinners before responding to a toast or picking up a fork, business people can take a cue from other people in the company. If the office comedian has lost esteem in the eyes of other supervisors, you can be certain that a more serious mood is in order.

Build relationships. Secretaries, switchboard operators, and even janitors with the authority to let you back into the building after hours can be lifesavers when you need an ally. Greet new people on the job and help them gain a first impression of a friendly company. That impression may stay with them throughout their tenure and will establish a mutually beneficial exchange.

Establish credibility. Be a person of your word.   Return phone calls. Answer letters. Set a tone that communicates the ability to follow through on assignments. Your reward will be less supervision and more autonomy as your boss sees an employee who can get the job done.

Maintain a professional attitude at all times. Any company function is an extension of the workplace. Never have too much to drink, tell off-color stories, or wear inappropriate attire if you want to be taken seriously in business. This does not mean wearing a conservative job interview suit to a company cook-out; however, remember that you make an impression on people with whom you work no matter what the occasion.

Adopt a conservative approach until you know your personal limits. Do not volunteer for too many committee assignments or projects until you have a solid idea of the time you will need to meet your current responsibilities. The fastest way to undo careful positioning is to develop a reputation for being ineffective.

Take pride in every task. Remember that the buck indeed stops with you and no amount of power can compensate for a job poorly done. Even if your power enables you to have a second or third chance, the eventual outcome in terms of lost productivity and position will not be worth the price.

Negotiate from a position of strength. Compile facts and figures to be able to document proposals. Try to evaluate the results of available options. If you see a need, be willing to discuss different viewpoints while stressing reasons why your solution is preferable.

Realize long-term applications. Too often business people misinterpret statistical data. Statistics may indicate that the average worker changes jobs every 3 to 4 years, but that job may be within the same company or in the same community. Build bridges instead of tearing them down. The person you antagonize today with a brusque comment or a witty put-down may be the person you need to follow through on a business deal later.

Treat the company's resources as your own. During business slumps, the people who will be valued are those who creatively stretch available resources and hold costs below generous budgets. A thrifty employee may have a position with the company long after budgetary cost have forced others to seek employment elsewhere.

Prepare, don't panic. Another popular way of stating this strategy is to act rather than react. With practice, you can develop analytical thinking. Mentally work out problems to their logical conclusion. Make a flow chart to visualize possible out-comes. If x, then y, if y then z or q, and so on until you have created a script in your mind for a predictable situation.

TAKING RISKS

Thomas Watson, former president of IBM, said, "Business is a game-the greatest game in the world if you know how to play it."

Security can be a prime motivator for many workers. They want a stable job and are content to do their jobs in an atmosphere in which no one causes trouble or challenges the status quo.

Security can turn to complacency without some risk taking. Once you have learned how to "play the game" in the context of your work environment, you will have the necessary information to seek opportunities and weigh risks.

One accountant had worked for a major oil firm for more than 10 years. Her benefits included full insurance coverage, generous vacation, and a stock option plan. When oil prices began to fluctuate, her job looked less and less secure. Rather than wait for her department to be phased out, she decided to open a private practice out of her home. At first, the salary cut and the less glamorous office surroundings made her think she had made a mistake. Eventually her old department was closed and several former co-workers were desperately seeking jobs whereas she had already begun to build her new clientele.

Part of assessing risks is to determine how much power you have over your job— and ultimately over your life— and how much power you want to have. Your job is more powerful (see Exercise 8-1) when you have

- ❑ Few rules
- ❑ Few routines or predecessors
- ❑ High variety
- ❑ Tangible rewards
- ❑ Flexibility
- ❑ Visibility
- ❑ Contact with senior officials
- ❑ Participation in problem solving
- ❑ Advancement prospects
- ❑ Central location
- ❑ Problem-solving input
- ❑ Decision-making ability

EVALUATING THE POWER POTENTIAL OF A JOB

One of the first clues to a job's potential power is the corporate chart discussed at the beginning of the chapter. Within that hierarchy, you can visualize the positions to which you can aspire.

Questions to ask in evaluating power potential include

- How many levels are between the CEO and me?
- Can I trace a career path from my job to the next level or will a lateral move be necessary in order to achieve the next promotion?
- Who reports directly to the CEO outside of regular office channels?

If the job seems to have reached a dead end according to the chart, try to determine what skills you can master by staying in the job, and try to find a challenge to avoid becoming resentful or bitter and ruining your chances for advancement.

If, on the other hand, the job seems to lead to a higher position, use that position as a goal. Spend some time each day working toward it. You may want to further your education or research past departmental performance.

Many times employees are passed over for important opportunities simply because they have not communicated their goal to anyone else. Telling co-workers you would like to be considered for the next management training seminar is not enough. Your goal needs to be brought to the attention of the person who can make the goal a reality.

Too often a person with flawless credentials silently wonders why she was not offered a job. When she asks she may be stunned to hear, "I had no idea you'd be interested. I wish I had known so you could have been considered with the other applicants." An administrative assistant was taking college courses at night in hopes of eventually expanding her responsibilities and paycheck. Her boss was proud of her accomplishments but saw no direct correlation between the courses and her job. When a mid-manager was transferred to corporate offices, the supervisor asked department heads to make suggestions to fill the opening. The assistant's name never came up in the discussions, and she was dismayed when she was asked to begin the paperwork to promote another employee. Now her only choice was to live graciously with the new manager and try to hide her disappointment, or to seek employment elsewhere based on her new skills and give up seniority and accrued benefits.

Supervisors cannot read minds. Although your family and friends may know that you would like to be the next corporate vice president, the people with the authority to make that decision will never know unless you articulate your goal. No one advocates telling someone else that you want his or her job, but you can conduct yourself in a professional manner and volunteer personal goals at appropriate times.

MOTIVES FOR POWER

Studies have shown that people who make it to the top are those who want power and admit it. These people readily accept opportunities and tend to be more productive. They have the political savvy to make rapid transitions when new situations occur and adapt their course to fit the new directive.

Four motives are readily apparent in the quest for power (Table 8-1). Although people will find a blend of all four motivations in themselves, one need will often dominate more than the others. Socially acquired motives for power are *affiliation, achievement, competence,* and *power* itself. No one motivation is better or worse than any other. All are learned behaviors determined by environmental influences. Most boys were conditioned to seek power whereas girls were conditioned toward affiliation. Read through each description and evaluate your personality based on the four motivations (see Exercise 8-2).

Affiliation

Affiliation motivates people to power based on relationships with other people. In this type of motivation, a person draws power from those around her, taking the support and nurturing attention they give. These people want to please others and they derive power from being popular, avoiding conflict, and caring for other people.

The behavior pattern can begin with positive reinforcement for good grades in elementary school. Pleasing parents results in a feeling of gratification that the student tends to want to constantly recreate.

Achievement

Achievement motivates people who want to always be the best. This person is goal oriented and often focuses on the challenge rather than the result. The climb may be more important than the conquest, for once the mountain climber reaches the summit, her mind will be on the next adventure.

Olympic athletes, military heroes, and many entrepreneurs may be examples of achievement-motivated people.

Competence

People driven by *competency*, are likely to be considered perfectionists by their co-workers. They want to do the best job at any cost. Sometimes they may forget the overall picture while concentrating on details. They may want to work alone and be reluctant to delegate authority, thinking that no one can complete the job to their satisfaction. They may not have the drive to be a leader, but any job they do will be a quality product.

Power

Power itself motivates people to seek greater power. These people have an overriding need to control their environment. They want to be sure their opinions are heard and their influence is felt by co-workers. They are more likely to volunteer their services as chair of a group or captain of a team because they perceive themselves as leaders. People motivated by power tend to be highly ambitious and masterful at office politics.

All these motivations combine and make us react the way we do. If you do not mind making decisions, or if you like competing, chances are you are acting out a preconditioned response. Looking at these profiles of motivation, try to identify your underlying motives.

Think of your boss, your spouse, or a friend and try to decide what motivates them to power. Once you have analyzed your need for power, you can better place yourself in a situation in which your conditioning adds to your power rather than detracting from it.

After you identify the motivation needs in employees, you can use certain techniques to obtain the best performance from the employee. Some of these methods are noted in *Supervision* (Gray, 1984).

For example, *if employees are motivated by affiliation*, try to make sure they are regularly assigned to jobs that allow for social interaction. When possible, allow them to choose co-workers or help develop the composition of a team. These employees appreciate a closer interpersonal relationship with their colleagues and supervisors. They need to feel appreciated and valued.

Table 8-1 Motives for Power

AFFILIATION	ACHIEVEMENT	COMPETENCE	POWER
Caring, social	Goal oriented	Detail oriented	Win arguments
Supportive, nurturing	Break records	Correct others	Dominate
Please others	Challenge	Seek recognition	Influence
Peer approval	Best job	Reluctant to	Change
Avoid conflict	Work well alone	delegate	Make things
Team member	Need feedback	Perfectionist	happen
Work in groups well		Work best alone	Take risks
Like to work and			Results oriented
interact with people			

If employees are motivated by achievement, they need the freedom to set individual objectives which can be accomplished through largely solo efforts. They may feel stifled in group projects where they have to depend on others for results. They need specific feedback on their performance. They will be highly motivated to work toward winning an award or reaching a quota.

If employees are motivated by competency, they will be motivated by a supervisor who allows them training opportunities to enhance their skills. They can use their attention to detail to advantage in planning meetings or conferences. Although they may lack the delegation skills necessary to lead a team, they can add strength to most team projects.

If employees are motivated by power, they want to be in positions where they can control information or resources. They respond well to a participative management style which allows them to have an influence on decisions. If they are assigned to a team effort, they will be more productive if they are given a leadership role.

CONCLUSION

Personal power develops over the course of a career. Try to resist the temptation to seek power for its own sake. Keep power in perspective and remember that power is to be shared.

These points are worth remembering as you test your power in the workplace:

Realize you will be tested. If you had no power, no one would challenge you. In confrontational situations, do not issue ultimatums, rather concentrate on results. Try to resolve the situation without making anyone feel as if they have lost.

Keep your options open. People change and so do their needs. If you are open to opportunities to gain and experience power, you will more likely be in a position for an interesting career move.

Generate your position. Seek ways to contribute to the organization. Analyze your budget or output quantitatively so you can express what you do in easily understood numbers. Use your information to initiate innovative plans that can safeguard your department from cutbacks or office politics.

Gain visibility. Let people inside and outside the company know who you are. Distribute business cards when possible and make it a point to showcase your skills when you get the opportunity.

Achieve something creative or out of the ordinary. Never stop thinking about ways to streamline production, save money, or increase productivity. Your next idea may be the million-dollar suggestion the company has been waiting for.

Finally, never lose your sense of humor. The ability to laugh at yourself will bridge many awkward moments when you are learning about your personal power.

SUMMARY

Power is the desire to be able to influence or create change. It is a skill that can be developed in management. Power can come in the form of position power, reward power, coercive power, expert power, and referent power. Building power requires understanding the different types of power and using strategy to enhance them.

Managers must assess the power potential of their job when evaluating their career goals. Motives for power include affiliation, achievement, and competence.

TERMS AND CONCEPTS

affiliation	generate your own position
autonomy	influence
big picture	perspective
coercive power	position power
competence	power
credibility	referent power
enthusiasm	reward power
expert power	visibility

REVIEW QUESTIONS

1. What are the top 10 qualities that people want in a job to-day?
2. List and describe the qualities powerful people share.
3. Define the types of power.
4. List five tips for building power most applicable to you.
5. Evaluate the power potential of your job. How can you increase it?
6. List at least four motives for power.
7. Compare the three socially acquired needs. Rank your strongest (1) to your weakest (3). Rank your supervisors.
8. How can appropriate humor enhance your power?
9. Explain the concepts used to generate your own position. Give examples of how you can generate this.

EXERCISES

8-1: RATE THE POWER POTENTIAL OF YOUR JOB

	Minimal 1	Moderate 2	Maximum 3
1. Number of rules	❑	❑	❑
2. Routines, predecessors	❑	❑	❑
3. Variety	❑	❑	❑
4. Rewards	❑	❑	❑
5. Flexibility	❑	❑	❑
6. Visibility	❑	❑	❑
7. Participation in problem solving	❑	❑	❑
8. Advancement prospects	❑	❑	❑

If you ranked 6 or more items "3," you likely have overall maximum power potential in your job; 4 to 6 indicates moderate power potential; and 1 to 3 indicates minimal power potential.

8-2: RANKING MOTIVES

Instructions: Use the following numbers to rank motives. (1) strongest, (2) somewhat strong, (3) least strong.

Your motives

1.

2.

3.

Boss's motives

1.

2.

3.

Person closest to you

1.

2.

3.

SUGGESTED READINGS

Coplin, W. D., and O'Leary, M. K., with Gould, C. *Power Persuasion.* Addison-Wesley, Reading, MA, 1985.

Cunningham, M. *Powerplay. What Really Happened at Bendix.* Simon & Schuster, New York, 1984.

Gray, J. L. *Supervision.* Kent Publishing, Boston, MA, 1984.

Greiff, B. S., and Munter, P. K. *Tradeoffs. Executive, Family and Organizational Life.* Mentor Books, New York, 1980.

Harragan, B. L. *Knowing the Score.* St. Martin's Press, New York, 1980.

Ilich, J. *Power Negotiating.* Addison-Wesley, Reading, MA, 1980.

Josefowitz, N. *Paths to Power. A Woman's Guide from First Job to Top Executive.* Addison-Wesley, Reading, MA, 1980.

Keidel, R. W. *Game Plans. Sports Strategies for Business.* Berkley Books, New York, 1985.

Kennedy, M. M. *Office Politics.* Warner Books, New York, 1980.

Kennedy, M. M. *Powerbase. How to Build It. How to Keep It.* Ballantine Books, New York, 1984.

Kennedy, M. M. *Office Warfare. Strategies for Getting Ahead in the Aggressive '80s.* Ballantine Books, New York, 1985.

Murray, V., and Gandz, J. "Games Executives Play: Politics at Work." *Business Horizons* (December 1980).

Naisbitt, J. *Megatrends*. Warner Books, New York, 1982.

Peters, T. J., and Waterman, R. H., Jr. *In Search of Excellence*. Warner Books, New York, 1982.

Sheehy, G. *Pathfinders*. William Morrow, New York, 1981.

9

STRESS MANAGEMENT

OBJECTIVES

- Understand the condition of stress
- Identify signs of stress
- Learn techniques to reduce stress
- Identify upward and downward organizational pressures
- Learn our basic reactions to stress
- Understand workaholic and burn-out syndromes
- Recognize symptoms of stress
- Provide relaxation exercises

DEFINING STRESS

Stress is a condition of strain on one's emotions, thought processes, or physical condition. To most Americans, stress is part of everyday life. *Stressors* are anything, real or imagined, that causes stress. Stressors may be internal, such as the drive to do a better job or to achieve the next rung on the career ladder, or external, such as a demanding boss or an approaching deadline.

Stress is usually expressed in negative terms. Doctors say that many of the diseases that plague modern executives stem from poor stress management. Ulcers, heart disease, and high blood pressure are found more commonly in industrialized nations. Stress is not inherently bad. A certain amount of stress may actually help propel us toward our goals. For example, runners report that they clock better practice times when they run with a partner instead of by themselves. The added pressure of competition—even in practice runs—brings out extra effort.

Most of the negative impact associated with stress comes from our reaction to stress rather than the actual stress itself. A great deal of stress comes from worrying about things that might happen. As Mark Twain said, "I've suffered a great many catastrophes in my life...most of them never happened." Think of something you spent time worrying about last month. How was the situation resolved? Was the outcome better or worse than you expected? Did the energy you expended in worrying have any impact on the situation's outcome?

When change is seen as desirable or is anticipated, a person is better able to handle the stress associated with it. Stress can be a powerful creative force that can improve your life or it can be a negative obsession that constantly blocks your future. We can become either masters or victims of stress.

SIGNS OF STRESS

Stress, like many of the diseases to which it is linked, is a silent killer. The human body shows an amazing capacity to internalize stress. Sometimes even close family members and friends are not aware of the stress we feel. A calm, controlled exterior remains highly valued in business situations. Professionals do not take their problems to work, rather they try to work things out on their own time.

Physical Signs

Although the workplace is not the appropriate forum in which to take stock of our stress, many busy managers forget to take time away from work to assess their mental and emotional strengths. One of the most important health investments a professional can make is an annual physical checkup. A dramatic rise in blood pressure may signal that the body is having to work harder to adapt to stressful situations. Many other physical symptoms, such as back pain, headaches, insomnia, or muscle spasms, may indicate that stress has begun to have an impact on your general health. Even shortness of breath or constant fatigue may be linked to stress.

If you discover that you have some unexplained symptoms of stress, use the technique of self-interviewing to see if you can determine the underlying causes for your ailment. Ask yourself

❑   When did I first notice the symptom?

❑   What else was happening in my job or personal life at that time?

❑   Have I changed my eating, sleeping, or exercise patterns recently?

❑   Have I been drinking more than usual?

❑   Have I started smoking or am I smoking more often?

Sharing any of these answers with your doctor will help the two of you form a stress-management team. If you cannot sleep, rather than simply taking a prescription for sleeping pills, thereby masking the symptoms, you and your doctor can try to determine your mental state and discuss specific problems that may be causing stress.

Mental Signs

Mental signs of stress may be harder to spot. Some of these are normal reactions to everyday frustrations. But when the signs continue over the course of several weeks or even months, they indicate serious problems in dealing with stress. Seven common signs of stress are

1. *Irritability.* A person who generally has a positive outlook and demeanor may find herself snapping at family members or co-workers and having to apologize for uncharacteristic outbursts.

2. *Short attention span or boredom.* You may find yourself daydreaming during meetings or conversations. Things that

used to interest you, such as attending meetings of your professional society or a hobby group, now seem boring.

3. *Inability to cope with routine problems.* Items such as a missed delivery of sales items or an incorrect billing, which you have always accepted as routine delays, now seem overwhelming. You may even find yourself asking for help on tasks you formerly performed alone.

4. *Anxiety about money.* Money never stretches far enough, but constant worry about money may signal deeper stress. Are you worried privately about losing your job as a source of income? Are you afraid that the company may close or move? Have you taken on unrealistic financial obligations with no way to repay them?

5. *Suppressed anger.* Women are conditioned from youth to believe that being angry is not ladylike. Boys are encouraged not to cry but to be tough. Girls, on the other hand, usually find crying more socially acceptable than getting angry. If these societal conditionings carry over into adult life, both personal and professional performance will suffer. If someone does something you do not approve of at work, let them know with an appropriate response rather than turning the anger inside or taking it out on friends or family members.

6. *Loss of sense of humor.* Taking everything seriously signals stress. The ability to occasionally laugh at our mistakes or weaknesses is an important coping mechanism. In times of stress, a co-worker's comment, such as "You look tired today," may make us worry needlessly about what people think. In less stressful times, you may be able to reply with a sense of humor, such as "Don't let my looks fool you, today is going to be a great day!"

7. *Creeping negativism.* An otherwise optimistic person may suddenly start making statements such as "I don't think I can handle this" or "No one seems to care." Before the stressful situation occurred, a person might see a change at work as a challenge; under stress, that same person would view the new way of doing things as a threat.

TYPE A VERSUS TYPE B

Although there are as many personality types as there are people, researchers have divided the population into two general groupings to study ways in which people react to stress: *Type A* and *Type B personalities* (Table 9-1).

Table 9-1 Type A and Type B Behavior

TYPE A								TYPE B
Overachievers								Patient
Ulcer prone								Calm
Competitive								Enjoyable
Nervous tension								Balances personal and professional life
Impatient								Sensitive
Worries								Realizes time limits
Guilty when relaxing or waiting								Worries less
Workaholic								Accepts circumstances

Place an "X" on the above scale to show where your type of behavior fits in the Type A - Type B range.

Place a "✓" by your boss's behavior

Type A people are the world's overachievers. They are the ulcer-prone, competitive people who are in a constant state of nervous tension. A profile of *Type A behavior* people indicates they

1. Try to accomplish too many tasks in too little time
2. Lack patience and resist people or things that represent obstacles
3. Worry about everything and are likely to become irritated over trivial matters
4. Become obsessed with success and achievement in their careers as well as in their personal lives
5. Feel guilty when relaxing or waiting

Type B people tend to be more passive than active in confrontational situations. This group shows more sensitivity to the feelings of others in their dealings. Whereas the Type A person might be a workaholic, the Type B person will more likely balance her personal life with her work. A profile of *Type B behavior* people indicates they

1. Realize time limitations and are more realistic in their estimates of the time required to complete a job
2. Have patience with other people and unexpected interruptions
3. Maintain a calm attitude with fewer worries

4. Accept rather than fight circumstances and try to make the best of the situation

5. Take time to enjoy life

These personality types are broad stereotypes of a range of human behavior. Most people fit into one type more than the other, although some people will exhibit different reactions based on the amount of stress they are experiencing. Looking at the behavior profiles, try to decide which personality type fits you. If your reactions always fit into the Type A category, this may be a signal that you need to learn better ways to manage your stress.

STRESS AT HOME

The woman manager does not experience only work-related stress. Although most professionals are successful in putting aside personal problems during the workday, stress at home may keep them from achieving their full potential. Before you can concentrate on controlling stress on the job, you must resolve personal conflicts.

At a recent meeting of a professional women's network, members voiced some of these complaints:

❑ "Everyone at work is married and when we have an office function, I feel out of place because I'm single."

❑ "My husband won't help me around the house although I work as many hours as he does and earn as much money."

❑ "My babysitter just told me her husband is going to be transferred to another city."

❑ "By the time I do all my chores after work, I'm too tired to think."

Some of these women's complaints reveal serious problems at home. Within the framework of their network as a support group, they may be able to offer solutions to some of the crises. Hiring household help or sharing names of babysitters might be helpful. However, a few of these stressful home situations stem from the inability to mesh professional life with personal life.

Let's look at the different family situations these statements reveal. The first speaker, who is single, has to balance a social life with a corporate world in which many of her co-workers are married. The second woman obviously has a well-paying job that she views as equivalent to her husband's. She wants their professional equality to extend to a partnership in the home. The next two women are working mothers who struggle with feelings of guilt over time away from their children and who worry about child care arrangements. The last speaker reminds us that women generally have obligations at home as well as work responsibilities.

Dealing with serious stress in the family may require professional counseling. Indeed, some dual-career marriages fall apart under the stress.

For day-to-day situations, some techniques may reduce stress at home:

Decide what is truly important. Adjust standards of household responsibilities to what is comfortable for you instead of what others expect.

Form a team. If possible, discuss promotions, transfers, and additional work responsibilities with other family members. Let them know that you may have to trade some nights and weekends of work for a career opportunity.

Delegate responsibility at home. Encourage family members to be more self-reliant in routine jobs so that everyone has more leisure time.

Use professional and personal contacts to make your life easier. Ask friends to recommend babysitting services or other services you need.

Schedule time for yourself. If you are single or married, you need time to work on personal goals and take a break from work.

STRESS AT WORK

Getting ahead in business seems synonymous with stress. Stress in the workplace is not limited to the upper echelons of corporate life. Indeed, many entry-level employees face equal amounts of stress in the context of their jobs. Whereas the CEO of a company may be under stress due to falling corporate profits, a mid-manager may be worried about her chances for receiving a promotion and a new employee may be concerned about passing a 3-month probationary job evaluation.

Job pressures can originate either inside or outside the organization. *External pressures* include family or personal problems as well as pressure from competitors, economic cycles, and the marketplace. Success does not ensure freedom from stress. Since it is often more expensive to start a new company than to acquire an existing business, many successful businesses have the added worry of unfriendly takeover attempts and mergers.

Internal pressures can come from top levels of management down or from employees up to the supervisor. Examples of downward pressure include

- ❑ Unrealistic deadlines from a supervisor
- ❑ Insufficient resources to do an adequate job
- ❑ Entrapment in a dead-end job with little chance of promotion
- ❑ Office politics among competing departments or supervisors
- ❑ Uneven distribution of workload or favoritism to certain employees

Sometimes the upward pressures are more subtle in the workplace; although we may expect to have demands placed on us from above, we have been conditioned to think that being the boss puts us in control. Realistically, a supervisor cannot expect to control every aspect of an organization. (See Exercise 9-1.)

Even though the supervisor will have ultimate control through her ability to hire and fire employees, a few common sources of upward stress are

- ❑ Incompetent employees
- ❑ Low morale or pervasive negative attitudes from subordinates
- ❑ Undependable employees or workers who are chronically tardy, absent, or ill
- ❑ Personality conflicts among workers
- ❑ Overly ambitious or aggressive employees who may threaten your job

FIGHT OR FLIGHT?

Although we think of ourselves as an advanced society, the way in which the human body adapts to stress has changed little over the centuries. When we are faced with an enemy—either real or imagined—nature sends impulses to the brain alerting us to either confront the situation and resolve the conflict or run away from it. In animals, we might call this a survival instinct. However, in people the surge of adrenaline associated with the fight-or-flight mechanism can cause internal stress, since it often occurs at times when it would not be socially acceptable behavior to either fight or flee.

For example, Joanne's boss asked her to work overtime when she had made other plans. She felt herself getting angry, yet she knew that any arguments might reflect on her job attitude. Rather than air her feelings, she suppressed her anger and left work seething about the situation. Her unresolved anger eventually led to headaches and other physical symptoms, as well as unexplained arguments with family members and friends over seemingly trivial matters.

THE WORKAHOLIC

A specialized reaction to on-the-job stress is the workaholic syndrome. A *workaholic* is addicted to work in much the same way an alcoholic is addicted to drinking. However, unlike other addictions, workaholism is sometimes considered a virtue, and workaholics are happy with the situation. They have intense, energetic, driven personalities, prefer work to leisure, and can do work anywhere at anytime. Most workaholics are Type A personalities. They have chosen to throw themselves into their work for any number of reasons. They may fear failure and resolve to give their job all their attention in an attempt to camouflage their insecurity. Some workaholics retreat to their desks rather than face a dismal personal crisis or function in a social atmosphere, believing that work is so much fun they would do it for free; they look forward to Monday.

Conscientious employees might exhibit workaholic tendencies during different stages of their careers. Learning new responsibilities, completing a large project, or filling in during another employee's absence may all be valid reasons for staying past quitting time. Workaholics blur the distinction between work and pleasure and maximize the use of their time. Employees need to be aware that although extra hours are appropriate for short periods of time, working too many long hours can be detrimental.

Workaholics risk early burnout, either slowing down or dropping out. *Burnout* is an extreme reaction to stress, ultimately characterized by lack of interest and feeling of worthlessness. It is psychological, emotional, physical, and spiritual exhaustion resulting from prolonged negative stress. The victim no longer cares as intently about work, relationships, and/or activities, that once interested her. Workaholics may see themselves as martyrs sacrificing their needs for the good of the company. When their efforts go unnoticed, their attitude plummets. Workaholics develop an unbalanced perspective about their world. Whereas co-workers can look forward to a relaxing weekend, a workaholic longs to be back at work and may even take work home or come into the office for a few hours when everyone else is off. Personal and family life invariably suffer as more time is invested in work than in building or sustaining relationships.

Self-awareness is the key to preventing burnout. Here is a 12-point checklist to help you identify and reverse its symptoms (Freudenberger and North, 1985).

1. *Stop denying.* Your body can give you clues about your level of stress. Admitting to pressure can be the first step.

2. *Avoid isolation.* Withdrawing from friends and family can intensify feelings of loneliness.

3. *Change your circumstances.* Determine the source of your burnout, whether it is a job, a marriage, or an overwhelming project. Seek creative solutions to your problems, but realize that leaving may be the only solution for chronic burnout.

4. *Diminish intensity in your life.* Attacking every problem or project at full intensity depletes energy. Save high energy levels for important tasks.

5. *Stop overnurturing.* Women tend to absorb the problems of others in their role as nurturers. If you are nearing burnout, try to find someone to nurture your needs instead.

6. *Learn to say no.* The principle of assertiveness training carries over into all aspects of life so that people no longer take advantage of you.

7. *Begin to back off and detach.* Try to delegate some of your responsibilities to lighten your load. Negotiate more realistic deadlines or reassess priorities for projects in light of your lessened energy.

8. *Reassess your values.* Decide what is truly important. Focus on what matters most, not what matters least.

9. *Learn to pace yourself.* Realize that you do not have to solve every problem you face overnight. Give yourself time to develop solutions with time for leisure and relaxation.

10. *Take care of your body.* Nutrition, exercise, and moderating smoking and drinking habits will build physical energy during times of mental fatigue.

11. *Diminish worry and anxiety.* If you can change something, change it. If you cannot, then no amount of worrying will change the outcome anyway.

12. *Keep your sense of humor.* The ability to laugh with others and at oneself can help you keep your perspective.

If workaholics maintain the physical stamina necessary to survive until retirement, they will experience feelings of uselessness, since their lives revolved only around work. Workaholics have long been stereotyped as men. Women now realize that workaholism–like other reactions to stress at work–knows no gender.

Soon after graduation, Sherry took a job as a systems analyst in a data processing firm with a national client list. Determined to build a career within the firm, she opted for high-visibility assignments to design computer systems for clients with increasing levels of automation. Since the new job was almost 1,000 miles away from her parents and college friends, Sherry often volunteered for overnight and weekend travel

Eventually her colleagues began to assume that Sherry would be available for any project that required working past 5 o'clock. The first time she protested that she had other plans, her boss seemed shocked. Eventually Sherry received her promotion, but soon realized that since she had made a habit of working 12-hour days, anything less seemed as if she was slacking off. After 3 years on the job, she realized she might have to give up the career she loved and start over at a new job in which she would not be expected to be married to the company. (See Exercise 9-2.)

If you sense that increasing job pressures are making you a workaholic, you can take *steps* to prevent the situations from controlling your life:

❑ *Take vacations when you have earned vacation time.* Some workaholics brag that they have never used all their vacation time. Long weekends can be rejuvenating. For one thing, they remind you that you are not indispensable since the office managed without you for a few days. They can also put you back in touch with social and personal relationships that may have suffered from working long hours.

❑ *Discipline yourself to an 8-hour day.* Getting to work a few minutes early or staying a few minutes longer than co-workers may increase your efficiency. But if you find yourself constantly staying extra hours when you have not been assigned overtime, you need to reassess your time management skills. Delegating or reorganizing the work may give you the break you need. If you find yourself taking longer than necessary to do certain tasks, ask yourself if you are using work to escape from other things that you do not like to do.

❑ *Plan your leisure time as you do your working day.* Working mothers who are responsible for their children's day care need no extra push to go home on time–generally their babysitter or child care center has strict rules about when parents must pick up their children. Single workers may find it helpful to enroll in an after-work exercise class to motivate them. If weekends are filled with hobbies and friends, you will be less likely to check your desk between Friday afternoon and Monday morning.

❑ *Make it clear to your boss and to co-workers that you do not mind occasionally working overtime as long as the assignment is temporary.* Don't let other employees take advantage of your being single or not having children to delegate evening or weekend responsibilities. Try to rotate out-of-town travel when possible so everyone takes a turn.

❑ *Develop friends from outside your company.* When employees are together, even for socializing, talk often returns to work problems. By expanding your circle of friends, you can avoid "shop talk" 7 days a week.

ARE YOU A WORKAHOLIC?

❑ Do you get up early, no matter how late you go to bed?
❑ If you are eating lunch alone, do you read or work while you eat?
❑ Do you make daily lists of things to do?
❑ Do you find it difficult to "do nothing"?
❑ Are you energetic and competitive?
❑ Do you work on weekends and holidays?
❑ Can you work anytime and anywhere?
❑ Do you find vacations "hard to take"?
❑ Do you dread retirement?
❑ Do you really enjoy your work?

If you answer "yes" to eight or more of these questions, you, too, are probably a workaholic (Machlowitz, 1981).

REACTIONS TO STRESS

Becoming a workaholic is only one reaction to stress. Depending on our personality and our general physical health, we all react differently to a stressful situation. Six common stress reactions are discussed in the following list:

1. *Withdrawal.* When faced with a stressful situation, some people use the flight reaction by withdrawing. Typically they do not express their concerns to friends or fellow employees. They become quiet and suppress their stress.

2. *Apathy.* Another form of fleeing from stress is to maintain an "I don't care" attitude. Generally the person's apathy is only a veneer, because they usually care very deeply. However, in the face of stress they find it easier to seem undisturbed than to let others know how stressful they really feel.

3. *Fixation or obsession.* Sometimes a distressing problem becomes such a great source of stress that a person can think of nothing else. Taking work home or constantly talking about a work-related problem can indicate fixation. The problem occupies all conversation and thought to the exclusion of day-to-day concerns.

4. *Displacement.* The human mind can reorder a situation so that we can deal with stress. Displacement may take the form of placing the blame for our problems on others rather than finding the cause in ourselves or assuming responsibility for the outcome. This kind of displacement is commonly known as scapegoating.

5. *Rationalizing.* Under stress, many people make up excuses for certain behaviors or results, attempting to give plausible, but not necessarily true, explanations for specific, often undesirable, behavior. This is a common coping mechanism that helps us avoid facing our own shortcomings.

6. *Physical disorders.* In a long-term stress situation, the body can succumb to pressure. Some of the previously mentioned signs of stress are merely reactions to unsolved problems. Internalized stress may manifest itself in headaches, digestive disorders, high blood pressure, skin rashes such as hives, and achiness or fatigue.

Uncovering Symptoms of Stress

When stress is having a negative effect on your performance at home or at work, you have two positive choices to manage your stress. One option is to solve the problem thereby ridding yourself of the cause. The other is to channel stress-produced energy into creative outlets.

If you face a known problem such as wanting to be considered for a promotion, the first option may be the best. The first thing you should do is to write down everything that you think is causing your stress. Include personal problems, financial obligations, relationships with co-workers and friends, and specific items related to your job. After you have listed the things that are bothering you, draw a line vertically down the page. Beside each problem, write possible solutions. For example, the solution to a dead-end job may be to find a new career or start your own business. A solution to a financial problem might be to work some overtime until the debt is paid or to take a second job to save toward a goal.

By naming the problems, you can come to grips with them. Instead of being overwhelmed by stress, you have broken down methods of relieving your anxieties into different tasks. Now you have the tools to begin a plan of action. You might even save your worksheet to chart your progress as you further analyze what needs to be done.

Some problems may not be so easily described or solved. Your financial situation may leave you unable to make a job change or you may simply be having trouble sleeping without being able to determine the cause. For this type of stress, some life-style changes may help relieve some of the pressure. Listed below are seven suggestions for curbing stress:

1. *Modify your diet to eliminate caffeine, alcohol, and refined sugar.* These chemicals may contribute to sleeplessness, which can result in feeling tired all the time. Lack of sleep depletes energy reserves that can help you bounce back from stress.

2. *Begin an exercise program.* Perhaps you have read stories about runners who develop a "runner's high." The body actually produces chemicals as you exercise that act as mood elevators. If running is too strenuous, check into YWCA or YMCA classes that offer beginning exercises. Even a daily brisk walk at lunchtime or after work is better than no exercise at all.

3. *Adapt to a healthy life-style.* The best advice is do not start smoking, but if you already do, check into smoking cessation programs. Many times health insurance benefits cover preventive programs such as weight loss or quit-smoking programs offered through hospitals.

4. *Develop a sounding board.* If you cannot talk to friends or family about your problems, seek out members of the clergy or low-cost counseling services funded through organizations such as *United Way* or a council of churches. Talking will not solve problems, but sometimes just knowing someone else cares or can relate to our problems offers an escape valve for pressures building inside.

5. *Learn to say no and do not overcommit yourself.* Learning more about the levels of stress you can comfortably handle will help you determine more about your limits. In the meantime, try to concentrate on one project at a time. If someone asks you to help on another project, explain that while you are flattered to be asked, you want to do your best and your time is limited.

6. *Balance your life to include time for work and play.* Hobbies, friends, and volunteer work are all constructive ways to invest time away from work. If you are new to a community, take weekends to explore local tourist or recreational attractions. Call the local Chamber of Commerce for a list of clubs or organizations in the area that meet your interests. Volunteer your time with a nonprofit group; you will meet people as well as make a contribution to the community.

7. *Plan time for yourself.* Think about things that make you feel good about yourself. This might include attending a seminar that gives your career a boost or seeing a wardrobe or makeup consultant to give you a new look. Even a new record album might be a well-deserved treat to remind you that you are your best asset.

RELAXATION EXERCISES AND OTHER STRESS-REDUCTION TECHNIQUES

Psychiatrists and psychologists have developed certain exercises that can help you gain control when you are feeling stressful. Some of these can be done in the privacy of your office. Others may be helpful when trying to wind down from the pressures of the day after work or before going to bed.

Breathing Exercises

When we are told to take a deep breath or count to 10, we are unconsciously practicing a breathing exercise. By concentrating on breathing in and out very slowly, you can get in touch with your body's involuntary muscles and regain control. Breathe in and count to 10 slowly and exhale at the same rate. The infusion of oxygen to the brain will clear your head as you calm down.

Biofeedback Exercises

Biofeedback means directing your body to do your will. Some researchers have reported amazing results with this technique, ranging from controlling pain to actually lowering blood pressure. With very little practice, you can use biofeedback to calm yourself as you talk to your body.

Find a quiet place in which you will not be disturbed. Try to wear loose or comfortable clothing and sit in a comfortable position. Close your eyes and try to block out any sounds or distractions that keep you from concentrating on your body. Starting with your hands, clench your fists and release the muscles as slowly as you can. Repeat each step twice for about 5 seconds. Bend your elbows and tense your upper arm muscles. Release slowly as before. Now wrinkle your forehead and relax. Follow the same exercise principle for other parts of your body. Tighten and relax the jaw, neck, and shoulders, stomach muscles, buttocks, thighs, calves, heels, and toes.

After doing every step twice, you should feel less tension in your muscles and a general feeling of relaxation.

Autogenic Messages

Just as biofeedback uses the mind to control the body, *autogenic messages* use the mind to control itself. Autogenic messages act to encourage us; they tell us "You can do it" or "Your mind is calm," even if your body has its doubts. If you are in a stressful situation at work, try to excuse yourself for a few minutes to reprogram your thoughts. Instead of accepting its instinctive messages to fight or flee, tell yourself "I am in control" or "I know they are just testing me." This will help relieve the frustration you feel, enabling you to act directly rather than making you do something you may regret later.

Creative Imagery

Creative imagery might be considered a grown-up version of daydreaming. Instead of taking a 15-minute coffee break, close the door to your office and use creative imagery. With your eyes closed, picture yourself doing something you enjoy. Even though your day may be filled with meetings and interviews, your break time can let you relive an enjoyable vacation trip or a moment of success. When it is time to return to work your mind will be clearer because you have had a mental break from the pressures at hand.

Visualization

Visualization is an extension of creative imagery. Visualization is the practice of seeing yourself achieving goals. Athletes, performers, and many executives use visualization to help them get ahead. Their theory is that if you can see where you want to be, you will begin to be comfortable with the idea of success. Just as computer programmers insert instructions into a machine to enable it to perform its calculations, proponents of visualization program positive ideas into their minds thinking they will come true.

When you are under stress, use visualization to think about where you want to be in 1 year or 5 years. Visualize your future and decide what steps must be taken now—even when you are feeling stressed—to achieve the goals. By looking beyond today's problems, you will alleviate the helpless feelings that often accompany stress.

Hypnosis and Subliminal Learning

We are just learning about the effectiveness of hypnosis and subliminal learning in tapping the human mind. *Hypnosis* involves going into a trance-like state and being given suggestions to alter behavior. Some people use hypnosis to stop smoking, to lose weight, or to modify destructive behavior. While this technique may not be for everyone, the power of hypnotic suggestion shows promise of being able to implant an idea deep into our subconscious mind.

Likewise, *subliminal learning* is learning that takes place at a level beyond our usual perception. Listening to motivational tapes as you sleep might be one example of learning outside the usual limits of the senses. Although the amount of information retained may vary from person to person, part of your brain will process the information for you to retrieve at a later time. Listening to soothing music or a tape of your autogenic messages exerts a calming effect to lessen stress.

CONCLUSION

To manage stress, you have to decide that you are the master of your destiny. Decide that you are in control of your life and take responsibility for it. Realize that you cannot change everything, but resolve to take the circumstances of your life and make the best of them.

SUMMARY

All modern managers will experience stress through a combination of things that happen at home and at work. Coping with stress is a skill managers must develop, because stress generally increases along with the responsibility of the job. Sudden behavioral changes can be signs of stress. Scientists have determined two basic personality types: Type A and Type B. Type A people tend to worry more and feel guilty when relaxing. Type B people more readily accept the limitations of time and space when accomplishing a task.

Reactions to stress range from becoming a workaholic to seeking relief from pressures with drugs or alcohol. More positive techniques for stress reduction include relaxation exercises, biofeedback, and meditation.

TERMS AND CONCEPTS

apathy	physical disorders
autogenic messages	rationalizing
biofeedback	stress
burnout	stressors
creative imagery	subliminal learning
creeping negativism	Type A behavior
displacement	Type B behavior
downward pressure	upward pressure
fight or flight	visualization
fixation or obsession	withdrawal
hypnosis	workaholic
meditation	

REVIEW QUESTIONS

1. What are some signals of increased stress?
2. How do Type A and Type B personalities differ?
3. What are some common reactions to stress?
4. Describe a typical relaxation exercise to use during a stressful time.
5. What life-style changes can contribute to a lower stress level?
6. What is the fight-or-flight reflex?

EXERCISES

9-1: HOW TO TELL IF YOU ARE STRESS PRONE IN THE OFFICE

Instructions: Rate yourself the way you typically react in each office situation listed below: 5—always; 4—frequently; 3—sometimes; 2—seldom; 1—never.

1.	Do you try to do as much as possible in the least amount of time?	❑ 1	❑ 2	❑ 3	❑ 4	❑ 5
2.	Are you impatient with delays and interruptions?	❑ 1	❑ 2	❑ 3	❑ 4	❑ 5
3.	Do you have to win at games to enjoy yourself?	❑ 1	❑ 2	❑ 3	❑ 4	❑ 5
4.	Are you unlikely to ask for help with a problem?	❑ 1	❑ 2	❑ 3	❑ 4	❑ 5
5.	Do you constantly strive to better your position or achievements?	❑ 1	❑ 2	❑ 3	❑ 4	❑ 5
6.	Do you constantly seek the respect and admiration of others?	❑ 1	❑ 2	❑ 3	❑ 4	❑ 5
7.	Are you overly critical of the way others do their work?	❑ 1	❑ 2	❑ 3	❑ 4	❑ 5
8.	Do you have the habit of often looking at your watch?	❑ 1	❑ 2	❑ 3	❑ 4	❑ 5
9.	Do you spread yourself too thin in terms of time?	❑ 1	❑ 2	❑ 3	❑ 4	❑ 5
10.	Do you have the habit of doing more than one thing at a time?	❑ 1	❑ 2	❑ 3	❑ 4	❑ 5
11.	Do you ever get angry or irritable?	❑ 1	❑ 2	❑ 3	❑ 4	❑ 5
12.	Do you have a tendency to talk quickly or hasten conversation?	❑ 1	❑ 2	❑ 3	❑ 4	❑ 5
13.	Do you consider yourself hard driving?	❑ 1	❑ 2	❑ 3	❑ 4	❑ 5
14.	Do your friends or relatives consider you hard driving?	❑ 1	❑ 2	❑ 3	❑ 4	❑ 5
15.	Do you have a tendency to get involved in multiple projects?	❑ 1	❑ 2	❑ 3	❑ 4	❑ 5
16.	Do you have a lot of deadlines in your work?	❑ 1	❑ 2	❑ 3	❑ 4	❑ 5
17.	Do you feel vaguely guilty if you relax?	❑ 1	❑ 2	❑ 3	❑ 4	❑ 5
18.	Do you take on too many responsibilities?	❑ 1	❑ 2	❑ 3	❑ 4	❑ 5

If your score is 18 to 30, you probably work best in nonstressful, noncompetitive situations, like to set your own pace, and concentrate on one task at a time. Interruptions drive you crazy. Stress is likely to hinder your performance rather than enhance it.

If your score is 31 to 60, you can handle a bit of stress and probably enjoy it as long as it doesn't occur in more than about 20% of your working hours.

(continued)

If your score is 61 to 90, look out! The people who work with you better look out, too. You need constant pressure in order to perform. You tend to stay up all night to finish reports or to expand tasks to increase pressure deadlines if the job's demands aren't stressful enough. You probably grit your teeth.

Adapted from Forbes (1981).

9-2: THE BURN-OUT CHECKLIST

Instructions: Answer the following statements as mostly true or mostly false as they apply to you.

		Mostly true	Mostly false
1.	I feel tired more frequently than I used to	_____	_____
2.	I snap at people too often	_____	_____
3.	Trying to help other people often seems hopeless	_____	_____
4.	I seem to be working harder but accomplishing less	_____	_____
5.	I get down on myself too often	_____	_____
6.	My job is beginning to depress me	_____	_____
7.	I often feel I'm headed nowhere	_____	_____
8.	I've reached (or am fast approaching) a dead end in my job	_____	_____
9.	I've lost a lot of my zip lately	_____	_____
10.	It's hard for me to laugh at a joke about myself	_____	_____
11.	I'm not really physically ill, but I have a lot of aches and pains	_____	_____
12.	Lately, I've kind of withdrawn from friends and family	_____	_____
13.	My enthusiasm for life is on the wane	_____	_____
14.	I'm running out of things to say to people	_____	_____
15.	My temper is much shorter than it used to be	_____	_____
16.	My job makes me feel sad	_____	_____

Interpretation: The more of these questions you can honestly answer mostly true, the more likely it is that you are experiencing burnout. If you answered 12 or more of these statements mostly true, it is likely you are experiencing severe burnout or another form of mental depression. Discuss these feelings with a physical or mental health professional.

SUGGESTED READINGS

Forbes, R. *Corporate Stress and Life Stress.* Doubleday, New York, 1981.

Freudenberger, H. J. *Burn Out. How to Beat the High* Cost of Success. Bantam Books, New York, 1980.

Freudenberger, H. J., and North, G. *Women's Burnout.* Doubleday, New York, 1985.

Kinzer, N. S. *Stress and the American Woman.* Ballantine Books, New York, 1980.

Kushner, H.S. *When Bad Things Happen to Good People.* Avon Books, New York, 1981.

MacDougall, A. K. "The Stress Test." *Success* (1981)

Machlowitz, M. *Workaholics. Living with Them, Working with Them.* Mentor Books, New York, 1980.

Schwartz, J. *Letting Go of Stress.* Pinnacle Books, New York, 1982.

Sehnert, K. W. *Stress/Unstress. How You Can Control Stress at Home and on the Job.* Augsburg Publishing House, Minneapolis, MN, 1981.

Tavris, C. *Everywoman's Emotional Well-Being.* Doubleday, New York, 1986.

Wanderer, Z., and Cabot, T. *Letting Go.* Warner Books, New York, 1978.

10

PROBLEM SOLVING AND DECISION MAKING

OBJECTIVES

- Identify barriers women face in proving themselves to be competent problem solvers
- Identify three basic strategies women can use to overcome stereotypes of women as poor problem solvers
- List factors that keep most people from making a decision
- Develop problem-solving skills
- Understand positive suggestions to take with employees who have problems that affect their work performance
- Learn how to prevent problems
- Learn three basic problem-solving techniques
- Learn six major points of problem solving
- Define problem-solving terms and concepts
- Identify common decision-making patterns
- Compare advantages and disadvantages of group decision making
- List six factors to consider when selecting a group
- List elements of a creative attitude toward problem solving
- Compare the two major types of decisions, programmed and creative

Managers face the daily challenge of recognizing problems, developing solutions, implementing the decisions, and analyzing the outcome.

This cycle repeats itself with alarming on-the-job regularity. New problems develop as old problems are being resolved.

Managers need the ability to recognize the problem, the judgment to solve the problem, the technical ability to implement a solution, and the strategy to analyze the outcome to reduce or eliminate future problems.

A *problem* is the difference or gap between a current situation and a desired or expected situation. It is anything that is "off target," unwanted, or urgent enough to warrant attention, analysis, or correction. *Problem solving* is the process of eliminating the gap and converting the current situation to the desired situation.

WOMEN AS PROBLEM SOLVERS

Women face additional barriers in proving themselves to be competent problem solvers and decision makers. Because they have traditionally had less experience in solving business problems, women may be perceived as needing extra help or being unprepared for decision making. Additionally, women have been unfairly viewed as making decisions based on emotions and sentiment rather than reason and logic. In reality, all managers, whether male or female, have to make tough business decisions without letting personal feelings interfere. In small departments or businesses, managers realize that their decisions affect people's lives and livelihoods.

To overcome this stereotype, women can use three basic strategies:

1. *Be aware of the stereotype without accepting its validity.* Stereotypes do not have to work against you if you are aware of them in advance and can mentally prepare to demonstrate extra competence. Being aware of the stereotype means that you can use it to your advantage. You can make an extra effort to put aside personal feelings or emotions and you can consciously choose to use words such as logic, factual, evidence and statistics, which cannot be refuted, rather than words that convey emotions, such as think, feel, hope, or wish.

2. *Master problem-solving skills.* As with any other business skills, problem-solving skills can be learned, practiced, and

strengthened. A few people may seem to have instinctive problem-solving abilities or inherent abilities to make decisions. Generally these people have studied and implemented the tactics developed by others to such a degree that the talent seems second nature.

3. *Act instead of reacting.* To act is to assume the power that comes from controlling circumstances instead of allowing circumstances to control the situation. Reacting is passive because you cannot react until something happens to cause your reaction. Taking the initiative in problem solving and decision making can give you added power because you will have an opportunity to advance your solution before others realize the solution is in the works. If you always wait to react, you risk having to constantly carry out the decisions and plans of others instead of your own.

Additionally, efficient prevention of a problem generally saves more time and money in the long run than correction.

THE MANAGER'S ROLE

Problem solving and decision making are major managerial functions. Managers are paid to prevent problems and to solve problems when they occur. The most basic role of a manager is to supervise employees. Without supervision to direct the work and see that deadlines are met and production is achieved, chaos would result.

As with almost all other managerial skills, effective problem solving begins with developing a positive attitude. Once you realize that problems come with the responsibility of being a manager, you can accept the fact that you will always be solving problems. Realizing problems are part of the job will help you build confidence because you no longer have to take problems personally. They are as much a part of the job as answering the phone or directing employees.

Six basic factors keep most people from making a decision. They include

1. Worrying about other people or what other people think
2. Getting too much advice from other people who may or may not be involved
3. Depending on other people to make the decision
4. Uncertainty about the desired outcome or what you really want

5. Fear of failure or of letting someone down who is counting on you
6. Inability to follow through once a certain decision is made

EIGHT MAJOR TRAPS TO AVOID WHEN MAKING A
DECISION (RUE AND BYARS,1986)

Trap 1   Making all decisions BIG decisions
Trap 2   Creating crisis situations
Trap 3   Failing to consult others
Trap 4   Never admitting a mistake
Trap 5   Constantly regretting decisions
Trap 6   Failing to utilize precedents and policies
Trap 7   Failing to gather and examine available data
Trap 8   Promising what cannot be delivered

These obstacles stem from an unrealistic problem-solving attitude. Managers must realize that no perfect solution exists to every problem. Every decision involves some positive and some negative consequences. The goal of effective decision making is to find the best possible solution with the least number of drawbacks based on information available at the time the decision is made.

People tend to view decisions as final. Effective managers view decisions with more flexibility. Too many managers see changing their minds as a sign of weakness or as having admitted making a bad decision. In fact, as soon as a manager realizes that a decision is not bringing the desired results, it is time to change course. Career decision makers know that the first decision is always the least costly one. If a decision seems to create a losing situation, it may be best to cut your losses and move on to the next decision rather than investing in a no-win situation.

Human beings are blessed with 20/20 hindsight. That is, looking backward, we always have additional facts or experience that would lead us to different decisions. Effective managers must look forward instead of backward and realize that some decisions will stand the test of time and others will not. Accepting the fact that some decisions will be better than others is a big step toward freedom from the fear of other people's opinions or of failure to make the correct decision. Every decision carries some risk, but without some risks, there can be no gains.

PROBLEM-SOLVING SKILLS

To keep decision making in perspective, managers can concentrate on twelve points that help build problem-solving skills:

1. *There is seldom only one acceptable choice in solving a problem.* Usually managers are asked to choose the best alternative among any number of proposed solutions that may come from colleagues, from superiors, from documents on another project, or from a creative exchange of ideas. Whatever the source, the manager must weigh the pros and cons of each to determine the best path. Even then, the chosen solution will be the one deemed best only for that particular circumstance and not necessarily the choice for future situations.

2. *Decisions should contribute to achieving objectives and goals within the company.* Objectives are the framework in which managers agree to operate; whether they express sales quotas or growth patterns, they form the basis of a work plan for a department or division. Decisions made without considering objectives are similar to quotes taken out of context. Although they may have merit, they add nothing to the total understanding of a problem. Objectives set boundaries for effective decision making within the current company goals.

3. *Feelings must be considered in any decision.* Although feelings should not be the overriding concern of a manager in making a decision, managers have to realize that companies are made up of people and those people have feelings. Even if you must make an unpopular decision, by considering people's feelings in advance, you can minimize the possibility of low morale or unproductive workers. Feelings and facts must be balanced whenever people are involved.

4. *Decision making takes time and energy.* Some decisions are made so quickly that they hardly seem to be decisions at all, such as deciding to take the stairs instead of the elevator or deciding to answer the telephone instead of letting another employee take the call. In reality, every decision takes time, and the more complex a decision, the more time it requires. If you know you must make a major decision, such as how to cut the budget or how to restructure the staff, schedule adequate time to deal with the problem in a place where you will have few interruptions. Select a time when you know your mind is fresh and you have enough energy to fuel the mental process of decision making. If you try to solve a problem when you are tired or busy, you may chance making crucial errors in judgment.

5. *Decision making improves with practice.* As with managerial skills, decision making builds on past experiences throughout your career. Discussing decisions with experienced managers, learning from good and bad decisions, and analyzing facets of current problems all become easier with time. Eventually, managers develop strategies for problem solving that blend management skills with their personal style to achieve effective results.

6. *Decisions will never please everyone.* Few decisions meet with unanimous approval. Almost every decision has its critics who contend that other solutions would be better or more desirable than the solution chosen. Sometimes, after a decision has stood the test of time, critics will agree that the course of action was wise. Meanwhile managers must realize that they need please only those in higher authority in making a decision. In democracies, majority rules; the will of the majority becomes law. In corporations, authority rules and the will of the appointed authority is final.

7. *Decisions do not occur in a vacuum.* Every decision starts a chain reaction that affects other people, other departments, and other decisions. In thinking through the consequences of different solutions to a problem, managers need to consider how decisions will affect those involved. Jill, a production manager, created a cost-cutting plan that greatly reduced her department's expenditures on copying memos and routing documents. Her supervisor was pleased and took steps to implement the plan. Barbara, a sales department manager, complained loudly after hearing about the plan. Barbara argued that without current correspondence from Jill's department, her sales force would lack up-to-date information for customers. Jill had failed to take into account how her decision affected other departments when she trimmed the budget.

8. *No one ever has enough time to make a decision.* You can always wish for time to investigate one more statistic, to ask one more question, or to analyze one more business cycle before making a decision. Business demands timely decisions based on the data at hand. Decision making carries risks and rewards. Delaying or deliberating over a decision can cost thousands of dollars as production lines are idled or shipments are delayed. Successful business leaders surround themselves with people who can give them the best resources in the time available for their decisions.

9. *At some point, every executive will be overwhelmed by either the enormity or the number of decisions made in a business day.* When you feel that the future of all your employees rests on

your decision or the fate of the business is in your hands, you risk being overwhelmed to the point of not being able to make a decision. Accepting the fact that you are doing the best job you can with the time, experience, and resources available will help give you peace of mind in making a decision. Few decisions are irrevocable. You can always decide later that you need to redirect a course of action or change your mind. Although you may lose some time or temporarily lose some confidence, these are small prices to pay for the overall success of a venture.

10. *Decisions must be made in spite of any real or perceived lack of support.* Waiting for others to support a decision really means you are waiting for their vote of confidence before making a decision. Managers do not have the luxury of waiting for a popular vote. Sometimes the solution to a problem will arise from a consensus. At other times, the manager will have to exert her authority to make the final decision and try to gain support for the plan. Even deciding not to make a decision is to decide.

11. *Decisions demand the strength of clear goals.* Having a reason for making a decision builds confidence. Sometimes you may want to share the reasoning with employees. At other times, you may want to remind yourself of the reason for the decision to keep the solution in perspective. In either case, decisions must be made in terms of the goals involved. If higher profits or controlled growth are goals, then decisions must be addressed in those terms. If higher morale or better training are goals, then making decisions will be easier if everyone understands that all plans must be considered in light of these goals.

12. *Once a decision is made, it requires commitment.* Commitment is the process of applying resources to a decision in order to see it through to its desired outcome. A decision without commitment is meaningless because commitment involves being dedicated enough to implement the alternative chosen. Managers set the tone for commitment when a decision is made. If the decision is announced with confidence, employees are more likely to see it as a positive move. If a manager announces a solution with uncertainty, such as "We're not sure if this will work, but" or "This is the best we could come up with," employees will know that the plan does not have the commitment of management. Without that commitment, employees will be less likely to give their best effort toward making the plan succeed.

WHOSE PROBLEM?

A fundamental issue in problem solving is deciding to whom a problem belongs. Too often managers waste valuable decision-making energy solving other people's problems or worrying about consequences of a problem that is not their own. Before you can effectively manage a problem through a decision-making process, you must determine where the problem belongs.

Becky was an office manager at an automobile dealership. Day after day her employees had to deal with customers who were unhappy about treatment they had received from their sales force or from the service department. She began to experience the effects of low office morale when employees started calling in sick more frequently and often reported late for work as if they dreaded hearing more customer complaints. Whose problem was it? Becky could take steps to implement tougher work rules regarding sick leave and tardiness, but that would not address the real problem. Unless the sales manager and service manager were willing to implement tighter follow through on quality control, Becky's employees would never escape the customers' wrath.

Managers must realize that some problems that affect their work are not their problems. The solution may be to determine where the problem originates and try to approach that supervisor or department head to make them aware that they have a problem that is affecting you.

If you have to speak to another supervisor about a problem, remember that your goal is not to solve the problem, but to alert someone to the problem so that it can be solved. Use tactful language so that you do not seem to be assigning blame. Avoid offering a solution, since this can be viewed as volunteering to solve the problem. Do not apologize for calling attention to the problem. If your motive is to alleviate a situation that is hampering some portion of the company's overall work, then you can take full confidence in delivering your message. Try to find the best time and the most private place to discuss the problem so that you do not make the other supervisor lose face in front of employees.

Sometimes employees have problems that affect their performance. In these situations, managers need to analyze where the problem belongs and deal with it on that level. A troubled relationship at home or tension about some facet of life outside of business is a good example of a personal problem that can sometimes affect a person's work. If supervisors suspect that an employee has personal problems that are contributing to problems at work, there are *four* positive suggestions to take without adopting the problem as their own:

1. *Remember that you are a supervisor and not a psychiatrist, psychologist, or social worker.* You have been trained for a

job that does not include functioning as a therapist for unhappy employees. You can talk about problems without offering to solve them. Ultimately the employee has sole responsibility for a productive career.

2. *Select a private place so you can let the employee know that the problem has now begun to affect the workplace.* If the problem had remained private, it would not have shown up at work in the first place. As a manager, your job is to alert the employee that the problem has now affected work in the office, not to try to build a friendship out of a business relationship.

3. *Try to get the worker to come up with a solution without your help.* Sometimes the talk itself will relieve the pressure building up inside an employee and will force a quick solution. Other times, the employee may need to be referred to the personnel department or to an in-house counselor who can give help in a certain area. You can give your opinion, but be careful that you do not take any responsibility for the problem.

4. *Never allow the employee to dump a problem on you.* A problem cannot belong to you unless you adopt it as your own. You can sympathize or even empathize, but you cannot solve someone else's problem. Your best strategy is to listen and hope for a positive solution while firmly pointing out the consequences if no solution can be found.

PREVENTING PROBLEMS

The only thing better than being known as a problem solver in business is having the reputation of being a manager who prevents problems before they occur. Although it may seem that managers who constantly have high-level conferences have the boss's ear, they may be losing ground if they always take problems into a superior's office. In the long term, most attention usually goes to the person who runs an operation quietly and smoothly. That is the person most likely to receive tough assignments or challenging work based on a reputation for solid, dependable work with few distractions.

Managers can foster an attitude of problem prevention within a department. One of the most effective ways to encourage staff participation in problem prevention is to reward employees. Safety awards are an example of spotlighting positive accomplishments to avoid the negative consequences that result from inattention to dangerous working conditions. Verbal rewards should be given when an employee has prevented a problem from slowing down work or inconveniencing clients. Managers can also set a strong example by focusing on the extra effort needed to prevent a problem rather than on the extra hours or work involved in solving a problem once it exists.

The climate of problem prevention can be communicated to upper management so that it reflects a positive sense of accomplishment about you and your department. Usually upper management hears only about negative problems— on-the-job injuries, high employee turnover, customer complaints— instead of creative solutions to preventing problems. If your division has gone 6 months or a year without a single on-the-job injury, draft a memo to the company's safety committee and the personnel department asking to have a plaque made to commemorate the achievement for your staff. Even if they do not grant the request, you will have sent an important memo documenting the fact that your careful attention is preventing problems. Let your bosses know that you are always thinking of ways to prevent problems. If you have questions about the success of a plan during a staff meeting, it is better to be a problem preventer and raise these doubts during the meeting than to wait until the plan is implemented and be forced to solve problems as the plan goes along.

PROBLEM-SOLVING TECHNIQUES

Whether a problem is simple or complex, arriving at the solution requires six basic steps:

1. Identifying the problem
2. Analyzing the problem
3. Setting goals and objectives that any solution must include or address
4. Searching for possible solutions to the problem
5. Planning the course of action based on the solution
6. Evaluating the solution as it is implemented either in stages or after its completion

In a complicated problem such as merging two companies, the steps will involve an enormous amount of time and human resources before adequate research can be done. In simpler problems, you may cover all six steps in a short conversation. For example, Elaine, a real estate agent, needed to attend a sales meeting at the same time she had agreed to meet a client at the airport. Realizing that she could not be at the airport on time if she stayed for the meeting, she decided that making a sale was more important than attending a meeting. Since her co-workers were going to the meeting, she asked one of them to tape record the speaker's remarks so she could listen to the tape later and still meet her client. On her way to the airport she felt relieved that she had been able to solve the problem.

Within the space of a few minutes, Elaine identified and analyzed the problem, set her goal of maintaining a strong client relationship, found a solution to the situation, and put her plan into action by involving a co-worker. Her evaluation involved weighing the pros and cons of her choices.

Within these basic steps, several specialized techniques have been developed for problem solving. Different problems will call for different approaches, but these three techniques may be helpful when you need additional information in one of the steps.

Brainstorming

Brainstorming is a creative process in which a large number of solutions to any given problem are suggested without regard to their effectiveness. It can be used with both simple and complex problems and is particularly effective when new solutions are needed. Brainstorming can be done alone or in a group. The three main rules of brainstorming are

1. *Write down every possible solution or idea* as quickly as it comes to you.
2. *Make no criticisms or judgments during brainstorming.* Brainstorming allows the brain to work at full creativity without having to consider all the reasons a plan will not work.
3. *Anything goes.* Creativity is the essence of brainstorming. Some of the most far-fetched ideas in a brainstorming session may hold the key to a new solution. Nothing is too radical to suggest during brainstorming.

In a brainstorming session, allow the ideas to pour out as long as the think tank is boiling. Once ideas seem to subside or you find ideas repeating themselves, it is time to analyze the suggestions and end the brainstorming session.

The DIGEST Approach

The *DIGEST approach*, as its name implies, reduces a problem to its simplest components, suggests alternatives to the problem, and finally selects an alternative to become a plan of action (see Exercise 10-1). The word itself forms an acronym to help you remember the steps: Define, Identify, Get the facts, Evaluate the alternatives, Select an alternative, and Take action. Steps in the DIGEST approach are

1. *Define the situation.* Write a one- or two-sentence description of the situation as you see it, or describe the desired outcome or objective in a clear, concise statement.
2. *Identify the problem.* What are the objectives facing the company or department? Being specific about the problem helps create parameters for solutions.
3. *Get the facts.* What happened? When did it happen? Who is involved? What policies or procedures enter into this situation? Has this happened before and with what consequences? The cause is what led to the problem. The consequences are what is happening or what may happen because of the problem.
4. *Set up tentative alternatives.* List different plans that might be solutions to the problem. Use publications, files, interviews, magazines, or any other resource that might help provide a solution. Be careful to always focus on the problem and not the symptoms when defining an alternative.
5. *Evaluate the alternatives.* Think of criticisms to each alternative and try to eliminate them objectively. Analyze the effect of different alternatives on the groups involved in the situation. Will the alternative solve the problem or meet the objective? If you can answer yes, you are ready for the next step.
6. *Select the alternative you consider best.* Defend your choice based on the logical reasoning developed during the evaluation step. Why is it best? How will it resolve conflict?
7. *Take action.* Establish specific timetables and goals for the plan to go into practice. Follow up at appropriate intervals to see that the plan is still working.

The Decision Tree

A *decision tree* is a graphic method of portraying and comparing possible outcomes of each of a number of alternative solutions or remedial actions. To make a decision tree, write down a possible decision and branch out from it by adding probable consequences.

The sample decision tree in Exercise 10-2 was developed by an executive trying to decide if she should accept a transfer to another city.

As an exercise, develop your own decision tree (Exercise 10-2). You have been asked to accept a job which has greater responsibility but would mean working more hours and doing some job-related traveling. Your boss has told you not to expect an increase in pay right now. Starting with the decision to accept the job, develop a tree that shows some alternatives which may occur.

The Delphi Technique

The *Delphi technique*, a more complex problem-solving technique, uses input from other people but it is a noninteractional approach. That is, the manager using the Delphi technique collects and tabulates other people's opinions without discussion or debate. The people involved are generally unaware of anyone else's participation. The Delphi technique is a problem-solving technique that relies on written answers and feedback to determine the best solution.

Advantages of the technique include having the benefit of several people's thinking without jeopardizing the integrity of their ideas through discussion or personality differences. In a discussion, listeners may be persuaded to accept a different point of view or may change their minds during the talk. Using the Delphi technique avoids this pitfall and gives the manager sole control of the data. Six steps are involved in collecting the data from a chosen group of people:

1. Individuals independently fill out a series of questionnaires concerning problems or issues.
2. Questionnaires are collected and tabulated. Factual feedback of results is given to the panel members.
3. If panel members ask for more information on the problem or issue, they are given additional data.
4. Individuals fill out a second round of questionnaires and receive feedback.
5. The process of questionnaires and feedback continues until the investigator achieves a significant agreement among panel members.
6. A final report is written that presents the results of the questionnaire process.

Obviously, the written exchange of information requires that a great deal of time be spent in designing questionnaires, compiling data, digesting feedback, and reissuing questionnaires to begin the cycle again. The Delphi technique should be used in dealing with large issues, such as setting goals for the next decade of a company's growth, forecasting a city plan, solving energy costs, or developing alternative resources.

In these situations, managers are willing to sacrifice the time to obtain more thorough and thoughtful solutions to problems or issues.

COMMON DECISION PATTERNS

When faced with a tough decision, many people choose the easy way out. Throughout school and later in business, we unconsciously develop certain patterns that seem safer than confronting a decision head-on, which might involve risks. Six common decision making patterns include

Default: Many decisions occur without anyone consciously having made them. Saying "things will work out for themselves" or "fate will take hold" actually conveys a decision by default. Default decision making involves letting something happen due to inaction. This is a weak form of decision making because it allows circumstances to control the outcome rather than direct intervention. Although default may seem safe in the short term, managers need a reputation for being able to overcome problem situations rather than letting the problems overwhelm them by surrendering to them.

Intuition: Snap decisions or choosing a course of action just because it seems right may not be sufficient grounds for decision making in business. Although a few people are inherently correct judges of character or strategies, most people require some facts or data to support a conclusion. If you are tempted to make a quick decision, try to step back and see if you are really perceiving a personality clash or the emotional side of an issue. If you are aware of the real reason for your inner feelings, you may have found the evidence you need to support a so-called snap decision.

Reactionary: Effective managers act rather than react, but reaction is a strong reflex in human nature. "You did this, so I'm going to do that" is a reaction that managers must overcome. Making a decision solely on the basis of someone else's behavior negates the process of identifying the problem and developing solutions. Instead it reduces the situation to an adversarial role that may lead to negative results rather than to a positive solution.

Management by crisis: Some managers fall into a trap of firefighting management, that is, they always seem to be putting out small fires or crises in the office with little time to devote to solving long-range problems or planning future projects. Although every manager at times will have to make a decision in a crisis situation, most decisions can be well thought out by identifying the problem quickly before the consequences cause a crisis to develop. Owing to a lack of time, a decision forced by a crisis cannot involve the basic decision-making steps of setting goals and devising solutions; things are happening so quickly that important steps may be overlooked.

Delegation: One pattern of decision making is to shift the responsibility of the decision to another person. Delegation may be appropriate when the authority rests with another person or another employee is equipped to decide, thus freeing the manager for other duties. If a manager delegates a decision to avoid negative consequences or to minimize risks, then the delegation is probably a sign of insecurity or inexperience as a decision maker.

Deliberate: Some people seem to take forever to decide what color ink pens to buy or where to go for lunch. In business, the deliberate decision maker tries to achieve thoughtful decisions but often pays the consequences of taking too long to decide. Decision makers must be willing to take problem solving one step at a time, but they must be equally willing to let go of each step after giving it reasonable attention. If you deliberate too long you may find a problem has reached crisis proportions and now requires a different solution than when you began the process.

TYPES OF DECISIONS

Just as there are types of decision makers, there are types of decisions in business. Two major types are *programmed* and *creative* (Table 10-1).

Programmed decisions are routine decisions that are made so frequently that certain procedures or methods are developed for handling them. Examples might be routing customer deliveries, taking incoming calls, or circulating memos. *Creative decisions* are decisions made outside the daily routine. These may be one-time decisions or short-term projects that may not occur often enough to warrant a policy. If the same situation occurs with regularity, the manager might try to structure the decision-mak-

Table 10-1 Programmed versus Creative Decisions

PROGRAMMED DECISIONS	CREATIVE DECISIONS
Routine	Outside daily routine
Handled frequently	One-time
Certain procedures	Short term

ing process so that other employees can have the benefit of past experience. In this way, a creative decision may become a programmed decision, freeing time for the manager.

GROUP DECISION MAKING

Group decision making often occurs in an office situation because most people believe input from two or more people is better than input from one in resolving a problem. In practice, group decision making has advantages and disadvantages (Table 10-2).

ADVANTAGES:

□ Group decision making gives managers a wider range of information as each person involved has different educational and technical skills.

□ Varied experience lends a creative approach as each person views a problem from a different perspective.

□ Group decision making involves people outside the individual manager, thereby improving communication.

□ As employees are allowed to share in the decision making that affects them, they generally have higher morale as a result of knowing their opinions have value.

□ Employees gain greater commitment to the solution if they have had a part in creating the plan.

□ Group decisions build a team spirit that can translate into higher productivity and a general desire to improve the quality of work.

DISADVANTAGES:

□ Every additional person added to the decision-making process adds extra time, which may take time away from other tasks. When time is of the essence, group decision making may not be feasible.

Table 10-2 Group Decision Making

ADVANTAGES	DISADVANTAGES
More information	Extra time
Different skills and experiences	Manager has ultimate responsibility anyway
Improves communication	One person may dominate
Higher morale	Implementation takes longer
Greater commitment	Hidden agendas
Builds team spirit	Risk alienation
	Costs may outweigh results

❑   No matter how many people help make a decision, the manager ultimately has responsibility for the entire group's decision.

❑   One personality may dominate the process. If a person is more talkative or has more experience, those factors may overshadow the participation of others.

❑   Implementation may take longer as each member of the decision-making process is involved.

❑   People in the group may have hidden agendas to further their own positions or authority based on the outcome. These factors may reduce the chances of the decision meeting its goals.

❑   The manager may already know the probable outcome of the process or the solution most favorable to upper management and may risk alienating employees if they participate in a decision that is overruled.

If you have weighed the positive and negative aspects of group decision making, you immediately face the question of who will be involved in the process. In *Moving Up! Women and Leadership*, Hart (1980) cites six factors to consider when selecting a group: authority, experience, education, timing, motivation, and climate.

1. *Authority.* Authority means having the potential to get results. With more authority in the decision-making team, you can ensure a solid follow-through once the plan goes into action. A few people may need to be involved solely because of their position of authority in the corporate hierarchy. Others may have authority because of their length of tenure or expertise in a certain area. Balance these types of authority to get effective results. Leaving out an important authority figure may hurt your plan's

chances of success, particularly if that person has the final authority to overrule your solution.

2. *Experience.* Few situations can be considered new. Most have occurred at some time in the past although a few of the details may have changed. Managers should never waste time reinventing the wheel when they can rely on the experienced mind of someone who has been there before. A more experienced manager may be able to see fatal flaws in a plan that looks perfect on paper. Experience is a great teacher, but learning from someone else's experience may save time in the long run.

3. *Education.* Just as experience can be helpful to a team, education can be an important factor. A recent college graduate who understands the latest technology may be as vital to a workable solution as a 20-year career veteran who has seen other plans come and go. Familiarize yourself with the resumés of other employees so that you will know who to call for a computer question or a statistical evaluation.

4. *Timing.* Timing is a more subtle variable in decision making. In deciding who can help you make a decision, be sure to find people who can devote the required amount of time to the process. Timing is also crucial in asking people to think about solutions and to give any action plan a fair hearing. Rushing the process will weaken the outcome.

5. *Motivation.* One problem may have a different impact on every group. For example, a decrease in sales may mean cutbacks in hiring, a freeze on buying new equipment, or a new marketing strategy to reverse the trend. When deciding who will help make a decision, a manager should assess what different people have to gain or lose by solving the problem. People directly affected by a problem will be more motivated to find a solution than those who see the problem as affecting only other departments or businesses.

6. *Climate.* Climate is another intangible factor. Before a group can function as a decision maker, the group must have an atmosphere conducive to problem solving. A group charged with making an important decision is no place for personality conflicts, uncooperative employees, or disruptive forces that could undermine the outcome. Try to select people who will put aside individual differences to work on the problem for the common benefit of those involved.

If you decide to use group problem solving, you must assume certain responsibilities as the leader of the group. In discussions, allow ample time for positive and negative comments on an issue. Ask for supporting evidence when a conclusion seems contradictory. Combine conflicting ideas when possible. Use straw votes to monitor the direction in which a group is heading. Once a decision is reached, summarize the decision and document plans as you follow through.

CONCLUSION

Once you overcome the psychological barriers to decision making, you can develop your own style of problem solving. Keep in mind these ten elements of a creative attitude toward problem solving:

1. *Desire* to make things better
2. *Alertness* to seeing the situation as it is as well as how it might be
3. *Interest* in finding solutions that may involve research and digging below the surface
4. *Curiosity* to constantly find new solutions and better ways of doing things
5. *Thoughtfulness* in reaching logical conclusions supported by facts
6. *Concentration* to think through possible plans of actions and to analyze solutions in depth
7. *Application* to give the time and energy required by decision making
8. *Patience* to solve problems in detail and involve others in the process when appropriate
9. *Optimism,* which leads to thinking that solutions will be achieved and decisions can be implemented with self-confidence
10. *Cooperation* or working within the system to achieve productive results

SUMMARY

Solving problems and making decisions are daily components of a manager's job. By planning ahead, acting rather than reacting, and overcoming stereotypes about female roles, managers can develop problem-solving skills. To keep decisions from being overwhelming, managers must keep them in perspective and realize that every manager will make some mistakes. Most problems can be solved by a six-step process of identifying the problem, analyzing the problem, setting goals for the solution, searching for possible solutions, planning a course of action, and evaluating the solution that is implemented.

Decisions may be made as a group or individually depending on the situation. In either case, managers may want to use proven decision-making techniques, such as using the DIGEST approach or the Delphi technique.

TERMS AND CONCEPTS

authority	Delphi technique
brainstorming	DIGEST approach
climate	group decision making
commitment	intuition
creative decisions	management by crisis
decision tree	problem
default	problem solving
delegation	programmed decisions
deliberate	reactionary

REVIEW QUESTIONS

1. How do stereotypes of female behavior reflect on a woman executive's ability to solve problems and make decisions?
2. What points can managers use to keep decisions from becoming too overwhelming?
3. Name the six steps in problem solving that can be applied to almost any situation.
4. What is the DIGEST approach and how does it work?
5. What situations would the Delphi technique be useful in addressing?
6. Compare the advantages and disadvantages of group decision making.
7. What factors should be taken into consideration when forming a group that will make a decision or solve a problem?
8. What is the goal of effective decision making?
9. What are three basic strategies that women can use to overcome stereotypes of women problem solvers?

EXERCISES

10-1: THE DIGEST APPROACH

A local computer store is changing its marketing plan from showroom sales to outside sales. Each sales associate has a certain professional group such as doctors or lawyers as prospects. Barbara is the only female associate. Lately, when she has come in to check her calls, her boss has asked her to watch the showroom until another associate arrives. Barbara is frustrated because time spent in the showroom cuts down on the number of calls she can make. Because she is paid on commission, she feels unjustly penalized when she cannot make her calls. The few customers she has helped in the showroom have not made large enough purchases to justify her time.

Define the situation in one or two sentences.

Identify the problem. Based on the written situation, state the problem in concise terms.

Get the facts. List at least five facts that relate directly to the problem.

1.

2.

3.

4.

5.

Evaluate the alternatives against the following criteria:

    Will it solve the problem?

    Will it meet the objectives?

    What effect will it have on the individual, the group, or production?

Select the alternative you consider best. Defend your selection in writing to show why it is the best alternative

Take action. Write down three main steps in implementing your plan.

1.

2.

3.

10-2: DEVELOP YOUR OWN DECISION TREE

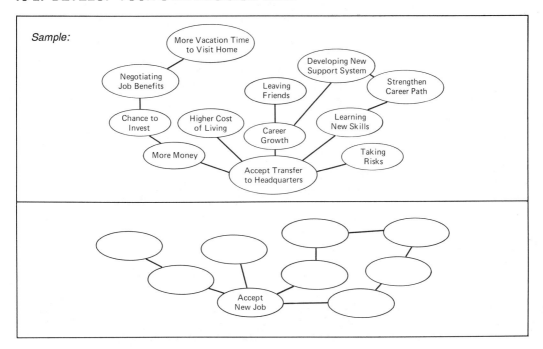

Sample:

Higher Cost of Living, More Vacation Time to Visit Home, Negotiating Job Benefits, Chance to Invest, More Money, Leaving Friends, Career Growth, Developing New Support System, Strengthen Career Path, Learning New Skills, Taking Risks, Accept Transfer to Headquarters

Accept New Job

SUGGESTED READINGS

Bay, T. *How to Turn Problems into Solutions: A Manager's Guide.* Prentice-Hall, Inc., Englewood Cliffs, NJ, 1980.

DeBono, E. *DeBono's Thinking Course.* Facts on File, NY, 1986.

Folger, J. P., and Poole, M. S. *Working Through Conflict. A Communication Perspective.* Scott, Foresman, Glenview, IL, 1984.

Hart, L. B. *Moving Up! Women and Leadership.* AMACOM, New York, 1980.

Huber, G. P. *Managerial Decision Making.* Scott, Foresman, Glenview, IL, 1980.

Ivancevich, J. M., Donnelly, J. H., and Gibson, J. L. *Managing for Performance* (3rd ed.). Business Publications, Dallas, TX, 1986.

Longenecker, J. G., and Pringle, C. D. *Management* (6th ed.). Charles E. Merrill, Columbus, OH, 1984.

Reitz, H. J., and Jewell, L. N. *Managing.* Scott, Foresman, Glenview, IL, 1985.

Rue, L., and Byars, L. *Supervision. Key Link to Productivity.* Irwin Publishers, Homewood, IL, 1986.

Sitterly, C. *Learning Guide for the Human Side of Organizations* (4th ed.). Harper & Row, New York, 1987.

Wonder, J., and Donovan, P. *Whole-Brain Thinking. Working from Both Sides of the Brain to Achieve Peak Job Performance.* Ballantine Books, New York, 1984.

11

TIME
MANAGEMENT

OBJECTIVES

- Think about time as a business resource, our greatest asset
- Prioritize
- Recognize time's internal and external traps
- Address procrastination
- Participate in and moderate an effective meeting
- Delegate and communicate more effectively
- Streamline paperwork
- Learn time-saving techniques

MANAGING TIME

For all the gains made by women through the last two decades, one area of management has always offered equal opportunities to males and females alike. Through time management, every employee—productive or nonproductive, effective or ineffective, man or woman—receives an equal number of minutes to work with each day.

Women may face a greater time management challenge because of extra responsibilities at home or in their communities, but they begin each day with 24 hours in their day's account. The effective use of allocated time is called *time management.* Effective time management enables one person to end the day with completed sales, edited correspondence, and a plan for meeting deadlines. Another person might use the same time to complete only one of these tasks. Women managers can strengthen their time management skills to enable them to make the most of each day's opportunities, personally and professionally. With the right skills, there is no such thing as a slow month.

Time as Money

Although you may be tired of hearing the statement, "Time is money," one of the first steps in effective time management is changing the way we view time. Analyze a busy person. Chances are that person organizes every minute of the day. She may be the person you see reading technical journals in an airport when others are complaining about canceled flights or she may be able to attend daily exercise classes after work when co-workers are stuck in a traffic jam.

When you begin to think about time as a business resource, you begin to realize the value of time management. Just as the right office equipment can simplify a complicated task, effective time management can create order out of a hectic work schedule.

Following the time-is-money analogy, use a simple diary to chart how you spend your time. Before you can start a financial budget, you have to know the dollar amounts available to you. Before you can plan your time, you have to be aware of how you currently spend it. Although each of us must work within the limits of a 24-hour day, the demands on a person's time change as responsibilities increase or decrease.

For example, two women share a similar job, a sales manager for an automobile dealership. It might seem that they have similar demands on their time and could benefit equally from the same schedule. However, a closer look reveals that one woman is trying to complete a master's degree in business administration during the evenings. She also travels every other week to meet her fiancé in another city for the weekend. The other sales manager and her husband have a preschooler and care for her elderly parents who live nearby.

Both women are in different situations as one plans for graduation and marriage and one mixes a career with child rearing and other family responsibilities. The prescription for better time management for each situation will be different. But the beginning method for charting time remains the same. Using an inexpensive notebook or tablet, keep a daily log of activities. Pay special attention to tasks so routine that you do not formally schedule them. Remember that even opening the mail or commuting to work is part of your 24-hour allotment.

After a week, the diary will form an outline of your life. If you have kept the diary with detailed discipline, you should be able to answer these questions about your time:

❑ Where does my time go?

❑ How can I use my time more effectively?

❑ Do my priorities fit my time expenditures?

Time's Net Worth

If you want to find out what an hour of your time is really worth, take your gross salary and divide it by 2,000. The resulting number is the value of each hour. For example, if a woman earns $50,000 a year as a gross salary, each hour of her time is worth $25 or 50,000 divided by 2,000.

Once you are aware of the value of 1 hour, you can begin to treat time as a commodity. For each hour you plan, experts estimate you save 3 hours, which further increases your time investment from the formula. Henry Ford said, "Thinking is the hardest thing to do. That's why so few people do it."

RANKING PRIORITIES

Every person thinks certain tasks are more important than others. From childhood we unconsciously begin to set priorities. Children who would rather continue playing than eat or sleep are indicating their priorities. For adults, priorities can usually be divided into two main categories: *work*, or professional demands, and *personal*, or family demands.

Making choices according to the perceived rank or importance of the task is setting priorities. By setting priorities, a manager ranks tasks from first to last or most pressing to least important.

Setting priorities is fundamental to controlling time, whether for a short-term daily itinerary or for a long-term research project. Priorities create a guide that tells us what must be completed first in order to achieve the desired end results. Supervisors have the additional responsibility of setting priorities for their staff members to keep the business running smoothly.

Written priorities are more effective than mental notes. Writing indicates a commitment to accomplish certain tasks and helps you visualize the job. Writing also enhances memory skills so that important details will not be forgotten. Once the list is on paper, you can begin systematically checking things off both mentally and physically.

Looking at the list, rank items from most important to least important. Designate which part of the list includes projects with an immediate deadline, or short-term implications, and which are parts of a larger long-term project.

Some items on your list may not actually be your job. As a manager, your responsibility is to see that your time, as well as your staff members' time, is used most effectively. If someone on your staff could perform the task equally well or if it is part of her job description, make a note in the margin of your list to delegate that item. Chances are at least one or two things on your list belong on another staff member's outline.

Charles Schwab, president of Bethlehem Steel in the 1930s, sent Ivy Lee, a founder of management consulting, a sizable check in appreciation for these tips:

- Set priorities
- Match time and resources to the relative importance of each task
- Rank tasks:
    1. Must
    2. Mid-range
    3. Routine

This concise list of points is still applicable for today's managers. Ranking the items on the list puts you in control of the agenda. Items may be ranked chronologically, according to which deadline is first, or topically, according to subject matter within a certain project. Other managers may rank items according to the time of day in which they can best accomplish them, such as when colleagues are most likely to be in their offices to return phone calls.

Your ranking system needs to determine which tasks are most crucial to the day's work, which must be done before the day concludes, and which can be postponed to another day.

After ranking the items, ask yourself, which of these items will make the most difference in my personal or professional life today? Be sure to save creative energy for the task you select.

After a few weeks of making a list and ranking the items, you should experience productivity gains as you check off each item as you accomplish the task.

TIME TRAPS

Once you know where your time goes, you can work on skills to help you avoid time traps (see Exercise 11-1). Time traps can be interruptions, unscheduled meetings, drop-in visitors, or anything that causes you to derail a well-planned day. A supervisor often begins the day with the resolve to complete a large project only to find herself robbed of her time by unplanned demands.

Think back to a day that became a time management disaster. Name three occurrences that caused you to stop concentrating on the main project. Distractions such as these may lead to ineffective time management practices. Time traps basically fall into two categories:

❑   Things you can control or internal time traps
❑   Things you cannot control or external time traps

Although you may not be able to change the behavior of others and completely eliminate *external time traps*, you can identify them so that you are aware of their effect on your schedule. External time traps include

❑   Telephone calls
❑   Meetings
❑   Visitors
❑   Paperwork
❑   Red tape
❑   Lack of competent personnel or lack of policies and procedures

Internal time traps are more subtle. These are personal traits or work habits that prevent effective time management. Although we may attribute these to our personality or our nature, most of these traits are learned behavior that we can modify. Internal time traps include

- ❑ Procrastination
- ❑ Inadequate delegation
- ❑ Failure to plan
- ❑ Poor scheduling
- ❑ Lack of self-discipline
- ❑ Attempting to do too much at once (unrealistic expectations)
- ❑ Lack of relevant skills

Procrastination

Procrastination may be the most common internal time trap. Almost everyone can recall a time when a job was postponed for some reason. Although we may say that we do our best work under pressure, most of us work best under pressure because we put off doing the task until we have no choice.

We seldom procrastinate on easy jobs. Usually the postponed job is too routine or boring or too overwhelming to know where to start. Rather than attacking the problem by breaking the task down into more manageable pieces, we are more apt to socialize with co-workers or spend our time with busywork to avoid the unappealing task.

Daydreaming, reading, avoiding delegation of routine tasks, subconsciously overloading your own agenda, or running away may all be symptoms of procrastination.

If the task seems too big, think about each step as a unit. Instead of writing down "complete annual report," write down the steps, such as "organize figures into profit and loss graph" or "send memos to directors asking for their message to stockholders." You can then concentrate on individual parts of the project rather than on the project as a whole.

Checking off an item on the list provides a feeling of exhilaration. Some managers may also build in tangible rewards, such as a coffee break after completing a rough draft of a letter or a short walk at lunch after a budget review.

Even with these controls in place, every manager occasionally faces an overwhelming task. When this happens, you can ask for help from a senior staff member or try to work out the problem on paper first. If you have a mental block about a problem, take a blank sheet of paper and draw a vertical line down the middle. In one column write down what happens if you complete the job and what happens if you do not in the second column. Look at the gains and the repercussions before you continue.

Save your most creative thinking hours for a large job. If you feel freshest in the mornings, concentrate on larger jobs early in the day. If you think most clearly after your first cup of coffee, do routine tasks until you are fully awake and then get down to more demanding work. Do not wait until you have only an hour or two before 5 PM to start a major task you would rather postpone.

Baby Ducks

Baby ducks are those less important details, tasks, and interruptions that nibble away at time required to complete key projects and responsibilities. For best results, discipline yourself to focus on those activities or projects that will make the greatest contribution, most significant difference, and greatest return on your investment of time and energy. For example, Kris was working against a pending deadline to complete a presentation to senior management. She needed a few hours to concentrate without interruptions. The public relations officer called asking for a new photograph for a news release, the mail arrived with an interesting seminar brochure, and her secretary dropped in to remind her she would be leaving for a long-standing dental appointment just as Kris was going to ask her to duplicate presentation materials. Kris took her copies to the photocopier only to find it was temporarily out of service again. Where was the repair number? Count the baby ducks. How many do you see?

TIME-SAVING TECHNIQUES

Making a *things-to-do list* is fundamental to controlling your time. Other techniques can be equally valuable when adapted to the needs of your day (Figure 11-1).

The second most important time management tool is a *calendar*. Office supply stores are full of calendars that provide a detailed hour-by-hour daily schedule or a year-long planning reference (Figures 11-2 and 11-3). You may need a calendar that fits in a purse or briefcase for reference during sales calls or a desk calendar on which to schedule appointments by phone. Select a style that fits your needs and write down deadlines and appointments.

Organizer systems that combine daily, monthly, and yearly calendars along with pages for goals, names and addresses, and notes have also grown in popularity. Some stores sell empty

THINGS TO DO!

Date: _____

Urgent   Done

❑   1. _____   ❑

❑   2. _____   ❑

❑   3. _____   ❑

❑   4. _____   ❑

❑   5. _____   ❑

❑   6. _____   ❑

❑   7. _____   ❑

❑   8. _____   ❑

❑   9. _____   ❑

❑ 10. _____   ❑

Notes: _____

_____

_____

_____

_____

_____

Figure 11-1 Sample things-to-do list.

	MONDAY	TUESDAY	WEDNESDAY	THURSDAY	DATE _____ FRIDAY
9 A.M.					
10 A.M.					
11 A.M.					
12 NOON					
1 P.M.					
2 P.M.					
3 P.M.					
4 P.M.					
5 P.M.					

Figure 11-2 Sample of a detailed hour-by-hour daily schedule.

	JANUARY	FEBRUARY	MARCH	APRIL	MAY	JUNE	JULY	AUGUST	SEPTEMBER	OCTOBER	NOVEMBER	DECEMBER
1												
2												
3												
4												
5												
6												
7												
8												
9												
10												
11												
12												
13												
14												
15												
16												
17												
18												
19												
20												
21												
22												
23												
24												
25												
26												
27												
28												
29												
30												
31												

Figure 11-3 Sample of a year-long planning reference.

notebooks and allow you to customize the inserts for special career or personal needs. Whatever your choice of system, it will only be as effective as you are in keeping entries up to date. A complete calendar will also give you a diary of activities for completing year-end reports.

Another time management aid is even less expensive than a calendar. Buy a set of 3-by-5 inch cards. Use one card to write down all your standing appointments for the month, such as a regular staff meeting, professional association meetings, civic club meetings, or family occasions such as birthdays. Refer to the card when scheduling trips or obligations.

On other cards, write down the names of co-workers or friends. Resist the impulse to call them about a small detail. Instead write the note on their card and plan to call them at a certain time to take care of several details. One organized phone call can save the trouble of drafting a memo or can replace several short calls.

Common sense is the best skill for time managers. If office policy permits, ask for a bulletin board at eye level from your desk. Use this space for reminders and messages to limit desk clutter. The bulletin board can also be used as a visual aid or improvised poster on which to diagram a project during an informal meeting.

If you cannot have a bulletin board, a flip chart is helpful in organizing projects. Use the chart to write down individual components of a large project.

One of the most useful of these techniques is the *PERT* or *Performance Evaluation and Review Technique.* PERT charts diagram the flow of activities from start to finish for a project. These may be heavily detailed or of a general nature.

Think of the PERT chart as a things-to-do list in chronological order. You can diagram the schedule and sequence of activities to coordinate the timing and identify the critical path to shorter project completion time. If plans call for you to consolidate a division, you would need to think through each task involved to reach that goal. The last step is obvious, since it represents the completed project, but how do you proceed?

Using a bulletin board or flip chart, write down each step in reaching the goal— no matter how trivial. Put each task on a small piece of paper as you think of it even though the steps may not be in order. Your chart might look like this:

❑   Meet with division heads
❑   Chart staffing needs
❑   Advise on relocation options

- ❑ Make public announcement
- ❑ Appoint transition team
- ❑ Complete division move by end of fiscal year

Now take your papers and arrange them visually in chronological order. If two steps must coincide for maximum effectiveness, place them on top of one another to avoid impeding the flow. After all the papers are on the board, you will have created a PERT chart for the project. Reduce your visual aid to a short memo and you will have a work outline to follow.

To make your model more complete, assign deadlines and use it as a performance checklist. Mark initials of staff members next to jobs to begin the delegation process. Share the chart with employees to give them a perspective on what their task means to the total project.

For some projects, parallel PERT charts for time effectiveness and cost effectiveness may be necessary before you decide on a plan (see Exercise 11-2).

TRIMMING MEETING TIME

Someone has said that the only people who want to attend staff meetings are those who have never been invited. The usual staff meeting is full of inefficiencies. Meetings generally neither start nor end on time. Often a prompt person is penalized by having to wait for latecomers. If staff members are unprepared for reports or agenda items, additional meeting time may be necessary. A few talkers may monopolize the time for their ideas while others sit silently until adjournment.

Yet with all these problems, meetings remain a primary tool for accomplishing business. When a memo, phone call, or informal conversation is insufficient for the needed results, you must convene a meeting. The secret of effective meetings is common sense time management. The only difference is that for a meeting you must manage the time of all participants rather than just for yourself.

Although other people in your organization may have a reputation for wasting time through inefficient meetings, you can use certain techniques to ensure that your meetings serve as a role model.

The most crucial time in determining how effective a meeting will be is not at the meeting, but during the planning stage. The first rule is to decide why a meeting is necessary. Try to summarize the need for the meeting into a clear, concise sentence. If you cannot verbalize the reason for the meeting, you may not need to go any further. You may, instead, need to make a phone call, write a memo, or research a fact.

Most meetings fall into a few general categories, such as *brainstorming, planning, organizing,* or *goal setting.* In a *brainstorming* meeting, participants are asked to come up with any suggestions they can think of to solve a problem or generate creative ideas. *Planning* meetings might be convened to develop a working outline for an upcoming project using participants' input to determine details. A meeting for *organization* might involve updating a project or pulling several different departments together toward a common goal. Finally, a *goal-setting* meeting would allow several participants to determine the future needs of a group or organization.

If you can determine which meeting fits your need, you can retain control by keeping the discussion on the central theme. Too many times a brainstorming meeting for a certain project digresses into a long-winded philosophical discussion more appropriate to a long-range goal-setting session. Do not let others derail your meeting. If, after some discussion, you decide another meeting is necessary, postpone inappropriate agenda items until that time.

An *agenda* or meeting outline is a useful tool in controlling discussion. Consider the agenda your homework before the meeting. A well-planned agenda includes names of those who will attend a meeting, the time and place of the meeting, and relevant items for discussion. Assign reports by placing staff members' names next to their responsibilities on the agenda. The agenda can do double duty as a reminder notice for advance preparation to save additional memos outlining report duties. An agenda should include the purpose of the meeting, objectives, decisions or questions that will be answered, and discussion topics. Note materials or preparation that are required. Rank the questions or discussion topics in order of importance. Note the number of minutes that can be allocated to each topic. Distribute the agenda before the meeting to allow participants to prepare.

SAMPLE AGENDA

❑ Planning Session for Ad Campaign
❑ 10:15 AM
❑ Thursday, May 15
❑ Second Floor Conference Room

❑ Attendance requested: Marketing Vice President
                          Corporate Secretary
                          Treasurer
                          Advertising Agency Representative

1. Introductions
2. Presentation of Campaign Budget—Treasurer
3. Agency Proposal—Advertising Representative
4. Discussion
5. Adjournment

In this example, the meeting was necessary because an outside firm, an advertising agency, needed to present proposals to key executives. Note the flexibility of the agenda to allow discussion. Some agendas may need to be more detailed or even include adjournment time or timed discussion items if a participant needs to catch a plane or a conference room needs to be vacated for another function. In more structured groups, the chairman may want to ask for voice approval of the agenda before beginning the meeting. By approving an agenda, participants agree to stay within the discussion items and a set deadline. They will be less likely to stray from a stated outline.

The agenda should state clearly the time and location. Both details are crucial to your goal of organizing a well-ordered meeting. Consider whether a morning, lunchtime, or afternoon meeting offers maximum participation. Sometimes a meeting at the end of the day encourages short reports. Start your meetings on time so as not to waste the time of those who respect the original intent of the agenda. After a while, people will realize that latecomers miss valuable discussion and have to catch up on their own. Choose the meeting room with equal thought. Comfortable chairs and refreshments have their place in certain settings, but may prolong a concise agenda. A stand-up meeting may accomplish the same results as a boardroom conference in less time. Let the agenda be your guide in deciding the place.

If a meeting involves only one person, go to that person's office so that you can leave when you finish talking. If the meeting is held in your office, you may be a captive audience until the person breaks off the conversation.

If you are on the receiving end of the agenda rather than the planning side, call the person who is convening the meeting to be sure that you know which parts of a report you are responsible for. If you are still unsure, submit a written draft of your report in advance. At the meeting, give a copy of your report to the secretary so that you get credit for being well prepared and your remarks are correctly entered into the minutes.

THE PAPER SHUFFLE

Although many offices are making strides in automation, paperwork remains critical to most corporate recordkeeping. Mail, memos, file copies, reports, invoices, and receipts all account for the mass of paperwork an office will eventually handle. In all cases, when in doubt, throw it out! Much office paperwork arrives via the mail. Therefore delegating the mail can be instrumental in cutting down paperwork. Delegate the mail to those familiar with the business. They can automatically separate junk mail from correspondence. Unless you are shopping for new equipment, instruct the mail clerk to file all catalogs and sale fliers for future reference; although these make interesting reading, they consume valuable working time. If a piece of mail carries no return address, it can generally be considered worthless. Put any duplicate mailings in the trash. If you wish to correct a mailing list, make the changes directly on the envelope that has the incorrect address and return it to the company so that you receive only one set of mail from the firm.

Buy a rubber stamp with an interchangeable date to process mail. The stamp helps keep track of the date you received the item, as well as the length of time it took to answer or file the material.

When possible, answer the letter on the letter itself. Then make a copy for your files. In most cases, this procedure relieves you of having to repeat major portions of the original inquiry. Your answer and the original letter take up only one piece of paper for future filing, thereby avoiding clutter.

Some letters may be answered with a telephone call. Jot a note of the call on your calendar if you need a reference. The rule of thumb is say it first in person, second on the phone, and third in writing to save work and the ensuing paperwork. If several people need to see a memo, mark it for interoffice routing rather than making copies.

Merle L. Meacham said, "Xerox is a trademark for a photocopying device that can make rapid reproductions of human error, perfectly."

If you have a computer, use it to create form letters and simple forms for routine items. Otherwise develop a file of standard letters to save dictation time when common situations or questions arise.

FILES

Files constitute a different type of paperwork than letters. Files become the permanent record of work and correspondence for the company. Although most files contain papers that have not been used in more than a year, certain files must be retained in order to reconstruct events or correspondence. Sometimes files become documentation in legal or financial disputes. At other times files serve as a collective memory in case a key person is no longer with the organization or an event happened before certain employees were assigned to the job.

Before clearing out a file cabinet, ask the accounting department and the legal department for guidelines on how long correspondence should be saved. Items pertaining to upcoming jobs, for example, should be kept even though they may be past a 3 or 5 year time limit. Some firms specify how long different items should stay in the files.

Once you know what items the company prefers to keep, separate files into current projects and completed projects. Completed project files may be stored in less convenient areas such as a central storage area or a room set aside for back files away from the main work areas. This frees valuable space for current files. Label back files adequately to save time when you must refer to their contents. Attach a note to back files showing the date you last used them. Once a year, throw out back files that no one has consulted in the last 12 months and that are no longer required by company filing policies.

When space is at a premium, many managers are tempted to ask for a new filing cabinet. A new trash can may be a better investment if your department has not sorted through existing files recently. Try to think of at least one reason for saving an item. Saving a letter from a famous person for sentimental reasons is perfectly acceptable. Just move it from the current correspondence file to a personal back file. If neither you nor any member of your staff can give a valid reason for saving something the company no longer requires you to keep, you are better off without it. In cleaning out files, give some thought to others in your firm who may have duplicate items on file. Try to consolidate these files into a central area to save storage space in individual offices or work areas.

Fewer files mean less paperwork to handle when you need to research a fact or review a letter. Less paperwork creates an environment that encourages effective time management. When you look at artists' concepts of the office of tomorrow, you see a near-paperless society. Computers replace file cabinets, desks function primarily as computer stations without drawers or typewriters, and computers record many messages not handled on paper. Even today, a neat desk and organized work area create an image of efficiency.

A good rule of thumb for making files is that when you have three pieces of correspondence pertaining to one project, you need to make a file. Otherwise general files such as correspondence and memos may serve your needs. One other essential file for business is a tickler file. This file can be set up with pockets for the 12 months or days in a month. In each pocket place notes to call prospects or meet deadlines. At the start of each month or day, check the file to retrieve that day's reminders.

Remember that a desk is not a place to stack items you want to remember. That is the job for well-organized files. Create a folder for leads or prospects. Create a business card file organized by cities, jobs, or people's names according to the way you best remember information. Place phone messages on a spindle or bulletin board. Simplify your workspace whenever possible.

COMMUNICATION

Paperwork is just one way to communicate in business. The telephone call has become more and more important when information is needed quickly.

Most businesses will have an operator or telephone receptionist to direct calls efficiently and screen out unwanted interruptions. For smaller firms, however, a telephone answering service or mechanical answering machine may be more economical. Although people resist a machine or answering service, most businesses have accepted them as a way to convey messages. If someone really needs to talk to you, chances are they will leave messages promptly.

If you have a secretary, free yourself of telephone answering duties. Schedule quiet time to work without phone interruptions and block out a portion of each day to return calls. Ask your secretary to handle as many questions as possible to cut down on telephone time.

One expert estimates that 80 percent of calls are made by 20 percent of the people—whether they are from friends, family members, or co-workers. Even if company rules permit flexible use of the phone, try to limit calls to 3 minutes or less as a mental discipline. Ask friends and family to call only at certain less hectic times of the day.

Schedule critical conversations as you would any other business appointment and allow no interruptions. Treat the call with the same attention you would give an in-person visit at your office.

Etiquette for business calls requires different rules than for personal calls. Try to get to the point of the call as quickly as you can without encouraging social comments. If a caller is long winded, ask them to call back at a less busy time.

If you are placing the call, use the time wisely. Make notes of questions that have to be answered. Save unnecessary call backs by consolidating several calls into one.

DELEGATION

Managers not only organize their own work but also the work of those they supervise. Delegation is the managerial act of assigning work to others, granting the subordinate the right to act or make decisions. Delegation, as with effective time management, is a skill that requires practice. At first, it may seem easier to do the job yourself—after all you know what has to be done and trust your work. However, if a manager constantly does the work of subordinates, work on the management level suffers.

Delegation begins by matching the task to the person. Try to determine who the best person is for a job based on speed of work, accuracy, or training opportunities. Match the employee's skills with the work that needs to be done. Realize that in order to be an effective manager, you must perceive yourself as one who delegates her authority rather than one who stays so busy with day-to-day tasks that she is unable to accomplish more important goals.

Avoid the temptation to continue doing routine jobs as you move up the career ladder, even though you may enjoy the security of doing familiar tasks. A good first step in delegation is to read your job description and the job descriptions of the people you supervise. If the descriptions are more than one year old, update them with new duties and responsibilities.

Next, list all the activities and responsibilities you have performed in the last few weeks. Break down these projects into individual tasks. Beside each task, place the initials of an employee whose job description includes similar activities. As you plan future projects, refer to the list before assuming a responsibility yourself. Thinking through the process of delegation helps a manager decide who should do a certain job.

If you resist delegation because an employee has not been trained, take specific steps to ensure that they will have adequate training before the project. Holding on to details is a strong temptation for managers who suspect they can do the best job for the company. However, only by training others to carry out details can managers free their time to achieve the objectives entrusted to them by the company.

SOME TRAPS TO EFFECTIVE DELEGATION

- ❑ "I don't have time to explain."
- ❑ "No one else will do it correctly."
- ❑ "I like this job so I'll do it."
- ❑ "This is an awful job, I can't give it to anyone else."

The person who receives your assignment must have technical skills, motivation, imagination, and dependability. You have to believe that the person will accomplish the task in order to let go of the responsibility. Think of delegating as a way to develop managerial skills in those you supervise.

When delegating, make the expectations clear. Spell out the degree of thoroughness, accuracy, deadlines, and quality of finished product you expect. Make the assignment in writing if you are concerned about details. Clearly delegate the work rather than making a suggestion. Ask the employee about concerns or questions before the project starts and clarify the procedures for reporting progress.

On the reverse side, if you are given a task, ask for clear instructions on how much time you have and how much responsibility you will have to get results. Delegation works best when both sides define the task and outline the scope of the work. New employees particularly may need feedback to understand the job and the reasons they were selected to carry it out.

Once a task is clearly delegated, you can discuss objectives, standards, time targets, and checkpoints. Be willing to answer questions, but watch out for questions that lead you into doing the job yourself. Instead, assume the role of consultant to offer support and encourage independence.

TIME BONUSES

As with any form of behavior modification, time management becomes a habit. Getting a full 24 hours from each day becomes a challenge. As you learn about your time expenditures, take some hints from others who have found common sense tips that simplify some tasks to give you more time for your important goals.

Plan ahead. Take advantage of free time to survey the next week or month and get a mental picture of the energy you will need.

Use a travel agent. Since they are paid commissions by airlines, they can function as a free staff travel planner. Their computer links save time and money in knowing the best fares and schedules.

Organize your work to do several tasks at once. You can read correspondence while you are on hold. You can pay bills after you balance your checkbook.

Use every service that you pay for indirectly as a taxpayer. Public libraries offer research departments that can locate facts in a hurry. A phone call may save a staff member hours of research time. Public universities often tie business courses to the community. For example, a marketing professor may allow students to do marketing research for local businesses as a class project.

Minimize errands by making lists before you leave home. Check the pantry before going to the grocery. Plan menus to have ingredients on hand. Shop at businesses located between your home and office.

Waiting need not waste time if you carry materials with you. Use waiting time to make notes or read short articles. A small package of stationery in your briefcase can be used to catch up on informal, handwritten notes of acknowledgment that you can do away from your desk.

Instead of reaching for an inflight magazine, take a technical journal on airplanes to catch up on reading. A small tape recorder can be used to play recorded books or dictate messages.

Subscribe to computer services or executive summary publications to receive up-to-date, condensed information. Scan titles and highlight passages to get more out of your reading time.

Shop at off times in stores for better service without crowds or order from catalogs. Buy in quantity, if you find something you like, to save time tracking down a favorite brand later.

Look for places that deliver free of charge or at a low cost. Personal shoppers, dry cleaning services, and grocery markets may be worth the extra cost if they deliver.

SUMMARY

All managers have the same amount of time each day. What makes the difference between an effective and an ineffective manager can be strong time management skills. Finding out what your time is worth emphasizes the importance of managing time. Setting priorities allows you to decide which tasks to spend the most time on and which tasks to complete first.

Although managers do not retain control over all aspects of their time, with practice they can minimize the interruptions and time robbers that contribute to inefficiency on the job. Making a things-to-do list can help organize tasks. Streamlining meetings can also open up additional work time during the week. Controlling paperwork and other communication can also reduce office clutter and inefficient work habits.

TERMS AND CONCEPTS

agenda   procrastination
baby ducks   time as money
brainstorming   time bonuses
delegation   time management
PERT   things-to-do list

REVIEW QUESTIONS

1. How can you determine what your time is worth in dollars and cents?

2. What are major pitfalls that occur in a business day that inhibit time management?

3. How can you overcome the temptation to procrastinate when starting a major project?

4. How can an agenda make a meeting more effective?

5. What is a tickler file and how is it used?

6. What are some traps to effective delegation of work?

7. What services available in most communities can offer time bonuses by freeing up a manager's time?

EXERCISES

11-1: TIME TRAPS

Instructions: From each list below, check the three great traps that most impede your ability to effectively manage your time.

EXTERNAL		INTERNAL	
Telephone	❑	Procrastination	❑
Meetings	❑	Poor delegation	❑
Visitors	❑	Failure to plan	❑
Paperwork	❑	Poor scheduling	❑
Red tape	❑	Lack of self-discipline	❑
Lack of competent personnel	❑	Too much at once	❑
Lack of policies	❑	Lack of skills	❑

Brainstorm: Identify at least two solutions for each trap identified from reading the text and discussion.

1.

2.

3.

4.

5.

6.

7.

8.

9.

10.

11.

12.

11-2: PERT CHART

Instructions: Prepare a diagram of a PERT chart for a project below or on a separate sheet of paper. Compare with other PERT charts. How did it affect your project?

SUGGESTED READINGS

Duke, B., and Sitterly, C. Work Smart. *The Secretary.* (June/July 1986).

Haimann, T., and Hilgert, R. *Supervision: Concepts and Practices of Management.* (4th ed.). South-Western, Chicago, IL, 1987.

Januz, L. R., and Jones, S. K. *Time-Management for Executives.* Charles Scribner's Sons, New York, 1981.

Lakein, A. *How to Get Control of Your Time and Your Life.* Signet, New York, 1980.

Mackenzie, A., and Waldo, K. C. *About Time! A Woman's Guide to Time Management.* McGraw-Hill, New York, 1981.

Mosrick, R. K., and Nelson, R. *We've Got to Start Meeting Like This.* Scott, Foresman, Glenview, IL, 1987.

Turla, P., and Hawkins, K. L. *A Personal Achievement Guide to Time Management.* Success Unlimited, Inc., Chicago, IL (no date).

Winston, S. *The Organized Executive.* W. W. Norton, New York, 1983.

12

FINANCIAL PLANNING

OBJECTIVES

- Recognize myths about women and money
- Develop attributes and challenges to control your finances
- Understand math phobia
- Determine your net worth
- Determine where and how money is spent
- Set financial goals
- List of information someone else should know
- Identify factors that affect your financial situation
- Establish a financial record-keeping system
- Learn mathematical formulas for financial record keeping
- Read an annual report
- Prepare a budget
- Choose an investment
- Select a professional team

WOMEN AND MONEY: THE MYTHS AND THE MYSTIQUE

Myths about women and money that American women have heard since birth include

1. The right man, Prince Charming or Mr. Fix-It, will come along and take care of you.
2. Don't worry your pretty little head about numbers.
3. It is not feminine to be motivated by money or to be rich by your own efforts.
4. Women should not compete with men for money or careers.
5. Money is a man's game.

Men are not by nature more financially capable than women, they are just expected to be. Women must recognize the stereotypes, overcome the negative conditioning, and take control of their own finances. Women should be prepared for the changes caused by divorce, death, catastrophe, and old age. Women are just as capable as men, and they have the right and obligation to protect their own financial interests.

In *The Women's Handbook for Financial Planning*, Rosenbaum offers four attributes to help control your own finances:

1. *Attitude.* You must want to take responsibility for your own finances and your future.
2. *Set career and life-style goals.* Where do I want to be 5 years from now? Ten years? Retirement age?
3. *Get financial training.* Acquire a knowledge of accounting, and set projections to become financially secure and to advance in your career.
4. *Develop a comprehensive financial plan.* A financial plan charts the steps you must take to reach your financial and career goals.

To develop a financial plan, women must meet these five challenges:

1. Accept responsibility for your own finances, present and future
2. Commit yourself to learning the basics
3. Set realistic goals for all aspects of your life, including your financial future

4. Choose a team of professional advisors
5. Establish a proper record-keeping system and keep files up
   to date

MATH PHOBIA

Math phobia describes a reluctance on the part of a person to work with numbers. Many times a woman will score well on math aptitude tests but will have deep-seated fears about failing math courses or making mistakes when doing computations. This concept of math anxiety is documented by Schenkel (1984) in *Giving Away Success*. A university professor noticed that many of his female students had mental blocks about learning statistics. In the same study, a social worker found that women, who otherwise would be considered high achievers, reacted to math activities with symptoms usually linked to phobias.

No evidence exists that math proficiency is a sex-linked trait. Yet many men and women in business and academic circles still accept this cultural myth. When boys fail in math, teachers and students attribute it to a lack of effort. When girls fail, they are more likely to link it to a lack of inherent ability.

More and more women who are free from or are unaffected by math anxiety are taking steps to fight the myth that money management skills are related to sex. Women must realize that financial skills, like all other management skills, can be learned and practiced to gain a level of expertise.

Once we address the myth that money is a man's realm and a man's game, we can start earning what we are worth and enjoying the success that money and money management can bring.

DEVELOPING FISCAL FITNESS

If the idea of money management seems too overwhelming, break it down into small parts. Divide your goal of developing skills in money management into stages, first learning to control your personal finances, then translating those skills into your job. Many women who have successfully run a $50,000 household budget or a $100,000 charity project might be surprised to find out how those skills relate directly to developing a budget for a business or writing an annual report. The Association of Junior Leagues has created a Volunteer Skills Portfolio designed to help women recognize skills developed at home or in volunteer work that can be included on a resumé when seeking jobs for pay (Association of Junior Leagues Inc., 825 Third Avenue, New York, New York 10022).

Many career women live from paycheck to paycheck and have no idea what they are really worth. They may be waiting until they get married to think about buying a house or waiting until they have dependents to discuss insurance needs. Tragically many women find out how much they are worth only when they have to replace their possessions after a burglary or fire.

Finding out how much you are worth can be as simple as adding your total *assets*, and subtracting your total *liabilities*. The resulting total is your *net worth*. *Assets* are the sum of all you own, including your salary, your car, your household furnishings, your clothing and jewelry, and any other property such as stocks or a house. *Liabilities* are your debts, the sum of all you owe. These can be bank loans, outstanding mortgages on a residence, car payments, credit card balances, or taxes that are due. One of the best ways to compute net worth is to fill out a *financial statement form*.

Blank financial statement forms are usually available free at any bank or savings and loan. Customers are generally asked to fill one out when applying for a loan or updating bank records.

The *financial statement form* is actually a detailed list of the most common categories for assets and liabilities. By filling out the form, you are less likely to overlook important information such as the cash value of an insurance policy or a collection of antiques. Once you have completed your financial statement, you have the background necessary for future financial decisions.

You may realize that you need to upgrade your insurance coverage to be able to replace your personal possessions. You may find out that your credit card balances added together have overloaded you with a debt that you need to pay off before you charge any more purchases. You may find that although you are making a good salary, you have little to show for it, and you need to develop a long-range financial plan.

Budgeting

Next to a financial statement, a *budget* is the working financial tool most used in business. A budget is really a summary of where the money goes. In preparing a family budget, first make a list of all fixed expenses, such as rent or mortgage payments, utility bills, taxes, insurance, loan payments, professional expenses such as dues, medical and dental care, and automobile expenses. These are called *fixed costs*, because they represent items that you must regularly pay, although you have little control over the cost. After you add these up, subtract them from the amount of your take-home pay. The difference is what is available for variable costs.

Variable costs may be essential, such as food, or nonessential, such as entertainment. Variable costs, in contrast to fixed costs, give the buyer greater latitude in making spending decisions. With food, for example, you may decide to eat at home or out. If you decide to eat out, you can choose between a fast-food restaurant or a full-service restaurant with a wide range of price options in between. In making a budget, all food, whether eaten at home or away, must be taken into account to get a realistic idea of the amount spent on food. Other necessary variable expenses might be unexpected car repairs, housing maintenance, and clothing to wear to work. Nonessential items include entertainment, whether renting movies from a video store or attending live theater performances, vacations, classes and lessons for recreation, furniture, and gift items. These nonessential areas should be included in a budget whenever possible as a way to reward yourself for working, but these also represent areas that can be trimmed in times of financial need.

Most people overspend because they want more than they can afford. They buy on impulse instead of considering their goals, or they have little idea about where their money goes. A budget can help solve these problems by presenting a realistic picture of how much it costs for you to live month to month and how much is left for discretionary purchases or investments (see Exercise 12-1).

How Do You Spend Your Money?

To find out where your money goes, review your checkbook and complete the following ledgers (from Rosenbaum, n.d.).

Categories should reflect your situation; you can change, add, or delete items as necessary to determine your priorities.

To complete the *daily ledger*, enter the amount of money spent in each category each day. Categories are rent, food, clothes, utilities, phone, entertainment, car, day care, maintenance, medical, miscellaneous, total, and in the last column enter income.

To complete the *monthly ledger*, add daily totals and enter for each month.

INCOME EXPENSES—WHERE DOES YOUR MONEY GO?
DAILY LEDGER

Date	Rent	Food	Clothes	Util.	Phone	Enter.	Car	Day Care	Maint.	Med.	Misc.	Tot.	Income
1													
2													
3													
4													
5													
6													
7													
8													
9													
10													
11													
12													
13													
14													
15													
16													
17													
18													
•													
•													
•													
27													
28													
29													
30													
31													

MONTHLY LEDGER

Date	Rent	Food	Clothes	Util.	Phone	Enter.	Car	Day Care	Maint.	Med.	Misc.	Tot.	Income
Jan													
Feb													
Mar													
Apr													
May													
Jun													
Jul													
Aug													
Sep													
Oct													
Nov													
Dec													

STARTING NOW: FINANCIAL GOALS

Some of your financial goals will require years to achieve. Others can be started immediately. In *The Woman's Financial Survival Handbook*, Perkins and Rhoades (1980) list six steps women can take today to build their financial foundation:

1. *Start a savings account immediately.* Many savings and loan institutions will open an account with an initial deposit of $50. Some companies have credit unions that you can authorize to deduct a set amount from each paycheck for savings. Put some money aside each month and forget about it. Even though a savings account is one of the most liquid investments, that is, the most readily converted to cash, the account should be used for emergencies only or to meet long-range financial goals.

2. *Find an attorney and have a will drawn up.* This accomplishes two simple steps in your financial plan. It establishes in writing where you want your money and possessions to go and it establishes a working relationship with an attorney in a non-stressful situation. Then, if you need a lawyer's advice for a di-

vorce, a business dispute, or a civil case, you will already have formed a business relationship.

3. *Buy adequate insurance.* Health and disability insurance may be available as a company fringe benefit. If not, you cannot afford to be without it in an age in which hospital and doctor bills can amount to thousands of dollars in a short amount of time. Insure your property even if you are renting rather than buying your home. Replacing all your possessions out of your own pocket would be a severe financial setback.

4. *Establish credit as soon as you are financially able and guard your credit as you would your reputation.* Women often have no credit on their own since most accounts are carried in their husband's or father's names, even though they are paying the bills. Apply for credit in your own name and pay bills promptly to ensure a good credit rating. If you are having trouble establishing credit, go to the bank or savings and loan in which you opened your savings account. Ask to borrow an amount that would be secured by the amount you have in savings. Then pay the amount back promptly and be sure that information goes on your report at the local credit bureau. Women have more rights to credit than ever before through the Equal Credit Opportunity Act. They can have access to their files, can know the reasons why credit was denied, and can have credit in a joint account or individually. If you know you are going to be late paying a bill, try to make arrangements ahead of time with the store or bank to avoid a past-due report in your file.

5. *Never sign anything you have not read thoroughly or do not understand.* Even if your husband or partner has read something, do not become responsible for something you do not want. Co-signing a note or agreeing to be the responsible party with a utility company or hospital means that you will be liable for any debts that go unpaid. No matter how simple an agreement seems, ask enough questions so that you understand the implications of having signed. If you are still confused, you may want to seek the advice of your attorney for clarification.

6. *Seek expert advice, then make your own decision.* Many banks offer women's services or seminars on money management either free or at a low cost. Courses at community colleges or universities can help demystify money matters. Financial planners can give you more personal advice. You can even seek advice from businesses that sell insurance or stocks and bonds, but remember that these businesses usually rely on a commission from sales to make their money; therefore weigh their advice against your own goals and ability to take financial risks.

INFORMATION SOMEONE ELSE SHOULD KNOW

1. Bank accounts: where they are and who can sign checks
2. Savings account: where they are and who can sign
3. Checkbooks: where they are located and how the checks are to be signed
4. Insurance policies and medical records: where they are kept
5. Will: where it is kept
6. Safety deposit boxes and P.O. boxes: where they are and who has access
7. Stocks, bonds, warranties, options, patents, copyrights, interests: where is the list, where they are kept, and who is your broker
8. Property in your custody that may belong to someone else
9. Notes that you owe: where they are kept, and to whom, and when are installments due
10. Routine bills to be paid: utilities, installments, etc.
11. Notes owed to you: where they are kept, who owes them, and when payments are due
12. Other debts
13. Real estate owned
14. Pertinent facts about your business and any ownership in other businesses
15. Name of your accountant, lawyer, financial planner, physician, and insurance agent
16. Funeral directions, and beneficiary or fiduciary
17. Where are your miscellaneous papers kept: car titles, income tax returns, etc., and personal belongings—jewelry, collections, etc.
18. Social Security number
19. Vehicles
20. Date of birth and birthplace

FACTORS THAT AFFECT EVERYONE'S FINANCIAL SITUATION

Investment decisions are affected by uncontrollable environmental factors. It is important to recognize and react to these factors when setting goals and developing financial plans (see Exercise 12-2).

Five factors that affect everyone's financial situation are

1. Inflation
2. Taxes
3. Uncertainty about the future
4. Variable job market
5. Changing roles

Inflation

Inflation is the rise in the price of goods and services. The rate of inflation is how high prices have risen over a given period of time. Take steps to increase your personal income to keep up with the rate of inflation. Invest in items that have a history of increasing in value faster than the rate of inflation.

Taxes

As your income changes, your tax liability may change. Even if you get a raise, the increase in tax percentages can reduce your spending power. This is called *bracket creep*. With bracket creep you are pushed into a higher tax bracket as your income goes up; as a result you suffer a net loss in buying power.

To cope with higher taxes

1. Reduce your taxable income by taking advantage of all possible deductions allowable by law
2. When selecting investments that increase your income, adjust the return for the resulting higher taxes
3. Keep abreast of new federal, state, and local tax laws

Uncertainty About the Future

Make the future work for you by taking calculated risks and learning as much as you can about financial planning now. Uncertainty about the future is something we must accept as a fact of life. We cannot afford to wait for inflation, taxes, or interest rates to decrease before we take the initiative to make a financial plan. Many experts recommend having enough money in savings to equal 3 to 6 months of your salary as a financial cushion.

Variable Job Market

Mergers, bankruptcies, salary cuts, cutbacks, freezes, layoffs, and terminations are a few possibilities that can affect our professional and financial well-being. Be prepared by saving, investing, and preparing a list of job contacts should you need to change jobs or companies.

Changing Roles

Changing roles, such as changing your marital status and forming a dual-career marriage, will affect your financial future.

Dual-Career Challenges

Money is power. The partner who handles the money in a relationship has greater control. Many arguments in marriages are caused by different spending philosophies or divergent financial goals.

If each partner maintains separate personal funds that do not go through the family account, resentment over money control can be alleviated. *Separate/personal funds* are funds that are outside the family budget; either partner can use these funds without seeking the other partner's permission and without the other partner's knowledge to allow for a degree of privacy about spending.

Some couples combine paychecks into one joint account and pay all the bills without regard to his or her money. Other couples retain two separate accounts and assign certain expenditures to each. Whichever system a couple decides to choose, it must fit their needs for independence and a feeling of general well-being about financial matters.

Money and Emotions

Money is an emotional subject. Avoid arguments by openly and honestly expressing your feelings about money. Try to recognize that cultural values and norms affect decisions. For example, if your family always paid cash, you may have negative attitudes about people who buy now and pay later.

Share decisions when possible. For example, if an expenditure is over $100, the family rule may state that you need to discuss the purchase in advance.

FINANCIAL RECORD KEEPING

A poor system of record keeping can actually cost you money if you overlook deductions you may be entitled to or omit a deduction because you lack documentation.

Household Files

Along with the tax records, you should file other important information. Information in these files should be accessible to a family member or trusted friend in case of emergency. Here are nine categories for files and examples of what they should include:

1. *Household inventory.* A detailed list of what you own can be invaluable if you need to make an insurance claim.

2. *Important telephone numbers.* In an emergency, family members may need to know the name of your lawyer, accountant, banker, or insurance agent to handle your business until you return.

3. *Bank records.* Keep a list of checking account numbers, savings account numbers, and locations of safety deposit boxes.

4. *Important papers.* Birth certificates, marriage licenses, death certificates, wills, military service records, citizenship papers, passports, and Social Security information should be compiled into one file. In addition to these papers, you should include property deeds, abstracts of titles, automobile titles and bills of sale, contract papers, mortgage records, and insurance policies. A safety deposit box is best for storage of these items. Warranties and guarantees go in a separate file folder. Keep these for all the items that you buy.

5. *Health records.* Health insurance policies, reimbursement forms, receipts for services, and doctors' and pharmacy's phone numbers go in this file.

6. *Canceled checks.* Canceled checks are often the best documentation of a transaction. After you reconcile your bank statement against the canceled checks, file them according to date.

7. *Tax records.* Always keep a copy of your completed tax return. The Internal Revenue Service has 3 years in which to audit Federal tax returns. However, this limitation may not apply in unusual cases. For example, if you failed to report more than 25 percent of your gross income, the government has 5 years to collect the tax or start legal proceedings.

8. *Funeral directions.* Since the will may not be read until after the funeral services, these records should contain certain instructions about the funeral service, the name of the preferred mortuary, deeds to cemetery property or information for burial arrangements, and any instructions for family or friends.

9. *Important keys.* Keys to your safety deposit box, post office box, or other lock boxes should be kept in your household file along with a description of the contents of any of these vaults.

Mathematical Formulas for Financial Record Keeping

INCOME STATEMENT FORMULAS (see Exercise 12-3)

❑   Total income equals the sum of all the money you earn.
❑   Total expenses equal the sum of all the money you spend.
❑   Net income equals total income minus total expenses.
❑   After-tax net income equals pretax net income minus income tax paid.

BALANCE SHEET FORMULAS (see Exercise 12-4)

❑   Total assets equal the sum of all you own.
❑   Total liabilities equal the sum of all you owe.
❑   Net worth equals total assets minus total liabilities.
❑   Total liabilities plus net worth equals total assets.
❑   Working capital equals current assets minus current liabilities.

CHOOSING AN INVESTMENT

In choosing an investment select something that

1. Will increase in value at a rate greater than the inflation rate
2. Will provide an income; determine when or how easily you can get your money out of your investment
3. You understand

Questions to ask to determine if an investment is good or bad for you:

1. What is the *return on investment* (ROI)? The ROI is a formula used to compare either the increased income or increased value of an investment.

$$\frac{\text{Amount Received}}{\text{Amount Invested}} = \text{Return on Investment (ROI)}$$

2. How do the tax advantages, if there are any, affect you?
3. What is my total liability?
4. Can I lose all or part of my money?
5. Is the return worth the risk?
6. Does the sponsoring group have a credible track record?
7. How accurate and realistic are the projections?

8. Does it feel right? Is it the best place for my money right now?

To be a successful investor you must choose an investment that will produce additional income through interest. *Interest* is the amount of money a financial institution pays you for "borrowing" your money and using it for their own purposes, while you leave it on deposit.

There are four considerations that will affect your decision to use interest-bearing investments: interest rates, tax benefits, safety, and liquidity.

1. *Interest rates* fluctuate depending upon legal limits, competition between financial institutions, and the money supply to the bank, which is controlled by the Federal Reserve Board.
2. *Tax benefits* are given to certain types of long-term savings accounts and financial investments.
3. *Safety* with interest-bearing investments is generally good, especially if the investment is backed by an insurance program such as the Federal Deposit Insurance Corporation which protects deposits in federal banks up to $100,000.
4. *Liquidity* is a term that expresses how easy or difficult it is to get your money out of an investment. You need a certain amount of money that you can get your hands on for emergencies or special occasions.

Putting Your Money to Work

In the 1940s and 1950s, many workers thought the Social Security system would take care of their retirement needs. Now most workers realize that Social Security needs to be supplemented with other sources of retirement income. Since few people can save enough to live comfortably during retirement years, the answer may lie in investing a part of your money to earn additional dollars.

Many avenues are open to investors, but most investments fall into two categories: *liquid* and *nonliquid. Liquid investments* are those that are readily converted to cash. For example, a passbook savings account allows you to withdraw your money at any time. *Nonliquid investments* may pay more return, but the value of the return must be balanced against the need for ready cash. For example, a rare coin collection may be a solid investment, but, in an emergency, you might not be able to sell it for its actual worth unless you could find a buyer in a short amount of time. Most experts recommend a combination of the two, particularly for people who are just beginning to invest.

In addition to liquid and nonliquid, investments also may be characterized by the amount of risk they involve. *Secure investments* pay lower dividends, but have a low degree of risk and are consistent over a period of time. A U.S. Savings Bond, government securities, bonds, and blue-chip stock from long-established companies are examples of secure investments. Other investments with more risk might be stock offerings from a new, unproven company; *commodity futures*, which speculate on the price of a commodity at some time in the future; or the purchase of a piece of art or antique furniture that you anticipate will increase in value. The higher the risk, the higher the return on your investment. Once again, combining security and risk will give you a diversified portfolio of investments to fit your financial needs.

More and more options are now available to smaller investors. Once you have saved $1,000 that you want to invest, research your alternatives based on your own goals for high yield versus low risk and your need for liquid assets. Mutual funds are one example of an alternative for smaller investors. A *mutual fund* pools the resources of its investors to buy stocks and bonds in greater quantities than an individual could possibly afford.

As an investor, you have to do your homework. Follow your stocks in the newspaper so that you know when you need to sell. Familiarize yourself with trends in interest. Even if you do not have a loan from a bank, the amount of interest the bank pays relates directly to the amount it can charge its loan customers. Keep up to date on current tax legislation on federal, state, and local levels. Knowing which investments will give you a favorable tax incentive can be a deciding factor in your overall financial plan.

SELECTING YOUR PROFESSIONAL TEAM

You are a professional in a particular field of expertise. Your time is best spent growing and expanding your knowledge within the parameters of that field or special interest. If you needed the services of an attorney, you would retain an attorney. If you have plumbing problems, you would simply hire a plumber. The same applies to your financial team. Certified/qualified financial planners have spent years educating themselves; because of the ever-changing tax laws, consider enlisting the services of a financial planner, accountant, banker, and attorney.

When selecting professionals, ask the following questions:

1. How are they paid? Flat fee? Commission? Percentage of what they help you earn?
2. What is their area of expertise?
3. What is their experience?
4. Are they willing to work with other professionals?
5. Do they have a proven history of success?

Short courses offered by brokerage firms or colleges and universities will greatly enlighten you regarding your current and future financial direction as well as enhance your communication skills in planning your own financial future through a professional.

MONEY AT WORK

Now that you have compiled a financial statement, developed a budget, written financial goals, systematized record keeping, and investigated alternative investments, you have a grasp of many of the tools used in managing a company's financial resources. Whether a job involves you directly with financial matters or not, managers must have some idea of where the company stands financially and how they can help the company make or save money as part of their job. One of the best ways to get an overview of the company is to study its annual report.

Unlike most financial information that is highly confidential, annual reports are generally available to the public. Firms spend huge amounts of money on interesting photographs, eye-catching graphs, and well-researched copy to portray the company in a light that appeals to stockholders, potential investors, employees, and the community. Generally the personnel department or public relations department will have extra copies of an annual report. If you want to compare your company to a competitor, check the local public library, which may have copies of annual reports on file, or write to the other company requesting the information.

Reading an Annual Report

In an article for International Paper Company entitled "How To Read an Annual Report," Quinn (1982) advises the following:

Start at the back of the annual report. First turn to the report of the certified public accountant who functions as an objective third party to audit the report. It should state whether the report conforms to *"generally accepted accounting principles"* or is "subject to" other variables. Generally accepted accounting principles means that the report is consistent with other reports bearing the same information. The "subject to" notation may indicate that a number is questionable or that the auditor needs more information before the number can be accepted.

Read the footnotes. Footnotes might explain wide variations in figures such as the sale of assets that meant high profits this year but should not be expected again. Footnotes also tell about revised accounting procedures or tax changes that may have affected earnings. The footnotes should be taken into consideration when viewing dramatic increases in either profits or losses.

Next, read the annual report's letter from the chairperson. This gives an overall summation of the contents of the report and analyzes reasons for the company's performance. The letter sets the tone of the report whether the chairperson brags about the profits for the year or tells why profits declined. The letter also provides insight to the chairperson's personality and thoughts for the future of the company.

Finally, read the numbers. Most people turn to the numbers first and miss the necessary background. The balance sheet should resemble a financial statement with assets on one side and liabilities on the other side. *Current assets* are those that can be quickly turned into cash. *Current liabilities* are the debts that are due in 1 year which are paid out of current assets. By calculating the difference between current liabilities and current assets, you get the *net working capital.* If working capital shrinks, the company may not be able to keep paying high dividends. The difference between total liabilities and assets is *stockholders' equity.* This is the presumed dollar value assigned to stock owned by stockholders.

Other key terms to understand in an annual report are

Long-term debt. As its name implies, this is debt still owed but not due within the current year.

Income statement. This statement shows the amount of money made or lost over the year. It includes a net sales figure. Adjust the net sales figures against the annual inflation rate to see if the company's real sales are staying healthy.

Net earnings per share. This number shows how much each share earns. Although this is vital to stockholders, check it carefully to see if footnoted information explains any sudden rise or fall.

Debt-to-equity ratio. This number divides the long-term liabilities by the stockholders' equity and gives a picture of the company's overall debt. Firms in a high-sales or high-growth phase can handle a high ratio; other firms may not be as fortunate. In analyzing this number, it helps to know how similar sized competing firms are performing.

An annual report may tell you how a company is doing, but it cannot predict its future or even indicate whether its stock will rise or fall. At best an annual report is a summary of the history of a company for 1 year; the information it contains helps you to form your own judgments. (See Exercise 12-6.)

CORPORATE BUDGETING

Directly related to the profit and loss statement is the *company budget.* A *budget* is a guideline that shows how much a company expects to spend and how much it expects to make. Just as the family budget can be a planning guide, the corporate budget can be an effective management tool to monitor the company's expenditures.

Budgets help control costs, anticipate expenses, and improve coordination between departments and divisions by giving an overview of operating needs and priorities. Although each department may have its own budget to consider, the groups are interdependent on all financial matters. For example, if the sales department cannot sell an expected amount, there may be less money to contribute to the overhead of the administrative division.

Two basic types of budgeting are *top-down* and *bottom-up.* These terms describe the origin of a budget. In a *top-down budget,* management sets financial goals and determines the amount of revenue needed to reach those goals. These figures are distributed to department heads who must develop a budget for their group that leads to the revenue amount. In a *bottom-up budget,* the department heads are asked for estimates and forecasts about expenses. These projections go to a senior executive who coordinates the budgeting function. After a preliminary outline, department heads may be asked to make certain cuts to achieve a percentage of increase or decrease in the total budget. The executive then determines the final budget for the overall goals and financial plan of the organization.

Budgeting responsibilities can be important in learning the financial side of the company. Women managers should actively seek input in budgets for their areas when possible. For example, an office manager might ask to be in charge of the office supply budget as a starting place to gain on-the-job financial expertise rather than just relying on the controller or treasurer to apportion office supplies to her group. Being involved in the budget can help a manager

❑ Show financial aptitude and dispel myths about women being unable to handle money

❑ Gain confidence in her ability to handle financial responsibility

❑ Alert her about the best times to ask for raises or other fringe benefits, since she will know when the new budget is being prepared and goes into effect

❑ Gain perspective on the overall picture of the company rather than just doing her job

❑ Reinforce her power over staff members to grant raises or bonuses through her own budgeting

❑ Provide top management with bottom line results of her performance in keeping a budget balanced and operating a division within a prepared budget

Preparing a Budget

To prepare a budget (see Exercise 12-5), *start with last year's budget. Review actual expenses and compare them to planned expenses.* Resist the urge to pad the budget with unrealistic numbers. If you do not have enough information to budget in a certain category, ask a staff member to check current prices on needed items from three different sources so your information will be current with this year's market.

Collect statistics about costs. Cutting costs unrealistically will lead to frustration as staff members try to stay within the new guidelines. Cutting costs can be an effective way to balance a budget but only if the employees can function at that level and achieve the same productivity.

Isolate fixed costs. Just as families have some costs they cannot alter, businesses also have fixed costs. These might be taxes, utility bills, or rent that will stay the same on a fixed lease or agreement. These costs should be written into the budget as fixed costs, so that budget analysts know they cannot be cut.

Project a reasonable profit. If you set a profit too high, you will never be able to meet it.

Review the budget at regular intervals. This enables you to check performance and be flexible.

SUMMARY

Developing personal and professional financial skills is the responsibility of aspiring women managers. The process of creating financial goals and a budget to meet those goals can be translated from household to corporate planning. At home, organized record keeping can indicate how you are spending your money as well as save time and money when preparing taxes or future budgets. Budgets should include some money for savings accounts as well as investments that can supplement salaried or retirement income.

Financial information for nonfinancial managers is available from most companies' annual reports. Reading an annual report familiarizes you with business terms as you analyze the financial condition of the company. Managers should seek additional responsibilities in budgeting for their departments to develop financial expertise and to learn more about how their department fits into the company's financial picture.

TERMS AND CONCEPTS

after-tax net income	liabilities
annual report's letter from the chairperson	liquid investments
	liquidity
assets	long-term debt
bottom-up budget	math phobia
budget	mutual funds
commodity futures	net earnings per share
current assets	net income
current liabilities	net working capital
debt-to-equity ratio	net worth
expenses	nonliquid investments
financial statement	return on investment
fixed costs	secure investments
generally accepted accounting principles	stockholders' equity
	top-down budget
income statement	variable costs
income (total)	working capital
interest	

REVIEW QUESTIONS

1. What is math phobia and how has it affected women as they deal with money and finances?
2. What are four attributes to controlling your finances?
3. What are the five challenges to develop a financial plan?
4. How do you compute ROI?
5. What factors affect your financial situation?
6. What items should be kept in a safety deposit box?
7. What questions should you ask when selecting a professional?
8. Where can you find annual reports about competing companies or companies in other cities?
9. What are the two basic types of budget preparation in companies?
10. What steps can women take to build their financial future?

EXERCISES

12-1: FINANCIAL PLANNING WORKSHEET

Instructions: Complete this worksheet on the current year and past year projected annual budget. Compare and note trends for next year's projection and for improved money management.

Income
    Take-home pay $ _____
    Child support   _____
    Interest, dividends   _____
    Other   _____
        Total $ _____

Expenditures
    Food   _____
    Mortgage, rent   _____
    Fuel, utilities   _____
        Oil, gas   _____
        Electricity   _____
        Telephone   _____
        Water   _____
    Household upkeep and repairs   _____
    Automobile   _____

Gas, oil   _____

Repairs   _____

Public transportation   _____

Insurance premiums   _____

Personal care   _____

Medical and dental   _____

Clothing   _____

Recreation   _____

Savings   _____

Miscellaneous   _____

Total $ _____

Major expenses likely this year

	Type	Amount
Personal	_____	_____
Your children	_____	_____
You	_____	_____
Other	_____	_____
Car	_____	_____
Education	_____	_____
Other	_____	_____
Total $	_____	_____

Assets

Cash $ _____

Checking account   _____

Savings and similar accounts   _____

Bonds, stocks, other investments   _____

Automobile   _____

Personal effects

Jewelry   _____

Art   _____

Home furnishings   _____

Clothing   _____

Miscellaneous   _____

Total $ _____

Liabilities

Car loan   _____

Mortgage balance   _____

Personal loans   _____

Credit card balances		_____
Other		_____
	Total $	_____
Insurance coverage		
Car		_____
Medical		_____
Life insurance		_____
From employer		_____
Own policies		_____
Other policies		_____
	Total $	_____

12-2: ARE YOU PREPARED?

Instructions: Review the list "Information Someone Else Should Know" on page 254. Place a "+" by each item you have completed to date and a "−" by those you have not completed. In the space below prepare a list of those activities that need completion with a target date for each

ACTIVITY	TARGET DATE

12-3: INCOME STATEMENT FORMULA

Instructions: Using the formulas listed in the text, compute the following transactions as they pertain to your financial situation.

Total income
Total expenses
Net income
After-tax net income

12-4: BALANCE SHEET FORMULAS

Instructions: Using the formulas listed in the text, compute the following transactions as they pertain to your financial situation.

Total assets
Total liabilities
Net worth
Working capital

12-5: BUDGET

Instructions: Obtain, compare and interpret your department or divisional budgets for the past 2 years. What trends/changes can you determine? Compare actual and planned expenses.

TRENDS/CHANGES:

ACTUAL EXPENSES	PLANNED EXPENSES

12-6: ANNUAL REPORTS

Instructions: Obtain the latest annual report from the organization in which you work or from another organization. Answer the following questions from the report.

1.	Does the report conform to "generally accepted accounting principles"?
2.	What do the footnotes reveal?
3.	Current assets?
4.	Current liabilities?
5.	Net working capital?
6.	Stockholders' equity?
7.	Net earnings per share?
8.	Debt-to-equity ratio?
9.	Income statement?
10.	Long-term debt?

SUGGESTED READINGS

Editors of *Success* Magazine. *Your Money: A Financial Planning Guide.* Success Guides. Success Unlimited, Inc., Chicago, IL (no date).

Hayes, R. S., and Baker, C. R. *Simplified Accounting for Non-Accountants.* John Wiley & Sons, Inc., New York, 1980.

Kelly, F. J., and Kelly, H. M. *What They Really Do Teach You at the Harvard Business School.* Warner Books, New York, 1986.

Passell, P. *Where to Put Your Money.* Warner Books, New York, 1984.

Perkins, G., and Rhoades, J. *The Woman's Financial Survival Handbook.* New American Libraries, New York, 1980.

Quinn, J. B. *How to Read an Annual Report.* International Paper Company, New York, 1982.

Rosenbaum, S. C. *The Woman's Handbook for Financial Planning.* Training by Design, New York (no date).

Schenkel, S. *Giving Away Success.* McGraw-Hill, New York, 1984.

Sivord, B. *The Working Woman Financial Advisor: What to Do with the Money You Make in 1987.* Warner Books, New York, 1987.

13

COMMUNICATION

OBJECTIVES

- Define communication
- Understand the process of communication
- List five elements (rule of five) for effective communication
- Identify blocks to communication
- Provide a communication checklist
- Enhance subordinate/supervisor communication
- Illustrate and interpret nonverbal communication
- Identify common body signals
- List characteristics of strong communication
- Enhance listening skills
- Deliver effective group presentations
- Develop interviewing skills
- Write business letters and reports more effectively
- Deal with mass media

ELEMENTS OF COMMUNICATION

Communication involves a transfer of information. By its nature, communication always involves at least two people: the speaker and the listener, as it links minds through the spoken or written word. In the case of mass media, communication may involve millions of people all watching the broadcast of a Super Bowl or a presidential inauguration simultaneously.

Although many people may watch the same event, each will receive a different message. Some may be more interested in details, others may try to relate the event to something else they have experienced, still others may find educational or entertainment value in the program.

This illustrates a fundamental principle: communication is what the receiver understands and not necessarily what the sender says. In a perfect situation, it can be both, but most of us do little to improve our ability to communicate because we take communication for granted, or else we place the burden of understanding on the other person. In a perfect setting, both parties agree on the message, but many factors, including perceptions, experience, attitudes, emotions, abilities, and even the complexity of language itself, can be barriers to effective communication.

Rule of Five

For effective communication to occur, five elements must be present between the message sender and receiver. The receiver must

1. *Receive.* The message sender must connect with a second party. In business this could be a telephone call, a letter, or a casual conversation.
2. *Understand.* The receiver must be able to understand the message. Both people must avoid jargon or unclear terminology for communication to occur.
3. *Accept.* The message receiver must allow the communication process to continue. If the receiver decides to ignore the message, the communication link is lost.
4. *Use.* Information is worthless if it is not used. Every day the human mind receives hundreds of bits of information. Some of these will be used immediately and some will be mentally filed for later use.

5. *Provide feedback.* Feedback may be as simple as nodding agreement when someone is talking to show that you understand or as formal as responding with a business letter to document the answer to a question.

If any one of these steps is missing, communication will not occur. A case study may illustrate the need for each step in the communication process. Barbara, a real estate broker, needed to communicate with Janet, a real estate agent in another city. Barbara thought a phone call would involve less time than writing a letter. She tried to call Janet but found she had left her office for the day. Barbara asked Janet's answering service to have Janet call her back the next day with a date to close an upcoming sale. Several days passed with no call from Janet. Barbara decided the sale was off and wrote a letter to Janet expressing her displeasure over the unreturned phone call. When Janet received the letter she was shocked, because she had never received the telephone message.

Barbara could have avoided frustration if Janet had been available to receive the original message. Failing that, the answering service was negligent in not understanding the importance of the message Barbara asked it to convey. Since the message never reached Janet, she had no opportunity to accept the information and use it to fulfill Barbara's request. When feedback finally came to Janet in the form of Barbara's letter, Janet was able to unravel the misunderstanding.

BLOCKS TO EFFECTIVE COMMUNICATION

Almost everyone can think of an incident in which two people seemed to be communicating, but neither understood what the other was saying. The two people might as well have been speaking foreign languages. Assuming two people are attempting to communicate in a common spoken language, they must still overcome a number of barriers before they achieve effective communication. Eight common blocks to communication are

1. *Poor timing.* A message's timing may be as important as its content. If you are concentrating on one task, you may not be able to shift mental gears to receive another message. In business, strategic timing for communication may mean the difference between getting a raise or having your request denied. Many sales staffs try to avoid scheduling calls on Monday morning or Friday afternoon based on the theory that on Monday morning

most executives are just easing back into a work setting after the weekend and by Friday they are more interested in getting out of the office than answering another call. Whenever possible, try to convey important messages when you know people will be able to give them their full attention.

2. *Inadequate information.* Communication must be complete in order to be effective. You cannot return a phone call if a co-worker has written down a wrong number. You cannot make a business decision if you lack important details such as deadlines or cost factors. In our enthusiasm to convey information, we often pick up the phone too quickly or rush to another office without realizing that by waiting to compile extra facts, the message would be clearer.

3. *Inappropriate channels.* In broadcasting, a signal is beamed out; however, communication occurs only when a receiver is tuned into the correct channel to receive it. When you need to communicate, consider carefully who the most appropriate recipient of the message should be. Instead of starting a letter with "To whom it may concern," direct it to the attention of the head of the customer relations department and call the company to find out that person's name. By directing the message to the best channel, opportunities for effective communication increase.

4. *Excessive noise.* Modern society leaves few quiet places for people to concentrate on communication. Telephones ring, computers click, background music buzzes, and people chatter. All of these distractions can block communication. If you cannot hear someone above the noise, try to move to a more private place. Do not risk misunderstanding vital instructions or statistics. Instead, repeat important information back to the speaker to be sure there is no confusion.

5. *Emotional interference.* The pressure of day-to-day life may create inner blocks to communication. Personal problems can intrude on people's thoughts, and their minds may wander when you speak to them. If people are late to work or are trying to meet a pressing deadline, their nervousness or anxiety may make it difficult for them to concentrate on anything you say.

6. *Personal beliefs.* If people have strongly held beliefs on a certain subject, trying to communicate with them may be a waste of time. If Christopher Columbus had wasted his time arguing with people who thought the world was flat rather than sailing across the ocean, we might still be waiting for someone to discover the New World. Facts and figures may help you make a case for your argument, but some people will never be convinced.

7. *Premature evaluation.* An average listener can process 400 words per minute and we speak at 200 words per minute. As

soon as you begin talking to people, they begin sorting the information in their brain's computer based on past experience, beliefs, and previous knowledge. Sometimes they will reach a conclusion before you have made all your important points. By the time you finish talking, they may have already made their decision without any extra input from you. With this in mind, effective communicators try to organize their facts so that the most persuasive items are presented before the audience has an opportunity to reach an opposing conclusion.

8. *Selective perception.* This relates to the axiom that people hear only what they want to hear. If a speaker tells a group that it can expect 50 percent participation in a business promotion, part of the group will leave enthusiastically thinking that half of their colleagues will participate and part of the group will leave complaining that half of their co-workers will not.

A COMMUNICATION CHECKLIST

Planning can alleviate many of the obstacles present during communication. Here is a checklist that can be applied to both spoken and written communications.

Summarize the message. Decide what you need to communicate, both in terms of your purpose and objectives, as clearly and concisely as you can. Once you know what you need to say or write, you have the basis for communication.

Fill in the blanks. How much information needs to be presented along with your basic message in order to accomplish your purpose? Will the information be clearer in a spoken form or is a written message necessary for future reference files? What is the best place to deliver the message—do you need a private place or can you speak openly in the office? Answers to questions such as these can help you determine the best way to deliver your message.

Analyze your audience. Your message may be aimed specifically at one person or at a group of staff members. After considering the size of your audience, think about different ways listeners could interpret a message. Try to put yourself in their place and anticipate who might agree or disagree with major points. Select words that the audience will understand.

Evaluate yourself as a message sender. In different situations, you may want to appear formal or informal. Weigh the benefits of various approaches based on previous experiences. If you have anticipated objections, you will be more prepared to react to questions. Although you are familiar with the message you want to send, remember that your audience will be hearing the information for the first time.

SUBORDINATE/SUPERVISOR COMMUNICATION

Strong communication should be simple, brief, specific, open, honest, sincere, and direct. Managers who strive for these qualities are more apt to achieve their goal of effective communication.

Too many business letters and speeches rely on trite phrases that add extra verbiage without adding any meaning. Simple, clear messages lead to less confusion and lead to higher efficiency and productivity, because less time is spent explaining instructions. Use active verbs to emphasize your message and strive to use positive language whenever possible.

In a supervisory role, do not make a suggestion when you intend to give a specific instruction. Delegate tasks clearly with full information to the employee. Be clear about deadlines and other details or procedures you expect to be followed. Do not assume knowledge on the part of the employee unless you know from past experience that the employee has the necessary background.

If you are receiving an assignment rather than delegating one, be sure you understand what is expected of you. It is better to ask one more question than to risk poor performance because you were unclear about a part of a project. If you receive written instructions, file them for future reference while you are working on the project. If the instructions are spoken, take notes so that you can refresh your memory without intruding on your boss's time.

In management, try to develop a climate for effective two-way communication between yourself and your employees. If you build a relationship based on effective communication, your job will be much simpler. As a manager, try to adopt the employee's frame of reference and remember that other points of view exist when you are communicating.

Two basic methods of learning are by *rote memory* and by *experience* or association with experience. Both methods have a place in business communication. Some tasks will be learned only by having employees do them over and over again. Other tasks cannot be memorized. As a supervisor, you must help the employee understand why these tasks are important to the job and to the company so that you can both derive the benefits when the tasks are accomplished.

NONVERBAL COMMUNICATION

Although our words usually convey our message, nonverbal messages are also at work. Nonverbal messages can either support or contradict our verbal message. In addition to the spoken word, posture, tone of voice, and body gestures form part of the communication process.

Consider your own reactions to the body language of others. If they say they agree with your point, but they have their arms crossed on their chest or seem to be looking away, it is hard to believe that they are truly in agreement. To become an effective communicator, you must take control of all aspects of communication so that nonverbal messages reinforce what you are saying.

To appear confident, avoid fidgety, nervous behaviors such as examining your hands or nails, doodling on a scratch pad, looking away from the speaker, clearing your throat, or smoking a cigarette. To appear composed even when you feel stressful, open up your body language by slipping your hands in your pockets rather than crossing your arms and looking the speaker in the eye. If you must keep your hands busy, take notes that relate to the conversation. If you are seated, leaning slightly forward indicates interest in the speaker, whereas leaning back gives the message that you are pulling away from the speaker or that you may be bored.

Body language is the study of how gestures and postures combine to send messages. As with any language, the total message is a compilation of its parts of speech. Be careful not to oversimplify and interpret one gesture or stance in body language while ignoring other important signals. Some common body signals involve the following:

Head. Shaking the head indicates no, whereas nodding indicates yes. Tilting the head toward the speaker shows agreement, whereas leaning backward indicates the reverse.

Face. A smile denotes friendliness and a willingness to please regardless of what the spoken language conveys. A blank expression shows boredom and a tight face with clenched teeth or jaws shows tension.

Posture. A wide stance generally evokes a feeling of power as the person seems to take up more territory. Likewise, a cowering stance with feet together and arms close to the body signifies a person who takes up less area and assumes less importance. Erect posture shows confidence, whereas someone who is slumping seems to bear the weight of the world on her shoulders.

Hands. Calm hands indicate a person who is cool and self-possessed. Nervous hands betray an unsettled communicator. Open hands seem receptive, whereas fists can reveal either insecurity or a confrontational manner.

Different messages call for different body language. Be careful to have the nonverbal message reinforce the spoken message for added emphasis, rather than leaving the listener with conflicting verbal and nonverbal signals.

LISTENING SKILLS

Listening is an important component of communication. In a conversation, most people think of the speaker as the active participant and the listener as the passive recipient of the message. Effective listening, just like effective speaking, is a skill that can be developed. Whether you are part of a large audience or the only person being addressed, you can practice active listening techniques. In social communication, active listening reassures the speaker that you received the message. In business communication, the result involves much more than mere courtesy, because of the time, energy, and money saved by communicating a message correctly the first time.

Active listening begins before the first word is ever spoken. It demands an open, attentive attitude toward the anticipated message. If you have already formed an opinion about the speaker or the announced topic, you will block effective communication. Wait until you hear a statement before you judge it. If you are distracted by another project, noise, or a pending appointment, you may not give the speaker a fair chance to communicate. When someone addresses you, make a commitment to concentrate on the message.

Remember that body language as well as spoken language lets the speaker know that you are listening. Looking directly at the speaker shows concentration, whereas looking at a piece of paper or another person gives the impression that your mind is wandering.

Listen for ideas rather than concentrating on each word. If you can repeat the central idea of the message after the conversation ends, you have done an effective job of listening. Try not to interrupt the speaker unless you do not understand a word or a sentence that is crucial to the main point. If you fear that you are missing something, politely cut into the conversation and ask for

Table 13-1 Five Types of Listening Responses

1. The nod: nodding the head slightly and waiting

2. The pause: looking at the speaker expectantly, but without doing or saying anything

3. The casual remark: "I see." "Uh-huh." "Is that so?" "That's interesting."

4. The echo: repeating the last few words the speaker said

5. The mirror: showing your understanding of the speaker by reflecting what has just been said; "You feel that...."

a clarification. If there is no gracious way to ask a question immediately, write it down and ask it after the speech.

Take mental notes to retain key statements. If you want to remember the information for a longer time, write it down. If you find yourself drifting away from the speaker, go back to the last main point you remember and try to recapture the train of thought.

One of the greatest temptations in listening is to let your mind race ahead to formulate the next point you want to say. When you are listening, you must make the other person the main character in the scene. If you are busy rehearsing the lines you want to deliver, you risk missing the message. To give the speaker a positive response, a listener may nod in agreement, pause quietly, offer a casual remark, echo the speaker's words, or mirror the speaker's thoughts. (See Table 13-1 and Exercise 13-1.)

GROUP PRESENTATIONS

At some time in your career, you will be asked to give a presentation to a committee, address a large audience, or speak to a group of visitors. If you are like the great majority of people, your first reaction will be to list all the reasons why someone else should take the assignment. If you agree to speak, you may feel confident at first and then, as the time nears, become increasingly nervous.

Although a few people may profess to be born public speakers, most admit that they had to overcome similar fears and practice relentlessly before gaining the necessary confidence. Public speaking can enhance visibility in any job. Instead of convincing one person at a time that you have valid ideas, you will be using your speech as a forum to persuade many listeners.

Preparing for a speech or presentation begins with homework. The best defense against going blank in front of an audience is to be very well prepared. Use any resources you can think of to arm yourself with the needed statistics, facts, or theories for your presentation. Public libraries, college textbooks, and in-house research departments can all contribute. You might not use all the facts you accumulate, but you will be able to select the best points to convey your ideas.

The best speeches seem spontaneous rather than memorized. Reading your speech insults the intelligence of your audience and shows insecurity. Most seasoned speakers advise writing your speech in complete sentences and then going back and outlining main points. These main points can be transferred to small index cards to help your memory while you fill in the outline points conversationally. Write down numbers or figures for accuracy and underline main points you need to remember, but try to use your notes as guides rather than cue cards.

Rehearse your speech in front of a mirror with a tape recorder running. If you have access to a video camera and recorder, use that to make sure verbal and nonverbal messages agree. Play back the recording to note words that were difficult to enunciate. If you continually stumble over a word, substitute a synonym rather than take a chance on getting distracted during your presentation. Time the speech to see if it fits the allotted program time. If you seem to be racing through the words, tape the speech again as you concentrate on slowing down.

As with any communication, analyzing your audience will give you clues in deciding on the tone of your speech. In a small committee meeting of your peers, you may be more informal. If you are asked to repeat the same information to a larger audience, you may need to adapt portions of your remarks to fit a more formal setting.

At first you may need to stand behind a podium to gain confidence. Resist the urge to clutch the podium as if you were grasping for confidence. Use your hands to make gestures that emphasize or punctuate your main points. Gradually train yourself to stop using the podium, thereby creating a more open appearance, with no physical barriers between you and the audience. (See Exercise 13-2.)

INTERVIEWING

Interviewing is the process of obtaining information from another person or group by asking questions and monitoring responses. Interviews take place throughout the course of a business day. You step into an office and a receptionist asks your name or inquires about your visit: Whom do you need to see? Do you have an appointment? Whether you realize it or not, the exchange constitutes an interview, because the speaker asks questions to discern whether or not you have legitimate business with the company.

If you have an appointment to talk with someone about a potential job, you will experience one of the best examples of business interviews: the job interview. First you may complete a job application, which is a type of written interview. On the basis of those answers, a personnel officer will ask you additional questions and monitor your responses to see if you are a match for the company and the job.

If you pass the first interview, the personnel officer may introduce you to your potential supervisor, who will ask more questions. Although this may seem like a friendly exchange, it is probably a continuation of the job interview.

Once you have the job, you will meet your co-workers. Each of you will draw conclusions based on first impressions. The process of getting to know one another is also an interview process. You and your new colleagues will be deciding whether you like each other and whether you will have feelings of cooperation or conflict as you start your new responsibilities.

The interview process does not stop there. You close a business deal, and your boss asks you how you accomplished it. If your boss thinks you have made a mistake, you may be asked to explain how an event happened, and so on.

If you are the interviewee, you must employ all the skills of active listening to determine what information the interviewer really wants to elicit from your answer. Taking a few moments to organize your thoughts before you start answering a question will produce a more articulate response.

If you know you will be in an interview situation, such as a job interview, try to prepare some answers in advance based on typical questions. You can anticipate that you will be asked about your prior work experience, of course, but job interviewers also like to ask thought-provoking questions like "What are your career goals?" or "Which of your accomplishments makes you most proud and why?"

Many job applicants lose points during an interview because they have failed to do their homework about the company or the job they seek. Most major companies have annual reports that you can find at a public library. These reports provide you with vital statistics about the size of the company, its assets, and the type of work it is pursuing. If you do not have access to an annual report, check the newspaper office in the city in which the business is located to read recent clippings about the company. If you have any contacts in a similar profession or company, ask them about descriptions of jobs that are comparable to the position you want. Although every company is different, jobs on certain levels or in certain departments will serve similar functions.

If you are the interviewer, there are six key points to an effective interview:

1. *Commit your time to being a good listener.* Concentrating on the interview saves time and energy. If you use the interview to your best advantage by asking relevant questions and listening to the answers, you can quickly determine the direction of the interview. If you like what you hear, you may want to call the interviewee back a second time. In interviews for information, such as an in-house survey on productivity, you can quickly find out if the person has the information you need to draw your conclusions or if you need to talk to another source. (See Exercise 13-3.)

2. *Do your homework.* Just as the interviewee needs to be prepared, the interviewer can streamline the interview process by reading in advance information such as a resumé, a job application, or a work history. You may want to keep the information in front of you for reference, but you should have a working knowledge of the background as well as a mental list of questions you want to ask before the interview begins.

3. *Develop a genuine interest in other people.* This is most important if your job involves a great deal of interviewing, as in the case of a news reporter or a personnel manager. Even if you interview only occasionally, people can sense whether you are truly interested in their answers or whether you are only going through the motions.

4. *Make the interviewee feel important.* If you have done your homework and are practicing effective listening skills, you have a solid start on showing interviewees that you value their time. During the interview, allow the interviewee plenty of time to answer your questions. In an unfamiliar situation, everyone is nervous. Do not rush answers and miss the benefit of the interviewee's thoughts. If you are having trouble absorbing all the information in an interview, make a few notes. Taking notes reassures the speaker that you think enough of the ideas to want to remember them.

5. *Put the interviewee at ease by letting her talk about herself.* Whether we admit it or not, we enjoy talking about our-

selves, our feelings, our accomplishments, and our goals. Use this to your advantage in an interview to draw the other person out.

6. *Express ideas in a way that the interviewee can understand.* Business jargon, or words that are known only to someone inside your industry, will confuse the interviewee and block effective communication. If the interviewee is a recent graduate, relate ideas to a college setting. If the interviewee has had years of experience in a profession, you can feel comfortable using a business vocabulary. (See Exercise 13-4.)

WRITTEN COMMUNICATION

Business Letters

Although the majority of business communication is done orally, either in person or over the telephone, the communication that is most likely to be remembered is written, because it can be catalogued and filed for later reference. Because of its longevity, written communication requires extra planning and effort in order to be effective.

A piece of correspondence, whether an interoffice memo or a letter that goes outside the office, begins communicating from the time the recipient opens the envelope. Smudged stationery, misspelled words, or sloppy typing all reveal that the contents were prepared without attention to detail. Business letters consume valuable work time. If a business matter is important enough to warrant the time it takes to write a business letter, then it is important enough to make the letter serve as an effective ambassador of your message.

The best business letters and memos are *short* and *to the point.* Whenever possible, *edit* the letter so that it fits on a standard sheet of stationery. The recipient is more apt to read the complete letter if it looks as though it will not take much time.

Start your letter by making an *outline* of the main points you want to convey. In some cases, you may have to supply substantial background so that the recipient has full information. In other cases, you may be able to refer to a previous piece of correspondence on the same topic to save time or attach a photocopy of background material so the recipient can have ready access to the information without going to the files. The more promptly you answer business letters, the less history you have to supply and the more efficient you seem.

Organize the main points of your outline so they flow from one idea to another. Add material to the main points that will substantiate your position. When you are ready for the final version, be sure your information is specific and you have used plenty of action verbs to convey a liveliness to your writing. Trite business phrases such as "as per your request" and "re: your letter of" have become empty affectations in letter writing and take up valuable space. Instead try, "as you requested" or "your letter dated."

Make the letter interesting by using the recipient's point of view. Make it to the receiver's advantage to read the entire copy. Use humor if appropriate and be positive in expressing ideas. Use natural language and write as you would speak instead of using business jargon that makes your letters sound like other pieces of correspondence.

Give special attention to the salutation and closing. Most importantly, spell the recipient's name correctly. If you have to call and verify the spelling with that company's switchboard, do so. Misspelling the recipient's name creates a poor impression and can raise unfortunate questions about the accuracy of the letter itself. If you do not know the person's name and have no way to find out, address the letter to a title, such as Customer Service Director or Personnel Manager.

Do not make assumptions about the sex of the recipient that could be taken as an insult. Sometimes it is better to start the body of the letter immediately after the inside address rather than using Dear Sir or Dear Madam or, even worse, To Whom It May Concern.

In the closing, follow the conservative business practice used by others in the company. Sincerely and sincerely yours are acceptable business letter closings. Save anything more emotional for personal correspondence only.

Written Reports

Employees who can translate technical business information into easily understood written words are in high demand. Business people need to be able to convey their messages to stockholders in annual reports or to other companies in business proposals. Whether you are asked to write a report, a job description, or a public relations brochure, you can use the basic skills developed in writing business letters and build on them.

As with letters, the first step is to decide the purpose of the report. Try to condense this purpose into a single, topic sentence.

If you can do this, then everything you research, write, or edit should support this idea.

As you are deciding the purpose, consider who will read the report. If it is going to the public, you need to keep statements general in nature so that they are easily understood without prior knowledge of the company. If it is going to stockholders, you need to realize that they have a monetary interest in what they will read. If it is going to other workers, you can focus on ideas that will catch their attention.

Once you know the purpose and the audience, you can begin to compile information. Use all available resources. You might ask key people to write their ideas in memo or letter form to include in the report or to use in excerpting quotes. You can use the company or the public library to find historical data or statistics. If you are missing important elements in your research, ask for help from departments that might have those files. When possible, give credit to people who helped compile the facts. They will be more willing to cooperate in future projects if they know you share the rewards of accomplishment.

Keep all the rules of effective writing in mind. Keep it short, simple, and to the point. Use verbs and nouns for active writing. If graphs or pictures can convey the message with fewer words, design the report to incorporate them.

Always allow "cooling off" time for any written material. No one writes perfectly the first time. By taking a second look at what you have written before it is distributed or printed, you can avoid embarrassing mistakes. Ask a trusted co-worker to proof-read your work in case you are missing the same spelling or grammatical mistake over and over.

MASS MEDIA

Many companies are learning the value of visibility gained through positive exposure in mass media. Newspaper business pages, radio or television talk shows, or public community forums all provide opportunities to communicate positive information about a company.

Some companies purchase advertising to share successes or new policies with the public. Instead of advertising sale prices, they actually buy space to communicate a philosophy or public service message. Other companies regularly send news releases to media outlets in the hope of gaining recognition for accomplishments or breakthroughs.

Many large companies have public relations departments that handle all media contacts. If your company does not have a similar department, you and your firm do not have to settle for a low profile. If your company approves, you may be asked to prepare a release on an employee's promotion or the opening of a new branch office for your company.

If you are asked to submit a news release, remember that accuracy is paramount. Reporters cannot report facts they do not have. The tried and true formula for news writing— answering who, what, where, when, why, and how— remains the best checklist for your information. Be sure the release has a telephone number on it so that the reporter can call for more information. Not all releases are used because of time or space limitations but some releases may catch an editor's eye and become feature stories or human interest stories. If you have a phone number on the release, an interested editor can easily call to seek more information.

Before you send in the typed release, call the station or newspaper to verify the name of the editor or news director. When you are on the telephone, ask if the station or newspaper has deadlines for specific editions such as a Sunday paper that may be more widely read. If you are given a deadline, stick to it even though it may seem unnecessarily early. Generally there is a reason for a deadline and missing it may mean missing the opportunity to have an item printed about your company.

Ask if the paper can use photographs or if the news station can use audiotapes or videotapes. Try to supply the news professionals with everything they need to make their job easier. Your story has a much greater opportunity of gaining valuable space or air time if you streamline the production time.

Build contacts with local media personnel. They are the best guides as to what papers and stations will or will not use. If you do not know anyone in the communication field, try to watch local newscasts or read local papers to find out the types of stories the editors seem interested in publishing or broadcasting.

If you have the opportunity to be interviewed for a story, review all the rules of public speaking. Being prepared is the best defense for on-camera nervousness. For television, professionals advise wearing a solid color suit without distracting prints or colors. Remember that fidgeting hands or feet may be captured on film in addition to your face. Try to look at the interviewer rather than at the lights or cameras. Concentrate on answering the questions fully and briefly, since the interview will be edited to fit the allotted news space. Give the reporter a business card to ensure that your name and title as well as the name of your firm are spelled correctly.

Work with your company's public relations department to coordinate any publicity. In a large company, the public relations officer may need help in knowing what is going on in different departments. If an employee attends an important training seminar or completes an educational degree, send the public relations department a short note and offer to prepare a rough draft of a news release.

CONCLUSION

Communication may be across the room, across the building, or across the airwaves through satellite transmission. No matter how sophisticated the system, the basic methods of communication rely on the ability of the receiver to unscramble the message.

Without an understanding of the responsibility of communication both on the part of the sender and the receiver, communication cannot be accomplished. If both parties accept the responsibility, effective communication will produce the desired outcome.

SUMMARY

Communication is not simply what is said or written, it is also what the message receiver understands. Communication is a process that involves both the sender and the receiver. For effective communication to occur, the receiver must receive, understand, accept, use, and provide feedback for the message. Blocks to effective communication can include poor timing or inadequate information. Listening skills can be developed by taking mental notes and concentrating with an open, attentive mind. Business communication includes spoken and written words as well as unspoken or body language. Analyzing the audience is important in deciding the method of communication. A group presentation or a memo will require different wording depending on who will receive the message. Managers can also use mass media such as newspapers and television to convey messages and increase personal visibility.

TERMS AND CONCEPTS

body language	premature evaluation
communication	receiver
emotional interference	rote memory
experience	selective perception
nonverbal communication	sender

REVIEW QUESTIONS

1. What is the rule of five as it applies to effective communication?
2. How can poor timing block communication?
3. What are the qualities of strong communication?
4. What is active listening?
5. What can an interviewer do to make the interview more effective?
6. How should you open and close a business letter?
7. What are some techniques to make a group presentation go more smoothly?

EXERCISES

13-1: HOW WELL DO I LISTEN?

Instructions: The following test may help you identify some of your listening weaknesses. Read the questions and rate yourself on each item using the following scale: always—4, most of the time—3, rarely—2, never—1.

		Score
1.	I maintain an attitude of objectivity	_____
2.	I don't think about the next question while the speaker is talking	_____
3.	I focus on content of message, not delivery or physical mannerisms of the speaker	_____
4.	I listen for main ideas, principles, concepts, not details	_____
5.	I try not to get "turned off" by specific phrases or "red flag" words	_____
6.	I don't make value judgments until I've heard everything the speaker has to say	_____
7.	I don't take notes word for word	_____
8.	When I feel something is missing, I ask simple direct questions to get the necessary information	_____
9.	When I am unsure about what was said, I restate what I think I heard in the form of a question	_____
10.	I eliminate distractions by holding telephone calls and choosing a quiet place to talk	_____
	Total Score	_____

Scoring: 32+, excellent; 26-31, better than average; 21-25, improve listening skills; 20 or less, critical listening skills improvement needed.

13-2: GROUP PRESENTATION

Prepare and deliver an 18-minute presentation on a work-related topic. You may choose to inform or entertain.   Time, evaluate, and discuss presentations.   Each negative comment must be preceded by at least one specific, sincere comment.

13-3: ASSESS YOUR LISTENING SKILLS

Employees sometimes share these complaints about their supervisor's listening skills. After each situation, rate yourself if you sometimes, always, or never react this way.

---

1. Continue making notes or reading memos when an employee is talking.
    sometimes ❑   always ❑   never ❑

2. Look at the clock or check your calendar when an employee is in your office.
    sometimes ❑   always ❑   never ❑

3. Interrupt an employee by interjecting a different topic before the first conversation is resolved.
    sometimes ❑   always ❑   never ❑

4. Finish sentence for employees before they have a chance to make a point.
    sometimes ❑   always ❑   never ❑

5. Make an employee repeat an idea that you missed during a distraction.
    sometimes ❑   always ❑   never ❑

6. Check your pencil points, your fingernails, or paper clips while an employee is talking.
    sometimes ❑   always ❑   never ❑

7. Reject an employee's suggestion without taking time to investigate its effectiveness.
    sometimes ❑   always ❑   never ❑

If you marked never in each situation, your listening skills show employees you care about their information and questions. If you marked sometimes on more than four items, you need to practice active listening. If you marked always more than four times, you may be missing vital information from your employees.

13-4: INTERVIEWING

1. Two participants will role play a job interview utilizing the list of questions below. Complete the interview within 15 to 20 minutes. Observers will evaluate and discuss reactions. One participant will play the role of the interviewer and the other will play the role of the interviewee. Allow 10 minutes for the participants to prepare for their roles by reviewing the following list of questions.

2. Pair all class members by numbering each 1 or 2. All 1's will serve as interviewers and all 2's as interviewees. Each pair will repeat the exercise illustrated in the above scenario, and then reverse roles. Discuss reactions.

Directions: To prepare for job interviews, complete the following questionnaire for your personal use.

---

1. How would you describe yourself as a person?

2. What are you best at doing?

3. What are you worst at doing?

4. What are your two biggest accomplishments?

5. How would you like your obituary to read at the termination of your life?

6. What would be the ideal job for you?

7. Why do you seek employment with our firm?

8. What do you know about our firm?

9. What career advice can you give yourself?

10. Describe the two peak experiences in your life

11. What are your five most important values (things most important to you)?

12. What are your long-range work (professional) goals?

13. What are your intermediate-range (professional) goals?

14. What are your short-range work (professional) goals?

15. How realistic are your goals in terms of opportunity in your place of employment or in your field?

16. How well suited are your qualifications and skills for achieving these goals?

17. What do you want to achieve in your personal life?

18. Why did you select (a) your college, (b) your major?

19 Why are you leaving your present position?

20. Describe your last boss. Did you get along with your boss? Other employees?

13-5: BUSINESS LETTERS

Instructions: Collect, edit, evaluate, and correct six business letters over a 1-week time span. Letters over one page should be condensed to one page. What improvements were made based on the suggestions in the text?

SUGGESTED READINGS

Adler, M.J. *How to Speak, How to Listen.* Macmillan, New York, 1983.

Allen, S. *How to Make a Speech.* McGraw-Hill, New York, 1986.

Comstock, T. W. *Communicating in Business and Industry.* Delmar Publishers, Albany, NY, 1985.

Detz, J. *How to Write and Give a Speech.* St. Martin's Press, New York, 1984.

Doolittle, R. J. *Professionally Speaking.* Scott, Foresman, Glenview, IL, 1984.

Dumaine, D. *Write to the Top: Writing for Corporate Success.* Random House, New York, 1983.

Einhorn, L.J., Bradley, P,H., and Baird, J.E., Jr. *Effective Employment Interviewing. Unlocking Human Potential.* Scott, Foresman, Glenview, IL, 1982.

Huseman, R.C., Lahiff, J.M., Penrose, J.H., Jr., and Hatfield, J.D. *Business Communication. Strategies and Skills (2nd ed.)*. The Dryden Press, Hinsdale, IL, 1985.

Jacobi, E. *Writing at Work*. Ten Speed Press, Berkeley, CA, 1986.

Lehman, A. J. *Writing for Industry*. Holt, Rinehart and Winston, New York, 1984.

Paxson, W. C. *The Business Writing Handbook*. Bantam Books, New York, 1981.

Redding, W.C. *The Corporate Manager's Guide to Better Communication*. Scott, Foresman, Glenview, IL, 1984.

Stewart, C.J., and Cash, W.B., Jr. *Interviewing Principles and Practices (4th ed.)*. William C. Brown, Dubuque, Iowa, 1985.

Walther, G.R. *Phone Power: How to Make the Telephone Your Most Powerful Business Tool*. G.P. Putnam's Sons, New York, 1986.

Wells, W. *Communications in Business (4th ed.)*. Kent Publishing Company, Northridge, CA, 1985.

Wohlmuth, E. *The Overnight Guide to Public Speaking*. Running Press, Philadelphia, PA, 1983.

14

NEGOTIATION

OBJECTIVES

- Understand why you need to develop negotiation skills in order to succeed as a manager
- Define basic negotiation terms and concepts
- Evaluate and increase your negotiation potential
- List, define, and apply four win-win negotiation strategies
- Understand four basic negotiation skills
- List and apply win-win negotiation techniques
- Identify the two most common resistances to negotiation
- Identify win-lose techniques to avoid

Negotiation generally brings to mind images of labor unions and management stamping out the details of a new contract or governments deciding the future course for nations in a treaty room.

In reality, negotiation is a part of everyday life. *Negotiation* is the act of persuading or influencing someone else to adopt a certain course of action. When a teacher tries to convince a student to do homework or a salesperson tries to sell one brand of computers over another, negotiation is taking place.

A few things in life are not open to negotiation. When you have reached the highest authority or the symbolic court of last resort, you must accept that decision. However, most business and personal situations leave room for an effective negotiator to change the outcome.

If you like

❑   to avoid conflicts and confrontations
❑   to be popular and well liked
❑   to accept whatever is offered
❑   to avoid haggling over details such as money or titles

then you probably need to develop negotiating skills in order to succeed as a manager.

On the other hand, if you like

❑   to settle differences
❑   to think under pressure
❑   to express yourself and your opinions
❑   to challenge your communication skills to persuade others

then you are on your way to being a seasoned negotiator.

A MATTER OF ATTITUDE

Some people hear the word "no" and perceive finality. Others hear the same word and see an opportunity to turn the negative into a positive— or at least a maybe. In the matter of negotiating, adults can learn by studying children. One of the first words a toddler will say is "no." Adults may even tease that children say the word so well because they have heard it so often by the time they are 2 or 3 years old. Even though toddlers know the word, they rarely consider that it means negotiations are closed.

A typical exchange might be a youngster's argument about bedtime:

"Can't I stay up late?"

"No."

"But I'm not sleepy."

"I still said no."

"But I promise I'll get up on time."

"No. For the last time."

If two adults were engaged in such a dialogue, chances are that the conversation would have ended at the first or at least the second no. To regain that childhood persistence, we must first adopt an attitude of negotiation.

If someone tells us no, we need to learn how to supply information to change their point of view. We must see negotiation as a collaboration designed to bring us the desired results, rather than a confrontation that makes us lose ground. Negotiation can be the way by which we achieve a compromise that places both parties in a win-win situation, rather than a clash that makes one party a winner and one party a loser.

A positive attitude is vital for effective negotiation. You have to aim for something before you can obtain it. Think back to recent television news clips in which a lawyer came out of a courthouse declaring the intention to appeal a client's conviction or a labor leader vowed to stay on strike as long as it takes to gain certain concessions. Both of these professions require strong negotiating skills for success. The lawyer must convince judges or jurors of a client's innocence. A labor leader must convince management of the workers' worth. No matter how both feel personally, they must approach negotiation as a challenge within their grasp in order to get the results they seek.

Too many women have been conditioned to accept whatever they were given without arguing. They adopted a mentality of working hard and quietly waiting for rewards. Now women are realizing that people in business get raises not because they necessarily deserve them, but because they ask for them. They may base their requests on standards or accomplishments, but they must also actively seek more money and better positions without waiting for someone to read their minds.

WHAT DO YOU WANT?

As with every business transaction, negotiation starts with knowing what you want to gain. You may want a raise or a promotion. You may be asking for a chance to experiment with a new technique or method you have developed. You may want a few days off or a bonus based on recent accomplishments.

Using skills gained in the earlier discussion of goal setting, write down the best possible outcome of the discussion. Be as specific as possible in order to start verbalizing your needs or desires. This could be the $100 a week raise, the title of sales manager, authorization to proceed with your plan, or anything else you want to have after the negotiation concludes. Clarify your goal so that it stays foremost in your mind throughout the preparation and final negotiation.

Next write down your *"fallback" position.* A "fallback" position is the minimum area in a range of concessions in which you are willing to compromise in the negotiation process. If you do not get everything you ask for, but at least get to this position or area, you will have gained something from the process. If you ask for a $100 a week raise, your boss may counter that the company cannot afford that amount right now. If the boss asks what it would take for you to stay, you can counter with your fallback position of $75 a week or an additional week of vacation or something else that you suspect is within the company's budget.

Once you have your win statement and your fallback position, the third part of the negotiation is to prepare mentally for the worst-case scenario. This imaginary scenario would be the worst thing that could come out of the negotiation. Usually the worst thing that can happen is to be told no and leave knowing that at least you had the courage to initiate negotiations. In imagining the worst-case scenario, be careful that you do not let it change your attitude from negative to positive. This important step should be part of the mental exercise only to toughen your skills before negotiation. By thinking through the worst, you can be prepared for objections you may face as you negotiate. To prepare for the negotiation and to better sell your idea or proposal, identify and list every possible objection and prepare countersolutions to each.

NEGOTIATION POTENTIAL

Part of analyzing negotiations in advance is to evaluate the negotiation potential of each person or each situation. *Negotiation potential* is the ability of a person or situation to affect a change. A person has negotiation potential if she has the opportunity to ask for a raise or the authority to grant one. If you are in a position to deal or to offer something in exchange for receiving something else, you have negotiation potential.

Consider the stakes of the negotiation—what do you have to lose and what do you have to gain? Draw a line down the middle of a sheet of paper. On one side, list what will happen if you win your raise or some other request. On the other side list what will happen if you do not. Chances are the worse thing that will happen is that you have to return to your present situation. Even then you may have won ground by making your opinions known to your superiors or planting a seed of an idea that may help you later. If you have been businesslike in your negotiations, you can enhance your career image, even if you do not receive everything you want.

As you develop your negotiation potential, you should study the overall picture of your company. Do not be content to know your department inside and out. You must know as much of the financial picture, the marketing strategy, and the projected growth plans as you can in order to mesh your plans with that of your superiors. Learning about the company increases your network of interoffice colleagues. Whereas others may know only those they work with daily, you will develop resource people in all parts of the company. By compiling information from these sources, you can create a larger demand for your services, which in turn gives you more negotiation potential.

Become identified as profit oriented. Learn the problems and needs of other departments. Then if you have to negotiate with that person, you can speak knowledgeably about the outcome of a certain plan. If you know the facts, you will be less likely to be intimidated by so-called pros or experts. Instead, you can address the problem by talking about real people rather than hypothetical situations, because you are acquainted with the background.

Another way to increase your negotiation potential is to visualize success. If you can use your imagination to see yourself as persistent, calm, rational, and persuasive, you may gain the edge in negotiations. Visualize yourself already enjoying the benefits of a pay raise or a new office with a new title. This exercise will help you reinforce your need to negotiate and plant the idea for success in your subconscious mind. Remember that if we want something badly enough, we may lose our objectivity; your imagination can help you detach yourself from the situation so that your objectivity can be retained.

NEGOTIATION STRATEGIES

To some business people, negotiation is similar to a verbal tug of war. Two sides pull against each other with the winner taking everything; the loser has nothing to show for the skirmish. Effective negotiators know that the interaction more closely resembles a chess game. Each side gradually achieves a better position through long-term strategy. Although one side will be the eventual winner, the ongoing challenge may take weeks with a different player ahead after any given move.

Every negotiator wants to win, but our instincts tell us that for every winner there must be a loser. One of the best strategies for negotiation involves changing from a *win-lose* mentality to a *win-win* mentality. A *win-win* situation allows both parties to leave victorious.

Win-win situations can evolve in a variety of ways:

Compromise. Both sides leave the meeting after achieving at least one goal. Both sides have given in to at least one of the opposition's demands, but neither side has surrendered to every demand that was originally made. A compromise is actually a third plan created somewhere between each side's position. The main saboteur to compromise is entering negotiations with a mind closed to other opinions or solutions.

Save face. Both sides can feel positive about the decision since no one has to admit a previous bad decision or take blame for a certain course of action. Instead both parties can leave with the feeling of a moral victory because of a new plan or outcome. Issuing ultimatums negates any chance of saving face. Instead of ordering the opposing side to "do this or else," saving face means offering the other side a range of choices that all provide favorable outcomes for yourself.

Collaboration. Instead of embracing one solution completely, the outcome includes portions of each person's plan to make the outcome a joint effort. Both sides share in the new hybrid plan as a partnership instead of one person receiving the credit. Pride and ego can derail attempts at collaborations. Collaborations can work only if both sides are willing to follow a certain course of action without regard to who will receive the credit.

Trade-out. In a direct trade, each party agrees to give up something to gain something else. For example, a manager might forego capital improvements to the office in order to gain a cost-of-living raise for the department. A trade-out is more likely to involve tangible assets such as money, titles, equipment, office space or employment benefits than ideas. However, a trade-out can still be a win-win situation because both parties have something to use in bargaining. Both have the opportunity to complete negotiations in a better position than they started. The main pitfall of trade-outs occurs when either side fails to realize what is truly important to their cause or what they are willing to give up in order to receive something else.

Win-win remains the most desirable outcome of any negotiation. Anything less means that one party will undoubtedly harbor resentment that comes from a feeling of losing. That resentment may return in the form of tougher negotiations the next time or a total rejection of future negotiation attempts. Win-win helps ensure that the next time you need something, the avenues of negotiation will still be open to you.

NEGOTIATING SKILLS

Some of the skills necessary for negotiating include being able to assess timing, to research facts, to communicate and listen, and to monitor and read interpersonal reactions. Even a sense of humor can be applied to negotiating.

Timing

Knowing when to ask for something can be as important as knowing what you want. A good time to negotiate for a raise is during the company's budgetary process, when you can show that your division has brought in increased revenues and hence deserves some of the financial rewards. If the company has just announced record sales, you know management will be more receptive to requisitions for capital expenses such as new equipment.

If you have a choice about when to introduce a subject, select a time that will be conducive to a fair hearing of your demands. Cynthia had finally summoned her courage to ask her boss if she could attend a training seminar at company expense. She had prepared a proposal outlining the cost effectiveness of the seminar, reasoning that if the company invested in her training, she could share that information with other employees as well as being able to advance her own career with the company. After reading her proposal, her boss effectively built a roadblock to any further consideration of the plan by saying, "I think you make a lot of strong points, but, unfortunately, our training budget for this year has already received final approval. If you still feel strongly about this seminar next year, feel free to resubmit and update your proposal."

Had Cynthia used her interoffice contacts to learn more about the budget process, she might have met an earlier deadline to gain approval for her project. Her only hope now is to thank her boss for looking over the proposal and put a note on her planning calendar so the proposal will be turned in on time for the next fiscal year.

Sometimes timing can mean taking a break or backing off from a discussion. Use timing to take a recess if you see you are losing ground and need a moment to gather your thoughts. Get a drink of water or suddenly remember a file you left on your desk to give each of you some time to think. By walking away you show that you have the power to simply let the matter drop. When you return, you may find the listener more responsive to your position.

Researching

Before you can negotiate effectively, you must familiarize yourself with the facts or background pertaining to the situation. College debating teams know the full value of having current facts on hand to support an opinion. They arrive at the debate location carrying portable file boxes full of index cards that contain citations for legal cases, definitions of important terms, and statistical studies on different issues.

Generally, they know the topic they will have to debate, but they do not know whether they will have to support a position in favor of or in opposition to the topic. Their training, along with hours of practice and coaching, enables them to draw their position, review their files, and come out debating. By selecting case histories or statistics that support their position, the debaters try to sway the judges no matter how each team member feels personally.

Although few employees want to turn a negotiation session into a debate, the principle of researching a topic in advance remains valid. Pat was interviewing for a job as an engineer with a construction firm that specialized in developing resort properties. Impressed with her resumé and experience, the interviewer asked her a few questions and then surprised her by asking her what she hoped to earn as a salary in her first job. In college, she had been more interested in getting a diploma than investigating current pay scales. She quickly came up with a figure that was at least 20 percent lower than the company expected to pay. When the interviewer offered her a job at that salary, she accepted. After talking with her new co-workers, she realized she had placed a low price on her skills because of her lack of research.

Pat's mistake will intensify over time if she stays with the same company, because most raises are granted on a percentage of current pay. That means that if she starts out making 20 percent less than her co-workers, she will never close the salary gap since her raises will be based on a percentage of her lower pay scale. The inequity might have been avoided if she had checked with her college placement counselor to find out comparable salaries being paid in her field in cities in which she planned to interview. Libraries often contain recent surveys by the federal or state departments of labor that detail salaries as well as availability of jobs. By arming yourself with background data, you may be able to avoid costly career mistakes.

Communicating

Your timing may be perfect and your facts may be irrefutable, but you still have to be able to communicate your position persuasively to the other party before effective negotiation can occur. In business, communication skills form a foundation for giving and receiving information. In business negotiation, the purpose is enhanced because the speaker seeks a certain outcome. If you are negotiating on a controversial matter such as budget cuts or mergers which may affect job security, then the pressure of an adversarial situation may force you to communicate under stress.

Asking for a Promotion

Asking for a promotion is an example of negotiating that most professionals will use at some time in their careers. A step-by-step approach will help systematize the request.

Prepare a case for your proposal before asking for a meeting time. Think about the points you want to make and begin researching facts for the presentation.

Ask for sufficient time to make your presentation and tell your supervisor the reason for the meeting. If you do not state the reason, the manager may assume you are quitting.

Review the current status of your department, emphasizing ways in which it has improved during your tenure. Do not take credit for others' accomplishments, but show how you have made a positive contribution.

Provide facts, especially budgetary data, that explain why you deserve a promotion. Update your supervisor on recently completed training or college courses. Effective presentations link research with known company goals such as promoting from within or rewarding managers who stay within a budget.

If appropriate, thank your supervisor for support and training opportunities. Volunteer to help during the transition or to help select a successor if company policy permits.

If a supervisor asks for time to consider your request, be prepared to leave a copy of your proposal for future reference and ask for a specific time when you may expect an answer. Getting a definite answer, even if it is negative, is better than being put on hold.

Be ready to outline a fallback position rather than accepting an unconditional "no." Offer concessions one at a time, such as agreeing to a trial or probationary period or waiting until the end of the fiscal year for a raise.

Confirm the agreement in writing as soon as possible, allowing management to make the formal announcement of the promotion. The memo should detail the effective date of the promotion and any raises or title changes agreed upon.

Follow through by keeping superiors informed of progress to show they have made the right decision, and keep any promises made during negotiation. If you promise to keep your new salary and benefits confidential, do not take chances by telling anyone in the office.

Monitoring Interpersonal Reactions

In negotiation, remember that words are only one part of the communication equation; also included are tone of voice, inflection, body language, facial expressions, and supporting documents. Organize your facts as you would any persuasive speech by outlining main points and memorizing key points that emphasize your case. However, remember that once negotiation begins, you will not be able to progress from fact to fact without interruption, because your boss or co-worker will undoubtedly interject other facts and opinions or even arguments along the way.

Rehearse your main points with a trusted friend who will agree to play "devil's advocate." The devil's advocate tries to take the opposing side to any idea to help you think of ways to counter objections. By anticipating any arguments such as "We can't afford it" or "We've never done it that way before," you can be mentally prepared to diffuse verbal obstacles.

If time allows, rehearse your tone of voice and inflections to be sure that your voice adds appropriate force to your words. If your voice cracks, or your inflections make it seem as if you are asking a question or seeking approval, your argument will weaken. If you know ahead of time that you will be in a negotiation situation, plan to wear something that always gives you confidence. If you are comfortable, you will be more likely to assume an assertive posture instead of appearing insecure.

When you negotiate, use strong eye contact, a firm tone of voice, and make sure verbal and nonverbal messages are consistent. Inconsistent messages let your listener know that you can be easily intimidated or manipulated. Stay calm so that you maintain control over the conversation. Remember you are the one who has done your homework and analyzed the situation fully ahead of the meeting. In negotiations, even silences can be a form of communication. If the conversation hits a pause, use it to your advantage by looking over notes or looking the listener in the eye as you wait for an answer rather than fumbling for words to fill an awkward silence. Act during pauses rather than reacting to them.

Sometimes you may want to bring supporting documents into the discussion. These may be copies of a study that draws conclusions you can use as evidence for your cause or a chart showing projected outcome of a certain plan of action. Slide shows, transparencies on overhead projectors, or even demonstrations may all be part of persuading your audience. If you plan to use any props, prepare them with the same effort you prepare your speech. A sloppy chart with typographical errors will do more to undermine your case than help it. If you have any questions about the accuracy, clarity, or impact of a visual aid, leave it in your desk. Use only professional-looking aids that reinforce your business image.

Reading Other People

Since communication is a two-way street, you must not only be aware of how you are transmitting your message, but you must also be aware of how others are receiving it. Have you used too much business jargon and confused the listener? Does the listener feel attacked by your point of view? Have emotions started to change the meanings of some of your words because of a defensive attitude?

Face-to-face negotiation is a trade-out. Because you can see the person you are dealing with, you can see if they seem to understand or if you need to repeat certain points. You can also see if you need to soften or toughen your approach as you talk to gain the desired outcome. The trade-out comes because you risk arousing unwanted emotions on the part of the listener. If your message is misunderstood or your motives are misinterpreted, you may have to cope with hard feelings or suspicion later in your dealings. On the other hand, personal negotiations have an advantage over letters written back and forth over a certain issue. Letters preclude the opportunity for immediate feedback or spontaneous decision making.

In negotiating, turn your communication skills around to analyze any messages the listener is sending. Crossed arms, furrowed brow, and nervous mannerisms may indicate that you should break the ice first with a less important issue before going on to more important matters on the agenda. If you sense hostility or defensiveness, try to remind the listener that the discussion relates only to business matters or professional considerations and not to personal feelings. Using factual statements supported by statistical evidence is a good way to avoid using "charged" words or words that carry a hidden meaning or connotation.

Make a strong attempt to identify with the listener's needs in order to get what you want. Assess their values, knowledge, and experience in relation to yours and to the problem you are discussing. Ask yourself what the listener has to gain and lose from the discussion. What does the listener need that you can give or what does the listener really want?

If you can make the situation mutually beneficial, your chances of receiving your request improve. Showing how your plan will save money, increase productivity, eliminate waste, or use resources more efficiently will demonstrate to your boss that you have the company's best interests at heart rather than only selfish motives. Think of negotiation as a sale you want to make. Sell the idea based on its own merits rather than comparing it to other successes or failures, and remember to stress points in a positive way whenever possible.

However basic it may sound, negotiators need to listen. By listening you can identify a strategy that helps you learn the weakness of your opponent's arguments. If you hear a question that relates to one of your main points, jump ahead to that part of the argument and return to other points later. If you sense tactics of delay or postponement of a decision, ask questions to find out the opponent's thinking.

In negotiations, questions should be open ended or questions that cannot be answered by simply saying yes or no. Examples are questions that start with how or why. These questions force the opponent to reveal underlying thinking behind an argument. Once you hear the answers, you can meet the resistance point by point.

These points form the foundation for a successful negotiator. Building on that foundation, the negotiator also needs to develop a style of negotiating that fits her personality. A sense of humor can be vital in negotiating. It helps you keep negotiations in perspective. When the negotiation goes your way, negotiation can actually be fun. When it does not go your way, your sense of humor can help you be philosophical about what you learned or how to approach the problem the next time. Negotiators need to remember that although serious issues are being discussed, if you take yourself too seriously or identify too intensely with the problem, you may forget the agenda at hand.

NEGOTIATING AS SELLING

The analogy of buyer and seller can be applied to negotiations. For example, the person who wants a promotion must "sell" the idea to upper management. The manager in authority must "buy" the idea in order for the negotiator to receive a promotion. The following five steps will help you to sell your recommendation (Allison, 1984):

1. *Research:* Finding out everything you can before you make a recommendation. Examples include

- ❑ reviewing the success of previous projects
- ❑ analyzing financial factors that may affect the proposal
- ❑ checking your proposal against stated company goals

2. *Planning:* Organizing a well-thought out plan to present to management. Examples include

- ❑ writing goals and objectives for the recommendation
- ❑ listing benefits to the company if plan is implemented
- ❑ estimating cost and time effectiveness of any suggestions
- ❑ creating a fallback position in case your original ideas meet rejection

3. *Preparation:* Finding ways to communicate your plan in a presentation. Examples include

- ❑ scheduling a conference to make your presentation
- ❑ compiling written material for meeting handouts
- ❑ proofreading all handouts and charts before meeting

4. *Presentation:* Offering the recommendation to supervisors. Examples include

❑ introducing the idea generally and moving to specific concepts

❑ projecting confidence and enthusiasm in the project

❑ answering questions or agreeing to find answers if you do not know them

5. *Follow-up:* Charting progress of implemented recommendation. Examples include

❑ distributing progress reports to appropriate managers

❑ informing management as objectives are met

NEGOTIATION TECHNIQUES

Some managers seem to know instinctively when to ask for something or when to push their cause and when to back off for a later advantage. Part of that knowledge comes with experience, but there are several techniques you can employ to increase the chances of success in negotiations.

If you sense that your opponent is underestimating you because you are a woman or because you represent a minority, take advantage of the situation. Because women are often perceived as less experienced negotiators, they may more easily be able to gain the listener's confidence toward their position. Be careful that you do not resort to inappropriate office behavior that makes the listener view you as a daughter, wife, or sister. Although you may want to use the advantage of less experience, you always want others to perceive you as an equal in a business relationship.

Realize that being told no is not the end of the world. Mentally prepare yourself for negative arguments by reminding yourself that the disapproval is for the raise or promotion you have requested and is not intended for you personally. Working through fear of rejection helps take the anxiety out of negotiations.

Do not be defensive. Know that you are not alone in your uncertainty in facing negotiation. Most supervisors would also like to avoid confrontation by granting every request. Adults understand that would be an unrealistic business situation that would soon grow out of control, resulting in office chaos. Knowing that bosses also hate to say no helps you keep negotiations in perspective, since you know both parties share some of the same emotions.

Select your turf when you negotiate. Just as timing creates negotiation power as a skill, turf selection creates power as a technique. Territory such as your own desk or your own office adds to your security in negotiations. Tackle negotiations where the territory is to your advantage. Do you want to be able to plant an idea and walk away? Then you should go to the other person's office so you can leave at will. Do you want to be surrounded by your files and your persuasive evidence? Then ask the other person to come to your office. For informal negotiations, look for places that are neutral and put both parties at ease, such as a coffee shop or lounge area.

Keep control of everything that could affect the outcome. Avoid distractions such as ringing phones or interruptions by securing a private place to talk or asking a secretary to hold all calls. Stand up if possible to be able to look down at the other person. This lessens the chance that the other person will be able to stand up and leave at will. Be tactful and positive so that your statements cannot be taken out of context against you if you are quoted on them. Saying something positive often disarms even the most angry speaker and builds leverage that you can use in completing the negotiation.

Build from power. Expand your duties to include more responsibility. Learn new tasks and document accomplishments. Compile every evidence of a job well done, such as congratulatory letters, certificates of accomplishments, positive evaluations, and profit figures. With this power comes the confidence to ask for more money or a better job title because you know you have earned it.

When appropriate, try to get a decision on the spot. Giving the other person too much time may allow them to think of new reasons why you should not receive your request. If you want something specific, try to get an answer within a specific time. If the listener promises to consider the request later, keep pressing for a specific time, such as a month or 6 weeks, in which to have an answer. If you let the issue become indefinitely prolonged, you risk losing the negotiation to added red tape or other layers of a corporate bureaucracy. In addition, your arguments may become diluted or irrelevant after some time has passed. Restate the agreed upon time in a memo for written confirmation.

In business, the two most common resistances to negotiation are *money* and *policy*. Every supervisor can eventually fall back on money or policy when denying a request. If you are familiar with the company's profit and loss record, you stand a better chance of proving the company can afford a raise or a promotion. If you know that sales are up, you can show how your idea can increase them further and become cost effective. If the budget will be reviewed in 6 months, you might suggest a reevaluation of your accomplished objectives at that time. If you get a positive reaction, follow up the conversation with a memo detailing what you agree to do in order to be reevaluated for a raise. List the specific date of the conversation and of the review. Your memo will be documentation that your supervisor agreed to the principle if not the original request.

Likewise, if you have read the company policy manual, you will know what is company policy and what is a weak excuse. Sometimes company policy is just a way of saying that the issue is closed. If you know the company has no written policy on a matter or if exceptions have been made for other employees, you have a strong argument. However, be careful in citing specific situations. If you were not a party to those negotiations, you may not know what specific situations or circumstances led to the exception and your strategy may backfire.

Avoid ultimatums. If you ask for only one thing "or else," you may be disappointed when your opponent selects the "or else." By giving an ultimatum, you create a situation in which the opponent can select only one alternative. Many supervisors resent being backed into a corner with statements of "If I can't have a raise, I quit" or "If you are going to promote her over me, you'll be making a mistake." Each of these statements leaves no room for the supervisor to do the job the company authorizes, which is to hire and fire and to promote. Besides the resentment, you may have offered a plan that is impossible and then the supervisor has no choice but to accept your resignation on the spot.

If you get an offer of money, that is the time to discuss salary without delay. In negotiations, it is easy to come down from a top price, but you can never go back up once you have mentioned a lower figure. As long as you have done your homework and determined the normal salary range for a job, ask for the maximum in the range. If you are too far off the scale, you may be seen as ill informed about the current market trends. If you are too low, you automatically undervalue yourself. If you are confident you know the range, ask for 5 to 20 percent above it. If you are offered a salary you do not like, do not hesitate to say "I will think it over," rather than letting emotions take over.

Companies want to hire the best people for the least amount of money. Your challenge is to get the job with the best package of salary and benefits possible. If you do not like an offer, restate skills as if you did not hear the salary. If you know the company can offer no more money, ask for paid insurance or extra vacation days as part of your package. If you see that your tactics are too risky to get the job you want, you can always agree to a lesser offer, but once you have accepted the job, you may lose your negotiating potential and have to accept whatever the company offers all new employees.

THE TABLES TURN

On your way up the career ladder, you may have to negotiate your pay scale, your working hours, your job benefits, and even your title. Once you become a supervisor, the people in your department will also become negotiators. Just as you will initiate negotiations, others will negotiate with you to improve their situation or assets.

As a supervisor, you exercise control over your employees' work. This control extends to negotiations in which you can use it to the advantage of you and your company. If an employee asks to talk to you, try to find out the nature of the problem before you agree to a meeting. Although you may exercise an open-door policy for all employees, this does not mean you cannot postpone or reschedule a discussion. If a worker says, "I'd really like to talk to you privately today," you can ask your own open-ended questions, such as "What do we need to discuss?" or "About how much time will we need to plan?" These questions will help you know if you are about to be asked a simple question or if you are headed for serious negotiations.

If the employee tells you the subject, you can begin doing your own homework. Look over the employee's records including salary, past evaluations, and recent accomplishments. Even in a small department, these facts can refresh your memory so that you have a better idea of values, experience, and education when it is time for the appointment.

Listen thoughtfully to the employee's request. Take notes if you want to refer to specific points later. Try to remember that if you were in the employee's position, you would want the respect of your listener. Ask questions to find out what the employee truly wants. An employee who asks for a few days off may actually have a more serious problem that you could help solve rather than just granting a simple request that may or may not help.

Try to find some point of compromise. If you cannot grant everything an employee asks, try to find some middle ground so the employee knows it is worthwhile to attempt negotiations. If you do not have the authority to take action on a request, promise the employee that you will take it up with your supervisor and then follow through. In most cases, it is better for your career if you intercede on your employee's behalf to your supervisors rather than letting them go over your head. Your supervisors may view the employee's overstepping of bounds as a sign that you cannot control your department or that you are ineffective in handling the chain of command. If you promise to ask someone else, however, be sure to do so to retain your credibility with your employees. Report back to them within a reasonable amount of time to avoid raising false hopes or expectations that could lead to low morale.

If you cannot meet the request on any common ground, then you must learn to say no. Part of negotiating is learning to say the word so that it is firm, final, and unrelenting, with no excuses, apologies, or whining. When no is called for, it must be delivered unequivocally. If you have a reason to substantiate your negative response, you can share it or not as you deem appropriate.

Never apologize or retreat from saying no when that is the decision you must make. After you say no, you can soften the impact with a smile or some words to reassure the person that you are rejecting their idea or request, rather than the speaker as a person. You may even be able to think of an alternative that would lessen the negative impact. However, if a manager needs to say no, and cannot give any more information, she needs to feel comfortable with that power.

CONCLUSION

When you negotiate and win you feel great. But even if you do not get what you want, you have sent a signal that helps others recognize your worth. Women must learn that silence can be costly. Many times people are only waiting for you to ask for what you want.

As with all goals, negotiation starts by knowing what you want and setting boundaries. Eventually you will be able to translate your accomplishments into dollars and job titles with more authority.

The National Commission on Working Women estimates that women earn 64 cents for every dollar earned by men. Women will gain the rest not by demanding but by negotiating. When you want a job or a raise or a promotion, you can start by solving problems, meeting needs, reducing waste, increasing production, reducing costs, simplifying methods, and concentrating on the bottom line and tangible results.

You can negotiate or you can settle for less. (See Exercises 14-1 and 14-2.)

SUMMARY

Negotiation is the process of persuading or influencing someone to adopt a certain course of action. Negotiation starts with knowing what you want to gain. Strategies for negotiators include compromising, saving face, collaborating, or devising a trade-out by which both parties get part, if not all, of what they seek. Research, communication, and timing can be factors in successful negotiation.

Money and policy are the two most common resistances to negotiation in business. Effective negotiators meet objections rationally, point by point, to secure results. If you are in the position of power, you must learn to occasionally say no and not apologize or retreat from that decision.

TERMS AND CONCEPTS

collaboration	saving face
compromise	trade-out
fallback position	win-lose
negotiation	win-win
negotiation potential	

REVIEW QUESTIONS

1. How does the goal-setting process relate to negotiation?
2. What is a collaboration and how does it differ from a compromise?
3. What evidence can lend support to your negotiations in a group presentation?
4. How can you meet objections because of money or company policies in a business negotiation?

5. How can a supervisor prepare for a negotiation session with a subordinate?

6. Why are ultimatums to be avoided in negotiations?

7. What part does eye contact play in negotiations?

8. List at least five reasons why you need to develop negotiation skills as a manager.

9. Define the following terms and concepts: collaboration, compromise, fallback position, negotiation, negotiation potential, saving face, trade-out, win-lose, win-win.

10. List at least four win-lose techniques or strategies you should avoid.

EXERCISES

14-1: NEGOTIATE

Three-step approach to getting more of what you want.

1. Identify and describe one course of action, proposal, or asset that you are willing to negotiate for within the next 2 weeks. Describe the other party. Quirks? Hot buttons? Likes? Dislikes? What is at stake?

    Determine:

        Fallback position

        Facts

        Best time

        Win position

        Lose position

        Obstacles

        Turf

Visualize your success.

Give examples of collaboration, saving face, trade-out, compromise.

2. Role play with a partner.

3. Go for it! Apply your skills.

14-2: NEGOTIATION ROLE PLAYING

Instructions: Role play the following scenario with two volunteer participants with a 15-minute time limit. Observers will share reactions. Identify techniques and skills utilized.

Situation: Ad Art Advertising Agency revenues increased $1,950,000 this year; the staff has remained at 18 persons with 6 art directors. Currently, there is no Creative Head. As Art Director, Kris would like to negotiate a new position as Creative Director to manage all art directors and copywriters and oversee all the creative endeavors of the agency to ensure that quality control, client satisfaction, and image standards have met or surpassed the agency's goals. Kris expects a 20% salary increase, a title change, co-worker's cooperation, and top management support. Kris has set a meeting with Lynn, President, to discuss the proposed changes. Lynn has acted as Creative Head because of her ownership position.

SUGGESTED READINGS

Allison, M.A. *Managing Up, Managing Down.* Simon & Schuster, New York, 1984.

Brody, M.D. *Get Some Respect! How to Get What You Want on Your Terms.* Ace Books, New York, 1980.

Cohen, H. *You Can Negotiate Anything.* Bantam Books, New York, 1980.

Coplin, W.D., and O'Leary, M.K., with Gould, C. *Power Persuasion. A Surefire System to Get Ahead in Business.* Addison-Wesley, Reading, MA, 1985.

DuBrin, A. *Contemporary Applied Management.* Business Publications, Dallas, TX, 1987.

Fisher, R., and Ury, W. *Getting to Yes. Negotiating Agreement Without Giving In.* Penguin Books, New York, 1981.

Ilich, J., and Jones, B.S. *Successful Negotiating Skills For Women.* Playboy Paperbacks, New York, 1981.

Nierenberg, J., and Ross, I.S. *Women and the Art of Negotiating.* Simon & Schuster, New York, 1985.

Seltz, D.D., and Modica, A.J. *Negotiate Your Way to Success.* Mentor Books, New York, 1980.

Wall, J.A. *Negotiation: Theory and Practice.* Scott, Foresman, Glenview, IL, 1985.

Warschaw, T.A. *Winning by Negotiation.* Berkley Books, New York, 1980.

15

THE FUTURE

MANAGING FOR THE FUTURE

Too often people in business can think about only the next deadline, the next profit and loss report, or the current crisis. Few executives take time to think about technological advancements or demographical data. Yet technology is moving so rapidly that many new inventions are already obsolete by the time they reach mass distribution. By the time a computer goes on the market, a newer, faster model with more capacity is already on the drawing boards. In much the same way, population shifts may be shrinking a market that was formerly profitable. For example, if a company's traditional market share has been homemakers who did not work outside the home, it may be facing an impossible marketing challenge as more and more women enter the work force.

This new emphasis on studying the future through trends and implementing the information into a plan of action is called *futurism*. The importance of this science has led to the emergence of specialists called *futurists* who research, analyze, and chart the future. Their work impacts on managers in two ways:

1. Managers must stay abreast of changes in the marketplace to keep their companies competitive and profitable.
2. Managers must stay informed about trends as they affect their own careers if they seek a thriving career.

In "Managing for the Future—Now," Machlowitz (1981) traces the futurist movement back to the establishment of "think tanks," such as the Rand Corporation, around the time of World War II when defense concerns created the need for advanced technology. Some of the ideas, such as robotics and computers, seemed farfetched then, although we now take the concepts for granted. Change represented not only a costly investment but also a threat to the status quo. As a result, most businesses concerned themselves with day-to-day commerce, and if a long-range plan existed at all, it rarely addressed more than a 1- or 2-year period.

Looking backward, many companies might have predicted some of the success stories of the 1980s had they made correct assumptions about population trends. More working women with fewer leisure-time hours have created giant fast-food and day care industries. A lower birth rate in families means that parents have more money to invest in each child, creating a boom in educational toys and children's furnishings. By looking at these trends, schools and colleges can get an idea of how many students they will need to recruit and educate in order to keep their doors open.

A few large companies have developed future-oriented projects or departments that encourage futuristic thinking. Other companies have assigned these duties to existing departments, such as research and development or marketing. Still others have hired a futurist as a consultant or invited a futurist to give an intensive seminar to train managers in thinking beyond tomorrow. Futurism need not be left to highly trained specialists. No matter how sophisticated futurism sounds, futurists employ a few basic techniques that can be adapted to almost any business or industry.

FUTURING TECHNIQUES

Although no one can predict the future, by analyzing certain trends, people can plan for it. David Pearce Snyder, a consulting futurist with the World Future Society in Bethesda, MD, gives four basic techniques to futuring that can be applied to charting the future in a personal or business situation.

1. *Scanning.* Scanning is collecting all available information. Snyder recommends reading at least one local and one national newspaper, such as *USA Today* or the *Wall Street Journal,* each day to spot issues and trends as they develop. Magazines, journals, and best-selling books can also give clues about trends. For example, a popular movie usually gives rise to a spin-off as a television show and marketable retail products based on successful characters. Other important sources of data include census reports or United Nations reports that document population and economic shifts.

2. *Modeling.* Developing a mathematical model from the data is the next step. Just as objectives require deadlines and percentages for measurability, quantifiable trend statements need numbers and percentages to give them measurable predictability. Examples might be creating a model that tells how many units a certain factory should be able to produce in a year or how many hospital beds a community will have to have to accommodate its needs in a certain year.

3. *Creating scenarios.* Scenarios can be compared to screenplays for movies. A scenario is a description of different conclusions based on available data. One approach is to take a "worst-case scenario" and a "best-case scenario" that outline the most disastrous outcome and the most optimistic projection and then fill in with scenarios between the two extremes. Creating scenarios reminds planners of the number of variable factors in

any situation. Competition, climate, population, and marketability must all be taken into account when making decisions about the future.

4. *Setting goals.* In futuring, setting goals defines Utopia. Futuristic goals outline the way we want the world to be, not necessarily how it will be. Working with the future involves long-range plans and even dreams to be effective.

The companies that learn to use futurists in management will have an edge over companies that live from fiscal year to fiscal year. These companies can act while competitors are trying to react to trends. If your company does not have a futuristic strategy, there are still some things you can do as a manager to prepare your department and your own career for the future. (See Exercise 15-1.) Machlowitz (1981) advises the following:

❑ *Learn what is going on in your organization.* Know as much as you can about your own department and the overall work of the company. Try to get involved whenever possible.

❑ *Incorporate a "future" perspective into everything.* Think about population shifts when trying to determine the best place for a branch office. Analyze the educational level of the market before deciding on an approach for advertising. Realize that changes in the community either have impacted or will impact on your business.

❑ *Use available resources.* Government statistics or public information are generally the sources used by professional consultants. If you can analyze the data yourself, you can save the costs of consultants or services.

❑ *Overcome managerial myopia.* Myopic vision or nearsightedness is a common pitfall for managers who are concerned about today's performance instead of tomorrow's profits. Since the next century is less than 15 years away, planning for the year 2025 is not too farfetched.

TRENDS

Just as the assumptions about management have changed, so have the assumptions about society as a whole. In *Megatrends*, Naisbitt (1982) describes trends that are fundamental to our contemporary society. Yet many people miss seeing them as trends because they are experiencing only subtle changes. Individuals may think they are the only people being affected. Since they are so close to the situation, they may not be able to reach a perspective enabling them to see that the world is changing with them. Ten of the major trends Naisbitt outlines involve changes:

1. *From an industrial society to an information society.* In 1956, for the first time in the United States, there were more white-collar workers than blue-collar workers. Naisbitt says the new source of power is not money but information.

2. *From forced technology to high tech/high touch.* To balance the high levels of technology in society, there must be a human response. Self-help books, a return to religious values, and emphasis on family traditions or ethnic heritage are all part of creating the balance.

3. *From a national economy to a world economy.* Telecommunications and jet travel have combined to allow full freedom in both the flow of information and people. Companies that will prosper are those that see their marketplace as the world rather than their region or country, and work to use the best parts of each economic segment. Although some companies are lamenting the low cost of labor in the third world, others are using the ideas of twin plants or satellite plants to capitalize on an economic advantage.

4. *From short term to long term.* A 5-year plan that can be revised, updated, and expanded is a logical place to start for companies and individuals. Short-term plans ignore the need to project into the future and cause businesses to constantly try to catch up to trends instead of staying ahead of them.

5. *From centralization to decentralization.* From our economic system to our political system, people are choosing local solutions over national ones. More and more businesses are carving out market shares based on regional differences in economics and culture. Politically, people are voting for less government from Washington, D.C., and more voice at home.

6. *From institutional to self-help.* In the past, people looked to all levels of government to provide emergency aid, health benefits, and retirement income. People now realize that they must participate in decisions that affect their own lives. Grass-roots movements such as halfway houses, birthing centers, and hospices are examples of ways people are encouraging a sense of self-reliance in life and death decisions.

7. *From representative democracy to participatory democracy.* Power is gaining momentum from the bottom up instead of the top down. People are organizing into political action groups and advocacy groups to promote key issues.

Even in business situations, the leader is more likely to be a facilitator rather than an order giver.

8. *From hierarchies to networking.* Naisbitt says the failure of hierarchies to solve problems has led to the establishment of networks. Networks involve people talking to one another to share information or resources. This process allows communication in a horizontal direction instead of the vertical direction of hierarchies.

9. *From North to South and West.* The 1980 census showed that the South and West had more people than the North and East. Although the North and East have long been the sources of political and economic strength, the South and West have the numerical advantage to produce both in the future.

10. *From either/or to multiple options.* Before the 1980s, people generally followed one pattern for their lives. They went to school, got married, had children, and lived in nuclear family units consisting of mother, father, and children. Now people have unlimited options for their lives—they may or may not go to school, may or may not marry, and may or may not have children. Even if they make these choices, they still have many options as divorce is more prevalent and more students on college campuses are over the age of 25.

Summary of Trends

FROM	TO
Industrial society	Informational society
Forced technology	High tech/High touch
National economy	World economy
Short-term plans	Long-term plans
Centralization	Decentralization
Institutional help	Self-help
Representative democracy	Participatory democracy
Hierarchies	Networking
North	South and West
Either/or	Multiple options

Naisbitt's conclusion is that we are living in a time of parentheses, the time between eras. The familiar past still exists and people by nature resist change. Instead of seeing this as a threat, we need to view it as an opportunity to redefine our own vision of the future.

Visions for Women

In an article for *Working Woman* (November, 1986) the editors used the occasion of the magazine's tenth anniversary to catalog "How Working Women Have Changed America." Some of the findings include

- ❑ In 1950, there were fewer than 4 million married women with children in the work force. Today, there are over 15 million and they represent 62 percent of all married women with children.

- ❑ In 63 percent of married couples, both partners work and 5 million wives earn more than their husbands.

- ❑ Professional fields such as law, medicine, and accounting are changing as women make up greater and greater numbers of postgraduate classes.

- ❑ Women now outnumber men as eligible voters. Eighty cities with populations over 30,000 had female mayors in 1986.

- ❑ Women are delaying marriage and having fewer children as they establish careers.

- ❑ By 1985, 9.2 percent of working women were executives. The number of women managers and administrators more than doubled from 1975 to 1985, reaching 4.4 million or 36 percent of the total.

- ❑ Service industries represent growth areas for jobs, particularly in child care and maid services that meet demands of working women.

- ❑ In 1986, women owned one in every four businesses, nearly 3 million in all.

CAREER ASSESSMENT

After reading the experts' opinions on the future of our society, a manager might be tempted to return to school for a degree in computer science and immediately relocate to the South or West in search of a perfect career in a high-paying job with an unlimited future. Although that may be the correct course of action for some professionals, no one oversimplification of a trend statement will chart the future for everyone. To put societal trends into a personal context requires an ongoing process of career assessment. *Career assessment* is the process of analyzing yourself and external factors that affect career decisions in order to make the best possible life decisions. Career assessment, like futuring, should be a continual process. The perfect job today may lead to burnout tomorrow if managers do not work to stay challenged in their careers.

The career assessment procedure can be simplified into four major concentrations.

Self-Assessment

Before looking at external factors, a career woman must look inside herself. Questions to ask yourself are discussed in the following paragraphs.

What are my interests? If there are certain courses that you tend to spend more time studying and subjects that you avoid, these answers might help determine whether you would be happier pursuing a career in accounting or a career in writing. Do not limit yourself to traditional choices. Talk with counselors at the college placement center or interview a professional in a field you want to explore before eliminating your options. Take electives outside your major field of study to be sure that you investigate other career choices.

Do I enjoy working with people or alone? If you enjoy working as part of a group, you should find jobs with greater amounts of interaction, such as a counselor, a professor, a doctor, or a lawyer. If you prefer working alone, a career as a researcher, a designer, a computer programmer, or an artist might meet that need.

What are my strengths and weaknesses? A gift for learning foreign languages or interpreting statistical data might be a key to unlocking the best career direction for you. Teachers, friends, co-workers, and even supervisors can give you clues about your talents. Too often we cannot objectively evaluate our own performance and may miss important aspects of our potential. Many colleges have free or low-cost counseling services that can further help you determine personal and intellectual strengths to build upon when selecting a career. Even learning your weaknesses can be an asset, because by knowing areas in which you need work, you can plan to take extra training or education in those fields to balance your strengths.

What goals do I have for my personal life and how will they fit into different careers? More and more women are combining marriage and child rearing with their jobs. For other women, a career must come first and marriage and children may come later, if at all. "Having it all" or combining a successful job and personal life cannot be achieved without planning. For example, if your job requires a great deal of travel and you know you want to be a working mother, you will need to develop the support system of a spouse or family member or make enough money to hire babysitters so that you can maintain your career.

Where do I want to live? Some people prefer the fast pace of a large city with proximity to more cultural and corporate opportunities. Other people prefer to have a short commute to the office and live closer to recreational areas. Climate, family responsibilities, and availability of educational opportunities may also be factors in deciding where you want to establish your career. If you aspire to complete a master's or doctoral degree, you should plan to take a job near a university that offers a program in your field.

How do I feel about security versus risk? Some people enjoy the challenge of being on the ground level of a new venture because they know that if the project succeeds, they will grow with it. Others want the security that comes from joining a company with a proven track record and working their way to the top. No one situation is better than the other, but each calls for a different type of personality to make the best partnership of companies and individuals.

Career Identification

After knowing more about yourself, you can begin to narrow your choices for a career. Some factors that need consideration are the following:

Salary. The importance of salary and how much money you want to earn are major job indicators. If you want to earn a six-figure salary, you will need to research careers that give you a realistic opportunity to achieve that goal. If a need to help people through an altruistic career is more important than money, then you need to weigh that against your potential earning power. Good sources for salary information include the U.S. Department of Labor and the Bureau of Labor Statistics, which publishes the *Occupational Outlook Handbook*. Earnings data are also published according to regions, industries, and professions by the Bureau of Labor Statistics. To obtain information specific to women, *Working Woman* magazine annually publishes a Salary

Survey edition that gives expected salary ranges for a wide variety of careers.

Responsibility. Some workers want to work an 8-hour day and go home, leaving the office and its problems behind. Other workers aspire to be managers, knowing that they will occasionally be called at home or asked to put in extra hours. Knowing the amount of responsibility you eventually want can help determine your career path. If you want to be a manager by the time you are 30, you should choose a career that allows early advancement rather than a career that requires several years of postgraduate study or apprenticeship.

Opportunity for advancement. No matter how prestigious some jobs seem, they may be dead-end jobs. If you are an assistant to the president, you may be as high in the company as you can go without replacing the CEO. If you seek challenges in the form of career advancement, you need to select a career that permits change and growth. For example, if a bank generally promotes from a commercial lending department, a woman who aspires to be a vice president will be more likely to achieve her goal if she takes an entry-level position in that department rather than taking a mid-management job in the public relations or bookkeeping departments.

Power. For some managers, power and recognition are more important than salary or other job considerations. State and federal representatives and senators offer good examples of jobs that offer power, although most of the people elected to those positions could probably command higher salaries at jobs in the private sector.

Fringe benefits. A company car, paid insurance, a country club membership, or on-site day care or health club facilities may all influence where you want to work. In highly competitive fields, companies are offering more and more incentives, in addition to salary, to recruit and keep trained employees. Although no one should go into an interview asking about the vacation policy, you can generally receive a booklet or brochure outlining available benefits before you take the job. Benefits can be equally as important as salary, because they offer security in case you become ill or disabled or try to maintain quality of life.

Career identification is association with or relation to the requirements, skills, activities, philosophy, attributes, and characteristics of a career according to your own values, needs, goals, philosophy, and skills. High career identification enhances the probability of a successful career.

Company Identification

The next step in career assessment is to decide on companies that fit the profile of where you want to work. Job leads may come from classified advertising in a newspaper, employment agencies, state employment services, unions, school placement centers, or friends and relatives. Most job seekers send out resumés to any number of companies in hopes of getting a job interview. Many times they know very little about the companies until the actual interview. Learning more about different companies is an important step in making the best career choice.

Some techniques to research companies include

Reading annual reports. As covered in the chapter on finance, annual reports are an important source of information about companies. By reading an annual report, you can determine how well a company is doing financially before your financial future depends on it.

Talking to people in the company or in similar fields. You may get one side of the story from personnel departments or professional correspondence. If you are seriously considering going to work for a company, you need to investigate attitudes of others in the business community about the firm as well as talk to other people employed at the firm to get different perspectives. Do not be discouraged if you hear negative things unless you hear them from more than one person. If several people share a negative opinion, you may want to rethink your decision.

Checking other sources. Business newspapers, magazines, and business sections of newspapers can offer clues about a company. If a company receives an award for supporting a charity, that may mean that it values social involvement on the part of its employees. If a company is named in a large number of lawsuits, it may mean that the company is at disproportionate financial risk and may be hampered in its growth.

Visiting the offices. Often you may be able to take part in a public tour or informal visit before you are an official job applicant. This can be an important part of your homework, because it can give you first-hand information. If you have never toured a manufacturing plant, you may be surprised at the contrast in noise level, safety procedures, or other working conditions. If you have toured the facility before your interview, try to mention your tour in the job interview to show your interest, and bring up questions you may have based on your knowledge of the facility, such as where a certain department will be located or when a construction project was completed.

Company identification is association with or relation to the organization's requirements, philosophy, ethics, mission, focus, goals and attributes according to your own values, needs, motives, ethics, philosophy, goals, expectations, and skill. Strong company identification enhances the probability of a successful career.

Getting the Job

Only after you have analyzed yourself, identified career objectives, and selected certain target companies are you ready for the last step of getting the job. Approaching the job hunt as a job itself helps develop a professional business style that carries over into the first impression with a company.

Some tools that you will need to start your search are

Resumés A *resumé* is a written summary of your credentials (Fig. 15-1), including educational and professional experience as well as awards and other information, which is designed with the objective of getting a job. Many professional resumé services are listed in the *Yellow Pages* of telephone books in larger cities. Public libraries also have reference volumes on how to write resumés. University placement offices often will help you write a resumé free of charge as long as you are enrolled as a student.

Resumés may be organized chronologically, starting with your most recent job or schooling and going back to your first job or high school diploma. They may also be organized topically, that is, listing work experience under different topics or job skills that you possess.

Whatever plan you adopt, some writing tips to keep in mind include

Keep it brief. A one-page resumé is more likely to be read from top to bottom than a two- or three-page resumé. Use your resumé to generate interest in hopes of getting a job interview rather than including so much information that the personnel manager feels nothing more can be learned in an interview. Limit your resumé to accomplishments that can be directly related to work. Adding extra material may be distracting and give a potential employer the idea that you do not understand the functions of the job.

Use action words. Verbs such as planned, coordinated, implemented, or produced help tell a potential employer what you can do. Job titles may be impressive, but since titles vary from

Mary Smith
123 Franklin Lane
Boston, MA
(555)555-1234

Employment Objective: Creative Director

Experience

ART DIRECTOR, Frankenfield's Creative Ideas, 640 4th St., Boston, MA, 1984-1987. Supervised 25 designers and production personnel for projects totalling $2.2 million in billings annually. Major accounts included an automobile dealership, a hospital, three department stores, two jewelry accounts, and a shopping center.

HEAD DESIGNER, Smithville Design, 248 Harris Ave., Boston, MA, 1979-1984. Coordinated production and design of full-color annual catalogs for clients ranging from an office supply dealer to a jewelry store. Earned award from American Advertising Federation for best direct mail campaign generated in a small agency (less than 25 employees).

DESIGNER, Montgomery Advertising Agency, 789 Williams Rd., Boston, MA, 1975-1979. Presented and won bid for multi-media advertising campaign for grand opening of regional shopping mall generating $850,000 in billings for agency. Received Rookie of the Year award as best new designer.

Education

Graduated with honors, Tufts University, 1974.
Major: Advertising Art; Minor: Journalism

Memberships

Professional

American Association of Art Directors, Greater Boston Chapter
International Business Communicators
Massachusetts Press Women

Civic

Soroptimist International Women's Service Organization
Greater Boston Chamber of Commerce Cultural Council

Special Skills

Photography   Writing

References available on request.

Figure 15-1 Sample resumé.

one company to another, they may not give an adequate description of the actual accomplishments.

Be specific. Numbers on a resumé are impressive. Instead of saying you supervised a large department, quanitify your work by saying you supervised a department of five clerical employees and six technicians. Numbers give an employer an idea of the size job you can handle.

Create an attractive document. Accurate typing, clear photocopying, and well-spaced information help give a resumé visual appeal. Avoid trendy colored paper, but use the best white or beige-colored stock you can afford to make a good first impression.

Cover Letters Once you have written your resumé, your next writing task will be the cover letter. This is the letter you attach to the resumé to communicate your objective to the company. Review the hints for effective written business communication from the chapter on communication before you start a cover letter.

Key points to remember are

Be concise. Quickly introduce yourself in the letter and state your objective. Let the company know the job you seek and why you are interested. Do not assume the personnel manager will know that you want an interview. State your availability for an interview and let the reader know you will be calling soon to follow up on the letter.

Be accurate. Spelling the addressee's name incorrectly or routing the letter to the wrong person can be disastrous. Take the time to proofread your letter and be sure it conveys the image and tone you intend.

Never use a form letter for a cover letter. Resumés may be duplicated or photocopied, but each cover letter should be an original. If you have access to a word processor or a memory typewriter, you may be able to use similar wording, but always personalize a cover letter to the company to demonstrate your eagerness to work there.

A cover letter and resumé are often the first impression a company receives about you. Sloppiness, misspelled words, or poor grammar may mark you as a careless employee. Strive for excellence in your first encounters with a potential employer, whether the first meeting is on paper or in person.

Interviewing Just as there is an art to interviewing people, there is an art to being interviewed. Interview skills improve with practice. Sometimes role playing an interview situation with a job counselor or friend can help build confidence for the actual interview. Every detail counts in an interview, from what you wear and how you answer questions to your ability to handle the stress of an unfamiliar situation and your own questions about the company.

Before you arrive

Secure recommendations. Most experts agree that you should bring a list of references (Fig. 15-2) to the interview rather than including them on your resumé. Your potential employer will likely contact your previous employer as a matter of policy, but you may also give references of your own choosing such as professors or personal friends who may be influential in the community. Always call references beforehand to ask for permission to use their name. People do not like to be surprised by getting an unsolicited call from a potential employer. By calling ahead, you can get an idea of whether the person will respond favorably and help the reference understand why you are seeking a particular job.

Do your homework. Know as much about the company as possible. Review your resumé and try to think of questions you will be asked. Interviewers generally ask questions such as "What can you tell me about yourself?" or "What are your goals?" These open-ended questions are intended to give you a chance to discuss your qualifications and why you think you should get the job. Rehearsing answers will help you organize your thoughts in advance. Be prepared, for example, to give a starting salary if you are asked how much money you want or to ask a few questions yourself, since many interviewers end an interview by asking if you have any questions.

Dress conservatively. A navy or black skirted suit with an appropriate blouse is almost always a safe "uniform" for a job interview. Unless you seek a job in an artistic field, such as fashion design or advertising, flamboyant dressing will not gain many

---

Martin Wilson, Creative Director, Frankenfield's Creative Ideas, 640 4th St., Boston, MA (555)333-4545

Roland Smith, Smithville Design, 248 Harris Ave., Boston, MA (555)333-5678

Bill Montgomery, owner, Montgomery Advertising Agency, 789 Williams Rd., Boston, MA (555)333-9090

Dr. Jean Franklin, Chairman, Department of Journalism, Tufts University, Tufts Station, Boston, MA (555)325-3434

Figure 15-2 Sample references.

points. If you have visited the company before, try to dress like the people who already work there. Later, when you have the job, you can relax some of the dress code restrictions if company policy allows, but always dress appropriately for a job interview. Wear something that makes you feel as comfortable and confident as possible to decrease the potential stress of the situation.

When you arrive

Be prompt. Being early or late can be equally unnerving for the interviewer. Try to arrive no sooner than 5 minutes before your appointment so the interviewer will not feel the need to rush any pending work knowing that you are waiting. Allow plenty of time for traffic and parking problems. Being late for an interview may diminish your chances for equal consideration among candidates who arrived on time. If you must be late or cancel, be sure the situation is justified as an emergency and call as soon as you are able to notify the company of the situation.

Remember that listening is part of being interviewed. Try to remember names by repeating them back to people as you are introduced. Listen for details about the company and make mental notes in case you need to ask questions later. Listening also helps avoid the temptation to talk too much or overanswer questions.

Use positive body language. Look the interviewer directly in the eye and do not slouch. Sitting on the edge of the chair instead of getting too comfortable shows eagerness and a high level of interest. Avoid any nervous habits such as smoking, chewing gum, or checking your nails. These habits convey anxiety and may be construed as bad manners.

Show attention to details. A firm handshake is a strong introduction. Bring a pen to fill out a job application. Use legible handwriting and be honest about all details on the application. Dishonesty, whether intentional or accidental, on a job application can be grounds for immediate dismissal from the job when it is discovered.

After you leave

Follow up the interview. Depending on the situation, you may want to write a note thanking the interviewer for the time you were given. If the personnel manager made reference to calling you, you must wait for that call. If not, you might call the interviewer and ask if the company needs any more information about you.

Check with people whose names you used as references to see if they have been contacted. This accomplishes two things: it gives you a chance to thank them for letting you use their name in your behalf and it lets you know if the company was interested enough in you to check your references.

SUCCESS STRATEGIES

Once you have the job, you enter the next phase of developing success strategies. Seven keys to success on any job are

Commitment. Make a conscious commitment to succeeding. Approach each challenge in a systematic way to reinforce your commitment.

Goals. If you have not already begun the life-long cycle of setting goals and achieving them before going on to more goals, you should start on the first day of your new job. Communicate your goals to those who can help you reach them. Do not wait for people to read your mind about what you want.

Action. Part of gaining additional responsibility is taking risks through action. Make decisions and be ready to justify them. Use your experience and training to get results.

Perseverance. Sticking with a course of action can be tough. Realize that learning to take criticism is part of any job. Do not give up until you have reached your goal.

Self-image. Your personal traits of projection, ethics, style, and image are a part of how people perceive you. You can never divorce yourself from that image. Keeping a sense of professional visibility is vital to success.

Education. Never stop learning. Be open minded to new sources of help or information. Find a mentor or role model and learn on a one-to-one basis. Read everything you can to find new ideas and broaden your perspective.

Optimism. Keep a positive attitude about your career. Visualize your success as you work toward it. View obstacles as temporary setbacks and detours rather than dead-ends.

Job Hopping and Fast Tracking

Very few people find success in their first job or even at their first company. Current trends predict the majority of people change careers three times and jobs ten times, and will need to retrain five times. Two strategies that have been identified in analyzing career paths are job hopping and fast tracking.

Job hopping is the strategy of making several job moves that eventually place you higher on the career ladder. Some moves might be horizontal at first, but each is designed to move you closer to a long-range goal. *Fast tracking* is working your way up through the ranks at one company. In fast tracking, you pay your dues in order to be promoted from within the company. Both strategies can pay off for women. In either strategy, it is important to remember that you are in control and you never have to stay in one place if it is not meeting your goals.

Job Hopping

In "Getting Promoted," Fader (1986) writes, "A promotion is never a gift or an accident of fortune. Make sure you are the right person in the right place for that promotion." Part of being in the right place at the right time is knowing when to stay and when to leave a job. Six indicators that it is time to find another job include

- ❑ Dreading going to work in the morning or after a weekend's rest
- ❑ Feeling bored or lacking a challenge in your work
- ❑ Thinking that you are not receiving ample rewards such as pay or appreciation
- ❑ Having an unresolved personality conflict with your boss or another superior
- ❑ Receiving indications that women in general or you in particular have gone as high as you can go within the company
- ❑ Being overlooked for a promotion when you have made your desires known

Dancing in Place

Dancing in place is the practice of not moving forward, backward, or laterally within a job. Persons who dance in place either possess minimal promotional opportunities or low expectations and aspirations. They do not initiate career moves because either they discount that they are deserving or qualified, that greater opportunities are open to them, and that advancement is worth the effort, or they simply have never viewed their career as more than a job to meet short-term needs.

For example, Linda recently completed her eighteenth year with a utility company; she knows that the younger women may aspire to management positions, but believes that it is too late for her, not worth the effort, and to date only one woman has been promoted to a mid-level position.

Selling Out

Selling out is an adjustive reaction in response to a professional situation that results in a compromise, trade-out, or substitution of an original goal for another opportunity, denying personal standards for short-term gain. For example, Sherry completed all course work toward her doctorate degree, but when the dissertation deadline approached, Sherry discounted the importance of the degree; the initials Ph.D. meant little anyway. How we resolve the issues we face can often be more important than the issues themselves.

Any of these situations may be cause for changing jobs. However, before you turn in your 2-weeks' notice, be sure you have a plan in mind. It is generally easier to find another job while you are still employed. Know your reasons for quitting so that you do not inadvertently trade one bad job situation for another. If a promotion or a raise would change your mind, discuss that option with your employer. Be aware, though, that more money or a new title will not solve underlying problems on a job.

Fast Tracking

Fast tracking is selecting a series of positions that are characterized by promotability and visibility and that lead to upper management in less time than usual. Few corporations give employees the opportunity to move ahead as quickly as they would like. Often the climb to upper management involves many years of patiently doing a good job and taking promotions one at a time. Many times the success stories of women in today's headlines fail to mention many entry-level jobs and early career steps that made the achievement possible. In fact, analyzing the career of someone you admire may give you clues about your own career path.

FAST TRACK TECHNIQUES

1. Consider alternate career paths
2. Set long-term career goals
3. Give each job a fair chance
4. Take risks
5. Be realistic
6. Be responsible for yourself
7. Deliver excellence

To put your career on the fast track, here are some techniques to use:

Remember there is no one career path. CEOs have come from all aspects of an organization when people recognize talent. Choose an area you excel in and strive to be the best while achieving the visibility that you need to be spotted for a promotion.

Always keep in mind the long-term goals of your career instead of only short-term goals. Sometimes taking a horizontal transfer to a position with no greater responsibility can be a smart move if it helps you learn more about the company or the product. Even taking an entry-level job for which you are overqualified can be a wise decision if you start gaining experience with the right company.

Give each job a fair chance. Learning the behind-the-scenes politics or operations of a job takes time. Companies feel more comfortable promoting someone they have seen perform reliably and competently over a period of time. Allow employers a chance to get to know you and to create opportunities for you before moving on to greener pastures.

Keep taking risks. If you get too comfortable in a job or a company, you may never grow past a certain position. Learn new skills, seek more responsibility, and volunteer for projects that stretch your potential.

Be realistic. Before assuming that you are underpaid or overworked, check the current market conditions and find out how your job compares to others. Do not compare promotions in an up-and-coming field such as computers with more established industries such as manufacturing.

Be responsible for your own life. No one else can tell you when it is time to move on or move up. You know yourself better than anyone else. If you are unhappy, that is a good signal to reassess your goals and define a new strategy.

Excellence

One career strategy that remains equally important for men or women is the achievement of professional *excellence.* One of the must-read books on every executive's bookshelf in the 1980s is *In Search of Excellence,* in which Peters and Waterman (1982) write that successful companies share certain qualities that give them a passion for excellence among customers, employees, and their corporate competitors. They provide eight clues to excellence that can be applied on a personal or corporate level.

1. *A bias for action.* This means that excellent companies encourage action rather than simply producing reports or having meetings.

2. *Close to the customer.* Excellent companies never forget that the customer is their reason for being and strive to stay close to customers for ideas and better service.

3. *Autonomy and entrepreneurship.* Excellent companies foster a sense of innovation and openness to new suggestions from employees. They know new, profitable ideas sometimes come only from laboratory failures and concepts that at first seemed too far out.

4. *Productivity through people.* People on all corporate levels are treated with dignity and respect in excellent companies. They accentuate the positive on an individual level.

5. *Hands-on, value-driven.* The authors write that excellent companies have established a value system. In other words, they know what makes them most proud and have a group of dominant beliefs to follow.

6. *Stick to your knitting.* Excellent companies stay within the areas they know best.

7. *Simple form, lean staff.* For excellent companies, bigger is not better.

8. *Simultaneous loose-tight properties.* Excellent companies balance tight control with informal communication networks and flexible structures.

SUMMARY

Futurism, the study of trends and the implementation of the information into a plan of action, impacts on managers' careers as they attempt to keep abreast of changes and manage their own careers. Women can enhance careers by learning what is going on in the organization, using available resources, planning long term, and noting major trends.

Women must redefine their own vision of the future, utilize career assessment techniques, and apply success strategies to fast track into the 1990s. Job hopping, delivering excellence, writing effective resumés, and developing interviewing skills will also maximize future opportunities.

TERMS AND CONCEPTS

career assessment   creative scenarios
career identification   dancing in place
company identification   excellence

fast tracking	resumé
futurism	scanning
futurists	selling out
job hopping	setting goals
managerial myopia	success strategies
modeling	

REVIEW QUESTIONS

1. Compare the ten major trends in our society.
2. Explain four basic techniques of futuring.
3. Discuss some of the recent findings from "How Working Women Have Changed America."
4. Explain the four major concentrations of career assessment.
5. Interpret the statement "Strong career/company identification enhances probability of a successful career."
6. List seven keys to success on any job. Give specific personal examples of how you can apply each.
7. Summarize indicators that it is time to find another job.
8. Apply the eight clues to excellence to you, your position, and your organization. Give specific examples of each.

EXERCISE

15-1: FUTURING

Scanning: Scan newspapers, magazines/journals, and newsletters and collect four articles over a 1-week period that illustrate a future trend.

Creating scenarios: Select and role play one futurist event from the indicated trends as a worst-case scenario and best-case scenario. Observers should share their reactions and indicate whether role playing the scenarios has changed or influenced their views.

SUGGESTED READINGS

Blotnick, S. *The Corporate Steeplechase. Predictable Crises in a Business Career.* Facts on File, New York, 1984.

Bolles, R.N. *The 1986 What Color Is Your Parachute: A Practical Manual for Job Hunters and Career Changes.* Ten Speed Press, Berkeley, CA, 1986.

Botkin, J., Dimancescu, D., Stata, R., with McClellan, J. *Global Stakes. The Future of High Technology in America.* Penguin Books, New York, 1984.

Catalyst Staff. *Marketing Yourself.* Bantam Books, New York, 1980.

Catalyst Staff. *Upward Mobility.* Holt, Rinehart & Winston, New York, 1981.

Curran, A. *Working Woman Success Book.* Ace Books, New York, 1981.

Drucker, P.F. *Innovation and Entrepreneurship. Practice and Principles.* Harper & Row, New York, 1985.

Editors of *Success* Magazine. *Career Change.* Success Guides, Success Unlimited, Inc., Chicago, IL (no date).

Fader, S.S. Getting Promoted. *Working Woman* (July, 1986).

Garfield, C. *Peak Performers.* William Morrow & Co., New York, 1986

Henderson, C. *Winners.* Holt, Rinehart and Winston, New York, 1985.

Kennedy, M.M. *Career Knockouts. How to Battle Back.* Warner Books, New York, 1980.

Levitt, J. *Your Career—How to Make It Happen.* South-Western, Chicago, IL, 1985.

Lydenberg, S., Marlin, A., Strub, S., and the Council on Economic Priorities. *Rating America's Corporate Conscience.* Addison-Wesley, Reading, MA, 1986.

Machlowitz, M. Managing for the Future—Now. *Management Woman* (April, 1981).

Naisbitt, J. *Megatrends.* Warner Books, New York, 1982.

Naisbitt, J., and the Naisbitt Group. *The Year Ahead—1986.* Warner Book, New York, 1985.

Peters, T.J., and Waterman, R.H., Jr. *In Search of Excellence.* Warner Books, New York, 1982.

Rogers, H.C. *Roger's Rules for Success.* St. Martin's Press, New York, 1984.

Schenkel, S. *Giving Away Success. Why Women Get Stuck and What to Do About It.* McGraw-Hill, New York, 1984.

Sherwood, A. *Breakpoints.* Doubleday, New York, 1986.

Sitterly, C., and Duke, B. Breaking Out of a Career Rut. *The Secretary* (January, 1987).

Viscott, D. *Taking Care of Business.* William Morrow & Co., 1985.

Wareham, J. *Secrets of a Corporate Headhunter.* Playboy Paperbacks, New York, 1980.

ASSESS YOURSELF, YOUR GOALS, AND YOUR ORGANIZATION

THE CAREER AWARENESS INVENTORY [1]

Know Yourself

How well do you know yourself, your goals, and your organization? To gain some insight into these issues, answer the questions below.

1. List three things you would specifically like:

TO HAVE	TO BE	TO DO
a.	a.	a.
b.	b.	b.
c.	c.	c.

2. What position will you seek next?

3. What training workshops/courses will you enroll in next?

4. How can you increase your visibility and/or recognition in your organization?

[1] From Sitterly (1985) and Baron (1985).

5. What new tasks or responsibilities can you seek within the next 3 months?

6. List three professional goals; give a target date for each.
   a.

   b.

   c.

7. List three personal goals; give a target date for each.
   a.

   b.

   c.

8. List three educational goals; give a target date for each.
   a.

   b.

   c.

9. Name at least one organization that would be beneficial for you to join.

10. Name at least one volunteer activity that would be beneficial for you.

11. List two new activities or hobbies that you will learn within the next 6 months.
    a.

    b.

12. Name the primary situation that creates stress for you.

13. What is the best way you have found to cope with stress?

14. Name two strategies for reducing stress that you will apply immediately.

    a.

    b.

15. What is your primary time waster?

16. What two techniques can you apply to better manage your time?

17. Name the field, position, salary, and location you project for yourself 5 years from today.

    a.

    b.

    c.

    d.

18. Name at least two role models.

    a.

    b.

19. Identify three powerful or influential others in your organization.

    a.

    b.

    c.

20. How can you build rapport with each of these persons?

21. Name three books you will read within the next 3 months.

    a.

    b.

    c.

22. What is your "secret project"? What would you really like to do?

23. Why? Why not?

24. What are the three factors that would make a difference in your career?

25. Name at least one person who could serve as a mentor to you.

26. What are three objectives of your organization?
    a.
    b.
    c.

27. What are three objectives of your department?
    a.
    b.
    c.

28. Describe yourself as a person.

29. What are you best at doing? What are your strengths?

30. What are you worst at doing? What do you most dislike doing?

31. What are your two greatest accomplishments?
    a.
    b.

32. What do you like about your present job?

Assess Yourself

(Respond with Good, Fair, or Poor)

Do You?

___

Implement changes?

Persuade? Influence? Negotiate win-win?

Get your points across?

Find subordinates agree with you?

Perform evaluations?

Set priorities?

Meet deadlines?

Remain knowledgeable in industry, company, or field?

Seek training?

Understand technical reports?

Handle confrontations?

Make demands when necessary?

Know subordinate's strengths and weaknesses?

Encourage subordinates to further education, training?

Set and achieve goals? Long-range plans?

Know subordinate's attitudes?

Procrastinate?

Take risks?

Plan projects?

Organize?

Manage time?

Handle stress?

Know next job description?

Attend conventions, trade shows?

Enroll in courses, programs?

Send personnel updated credentials? Updated resumés?

Join women's organizations?

Volunteer for community projects?

Develop contingency plan?

Compete with self or others?

Increase visibility?

Stroke others?

Offer suggestions?

Undertake activities that will teach you new skills?

Stretch abilities?

Read?

Reassess? Reaffirm?

Maintain positive attitude?

What are your obstacles?

What are your greatest contributions?

Management Training Checklist

Do You?	**Yes**	**No**

Work well by yourself?

Always look for a better way to do your job?

Work at a steady pace without apparent effort?

Have neat work habits?

Manage time well?

Set priorities?

Seek ways to

      Save time?

      Cut costs?

      Reduce waste?

      Simplify procedures and methods?

      Improve organization?

      Generate customers?

      Increase profits?

      Improve customer service?

Make suggestions?

Solve problems?

Work as though you owned the business?

Ask questions?

Know how your job fits into the overall picture?

Cooperate with peers, subordinates, as well as
top-level managers?

Have an open mind to new people, equipment,
processes, ideas?

Listen?

Admit mistakes— correct, learn, and forget?

Separate business and personal relationships
satisfactorily?

Face problems and deal with them as they arise?

Refresh skills and learn new ones?

Volunteer for special projects?

Support your boss?

Know your boss's goals? Department's?
Organization's?

View position as a job or career?

Set, achieve, and share goals beneficial to you,
your department, and your organization?

Review those questions that received a **NO** answer.

SUGGESTED READINGS

Baron, R. *Behavior in Organization.* Allyn & Bacon, Boston,
1985.

Sitterly, C. (contributor) Instructor's Guide. *Promotable Woman*
(2nd Ed.). Wadsworth, Belmont, CA, 1985.

GLOSSARY

affiliation Socially acquired motives in which a person desires to work with people, serve on committees and teams, and smooth tensions.

after-tax net income Pretax net income minus tax paid.

Age Discrimination in Employment Act Protects employees between 40 and 70 years old from discrimination in hiring, firing, and other terms of employment.

agenda A meeting outline or an outline of goals or objectives that need to be accomplished. A hidden agenda is the underlying motive for an employee's behavior, which may not be readily apparent.

aggressive Expresses feelings in a dishonest, overbearing, pushy, inappropriate manner that violates the other person's rights.

angry assertion Express anger without placing blame or being aggressive.

annual report's letter from the chairperson Summarizes the report's contents and analyzes the reasons for the company's performance; sets the report's tone and provides insight into the future of the company and the chairperson's personality.

apathy Flight reaction to stress in which people's uncaring attitude and undisturbed appearance cover how they really feel.

assertive disengagement To postpone a discussion that would be more effective at a later date.

assertiveness Communication style; standing up for your rights or needs in honest, direct, and appropriate ways that do not violate another person's rights.

assets (total) Sum of all you own.

authority Potential to get results.

autogenic messages A stress-reduction exercise in which you use your mind to control your mind's messages. When you have doubts, reprogram yourself by sending positive autogenic messages reaffirming your abilities and belief in yourself.

autonomy Freedom to pursue an idea without the necessity of obtaining too many approvals.

baby ducks Less important tasks that nibble away at time needed for key projects and major responsibilities.

behavior modeling Changing your actions through understanding and applying a set of skills.

big picture Systems theory; ability to conceptualize the entire idea, project, organization, or end result in spite of details; ability to see how various factors, persons, or departments affect other factors.

biofeedback A stress-reduction exercise using your mind to direct your body to do your will, to reduce muscle tension and provide a general feeling of relaxation.

body language Study of how gestures and postures combine to send messages.

bottom-up budget Originates from the bottom. Department heads are asked for estimates and forecasts about expenses; these projections go to a top executive who coordinates the budgeting function.

brainstorming Compiling a large number of solutions to any given problem without regard to their effectiveness during the creative process.

broken record Repeating a statement to add emphasis.

budget Financial tool to show categorical projections of expenditures to help control costs, anticipate expenses, and improve coordination between departments by giving an overview of operating needs and priorities.

burnout Possible reaction to workaholic syndrome. Prolonged negative stress resulting in psychological, physical, emotional, and spiritual exhaustion so that the person no longer cares about work, relationships, and/or activities that once interested her.

bypassing Identifying who can provide the information, influence, or resources to assist you in your objectives and going directly to them for assistance, regardless of position or title; an alternate path.

career assessment Process of analyzing yourself and external factors that affect career decisions in order to make the best possible life decision through self-assessment, career identification, company identification, and getting the job.

career identification Association with, or relating to, the requirements, skills, activities, philosophies, and characteristics of a career according to your own values, needs, goals, philosophies, expectations, and skills.

climate Organizational atmosphere.

coercive power Power to punish, fire, or demote; reciprocal of reward power.

collaboration Win-win negotiation in which the solution includes portions of both sides' plans to make the outcome a joint effort and enable both sides to share in the new hybrid plan as a partnership.

commitment Process of applying resources to a decision in order to see it through to its desired outcome.

commodity futures Investments that speculate on the price of a commodity at some time in the future.

communication Process of reaching others with an effective transfer of information that the receiver understands.

communication skills To persuade; to present information clearly and effectively.

company identification Association with or relation to the requirements, philosophies, ethics, mission, focus, objectives, and attitudes of an organization according to your own values, needs, motives, ethics, philosophies, goals, expectations, and skills.

comparable worth Pay equity concept that asserts that women should be paid as much as men for performing tasks in other jobs that involve comparable but not identical skills, education, responsibilities, and effort.

compelling vision Ever-present "consciousness" about desired outcomes.

competence Socially acquired need that emphasizes achievement, feedback, goal orientation, and doing a job well.

compressed work week Shortening of the work week so that the number of hours per day increases for fewer days per week, such as a 4-day, 40-hour system.

compromise Third plan created somewhere between each negotiator's position.

concentration To focus attention on the desired outcome.

conceptual skill The ability to see the organization as a whole; to analyze, plan, forecast, integrate, and coordinate ideas, concepts and practices. Most important to top level managers.

confrontive assertion Resolve a problem by pointing out an agreed upon set of circumstances, explain a specific discrepancy, and ask for a response that commits the listener to a future action.

consulting style Situational leadership style in which the leader consults, supports, directs, and gives information without direct hands-on supervision, allowing followers the latitude over methods but retaining final authority over decisions.

control Managerial activity that is undertaken to assure actual operations go according to plan.

creating scenarios Futuring technique that describes different conclusions based on available data to remind planners of the number of variable factors in any situation.

creative decisions Decisions that require deliberation beyond the daily routine as a result of one-time, short-term, or sporadic occurrences.

creative imagery Stress-reducing technique in which you visualize yourself doing something you enjoy; structured daydreaming, a mental break from daily pressures.

creativity Success factor that utilizes imagination and good memory and proposes new solutions and ideas.

credibility Believable attribute of a person who follows-up, delivers expected results, and completes a job well and successfully.

creeping negativism A sign of stress; a reaction to frustration in which otherwise optimistic people view changes as a threat, questioning their own ability to handle situations, which under normal conditions would not be questioned.

current assets Assets that can be quickly turned into cash.

current liabilities Debts due in 1 year that are paid out of current assets.

damage control Reaction to an error or mistake in which you seek to lessen repercussions by admitting the mistake and informing the supervisor.

dancing in place The art of not moving forward, backward, or laterally within a job. "Stuck."

debt-to-equity ratio Divides the long-term liabilities by the stockholder's equity and gives a picture of the company's overall debt to know how similar sized competing firms are performing.

default Common decision-making process in which the decision maker lets something happen due to inaction, allowing circumstances rather than direct intervention to control the outcome.

delegation decision-making pattern Shifting the responsibility of the decision to another person. Authority shared rests with the person making the decision.

delegating style Situational leadership style with subordinates who require little active leadership. Leader generally delegates project, states the expected end result, and asks for updates.

deliberate decision-making pattern Tries to achieve thoughtful decisions, but often pays the consequences for taking too long to decide. Deliberating too long may allow the situation to reach crisis proportions.

Delphi A noninteractional problem-solving technique in that the manager collects and tabulates other people's opinions and feedback to determine the best solution.

DIGEST A problem-solving approach that reduces a problem to its simplest components, suggests alternatives, and selects an alternative that becomes a plan of action. Steps include *D*efine situation, *I*dentify problem, *G*et the facts, *E*valuate alternatives, *S*elect an alternative, and *T*ake action (follow-up).

displacement Reaction to stress in which the person places the blame on others rather than taking responsibility for the outcome; commonly known as scapegoating.

downward pressures Organizational pressures that originate from within the organization, filtering from top management downward.

dual-career marriages Both husband and wife work each day at demanding jobs.

emotional interference Communication block in which the communicator becomes distracted by personal problems, pressure, deadlines, or preoccupation with competing events.

empathetic assertion Acknowledging the listener's feelings while being assertive.

enthusiasm High energy level.

entry level First, lowest level of administrative hierarchy. Coordinates work of nonmanagers, but reports to managers.

Equal Credit Opportunity Act of 1974 Gives women equal access to financial services and prohibits discrimination in granting of credit.

Equal Employment Opportunity Commission Enforces antidiscrimination laws.

Equal Pay Act Prohibits employees from paying women less than men for the same work.

excellence Virtue; valuable quality; to surpass, go beyond the limit; intense effort for superior performance; collective commitment to a common purpose. Desire to be the best, to make a difference, insisting on top quality.

expenses (total) Sum of all the money you spend.

experience Learning method of providing on-the-job training through trial and error until results are achieved.

expert power Power from technical expertise or competence.

fallback position Minimum area in a range of concessions in which you are willing to compromise during the negotiation process.

fast track Career path that includes a series of positions leading to an upper management position in less time than usual.

female-intensive careers Jobs in which more than 60% of the employees are women.

female longevity Women live longer than men.

feminization of poverty A condition in which women who become single heads of households find that their earning power drops.

fight or flight Reaction to a stressful situation in which we either confront the situation or run away.

financial statement Statement that includes a detailed list of the most common categories for assets and liabilities to provide a background for financial decisions.

fixation or obsession Reaction to stress in which the person becomes preoccupied with a distressing problem to the exclusion of other day-to-day concerns.

fixed costs Expenses for items that you cannot do without, although you have little control over the cost.

flexplace An employment practice in which employees are allowed to work at home rather than at an office or plant.

flextime A condition in which employees may, with prior approval of their supervisor, alter their usual working hours.

fogging Avoid taking unjust criticism while agreeing in part with the speaker.

futurism Studying the future through trends and implementing the information into a plan of action.

futurists Specialists who research, analyze, and chart the future.

generally accepted accounting principles Indicates that a report can be trusted to be consistent with other reports bearing the same information.

generate your position Concept in which you seek results or innovations to contribute to your organization, to extend beyond what is expected as a standard of performance.

goal Desired outcome or planned result; long-term objective.

group decision making Creative approach involving people outside the manager to provide a wider range of information, perspectives, and commitment to the solution.

harassment Any unwanted behavior, whether verbal or physical, that either creates an implicit or explicit condition for employment or interferes with an individual's ability to work in an atmosphere free from intimidation.

health Success factor enabling someone to handle stress, fight off illnesses, and meet work demands.

human skills Ability to work effectively with, motivate, counsel, and guide people. Most important to the middle-level manager.

hypnosis Entering a trance-like state and being given suggestions to alter behavior.

impact To create a good first impression and to command attention and respect.

income statement Form that shows how much money was made or lost over the year, includes a net sales figure.

income (total) Sum of all the money you earn.

influence Cooperation without argument.

initiative To originate action.

intelligence Factor that increases success potential by reading, research, experience, and education.

interest Amount of money a financial institution pays you for "borrowing" your money and using it for their purposes while you leave it on deposit.

introversion/extroversion Success factor that is the balance of excelling in both individual and group pursuits.

intuition Common decision-making pattern utilizing inner feelings and judgments to make a quick decision because it seems right.

job hopping Strategy of making several job moves to eventually bring you closer to a long-range goal.

job sharing Approach to job enrichment in which two employees share a full-time position.

judgment Skill needed to reach a logical, sensible, well-founded conclusion.

leadership Ability to influence, persuade, get ideas accepted, to guide willing followers, and to create a positive team climate.

liabilities (total) Sum of all you owe.

liquid investments Investments that may be readily converted to cash.

liquidity Term that expresses how easy or difficult it is to get your money out of an investment.

little lady syndrome Reaction that discredits or discounts the contribution or potential worth of a woman based on the belief that women are inferior on the basis of sex.

long-term debt Debt not due within the year but still owed.

male chauvinism Male behavior that reflects a patronizing, condescending attitude, a result of social conditioning; judging females on the basis of sex rather than of merit.

management Effective utilization of human and material resources to achieve the objective of the organization.

management by crisis Fire-fighting management. Decision-making pattern in which the decision is forced by a crisis. Because events happen so quickly, important steps may be overlooked.

management by objective Simultaneous goal setting between supervisor and subordinate in which mutually agreeable and measurable objectives are set.

managerial myopia Nearsightedness, or concern about today's performance instead of tomorrow's profits.

managers People who carry out the responsibilities of management.

manage-up Supervisors' ability to size up their boss and to adapt their behavior to earn rewards that result from a positive boss-employee relationship.

math phobia Reluctance on the part of a person to work with numbers because of deep-seated fears about failing math courses or making mistakes when doing computations.

meditating Communing with a higher power.

mentor Sponsor who advises, teaches, coaches, and shares information to learn the complexities of business.

mentoring Practice of sharing information, counseling, advising, and coaching a new or less experienced employee to understand the complexities of business.

middle management or mid-management Middle level of administrative hierarchy. Managers coordinate work of managers and report to a manager.

modeling Developing a mathematical model from the futurist's data to quantify trend statements for measurable predictability.

mutual funds   Pool resources of its investors to buy stocks and bonds in greater quantities than an individual could possibly afford.

nature verses nurture   A theory that we either inherit certain qualities that make us different from birth or that we come into the world with equal abilities, but because of environmental factors, we develop different abilities.

negative assertion   Admit a mistake without becoming defensive or accepting guilt.

negative inquiry   Ask for a specific criticism to clarify an objective.

negotiation   The art of persuading or influencing someone else to a certain course of action.

negotiation potential   The ability of a person or a situation to affect a change, to deal, to offer something in exchange for receiving something.

net earnings per share   Shows how much shares earn.

net income   Total income minus total expenses.

networking   Using personal contacts to achieve a goal or objective; trade-offs to share information, business contacts, and support.

net working capital   Difference between current liabilities and current assets.

net worth   Total assets minus total liabilities equals net worth.

nonassertiveness   Suppressing needs or desires, appearing to avoid conflicts in a manner that violates personal rights.

nonliquid investments   Investments that cannot be readily converted to cash.

nonsupervisory worker   Subordinate who carries out technical work under the directions of a supervisor, and is evaluated on the quality of individual work.

nonverbal communication   All forms of communication other than written or verbal forms, including the use of space and body gestures.

objectives   Steps or activities that lead to your goal; building blocks of goals.

organization   Success factor that includes the ability to control yourself and your environment to the greatest possible extent; coordination.

organize   Managerial activity that results in the design of a formal structure of tasks and authority.

participating style   Situational leadership style in which the leader facilitates, moderates, and allows subordinates to participate in the decisions that affect them or their work.

person oriented   Democratic leadership approach, characterized by participation and consensus in decision making.

perspective   Ability to conceptualize the "end result" in spite of details.

PERT (Performance Evaluation and Review Technique)   Diagramming a project to schedule and coordinate the sequence and timing of activities and to identify the critical path to shorten project completion time.

pink ghetto Employment area comprising disproportionate numbers of women in lower paying positions that offer little chance for promotion.

physical disorders Reaction to long-term stressful situation, in which the body succumbs to pressure. Internalized stress may manifest itself in headaches, digestive disorders, high blood pressure, backaches, skin rashes, achiness, and fatigue.

plan To develop managerial activities, to set objectives, and to determine appropriate means of achieving the objectives.

positioning Developing strategies that put you in favorable situations, preferably closer to people with the authority to make decisions.

position power Legitimate power; ability to execute the assigned authority inherent in the job description, title, and specifications.

power To have impact, influence, effect change, make things happen, choose to change. Ability to achieve objectives and get results.

Pregnancy Discrimination Act of 1978 Extended protection of Title VII to pregnant employees.

premature evaluation Communication block in which the listener reaches a conclusion before hearing all the points.

problem Difference or gap between a current situation and a desired or expected situation; any situation that is "off target," unwanted, or urgent enough to warrant attention, analysis, or correction.

problem solving The process of eliminating the gap and converting the current situation to the desired situation.

programmed problem solving Routine decisions handled so frequently that certain procedures or methods are developed to handle them.

qualitative goals Goals that define how well an activity can be completed, how aspects of production can improve, or how workers can improve knowledge of their job.

quality circles Participative approach in which groups of employees meet to solve problems with the goal of enhancing the quality and productivity of their work.

quantitative goal Measurable goal expressed in a number or percentage that can be calculated, telling how much improvement is expected, how large a firm will grow, how much sales will increase, etc.

rationalization Common coping mechanism; a reaction to a stressful event in which the person attempts to give plausible, but not necessarily true, explanations for specific, often undesirable behavior.

reactionary Common decision-making pattern utilizing a human nature reflex to make a decision based solely on someone else's behavior, reducing a situation to an adversarial role that may have negative results rather than a positive solution.

receiver Listener who receives and understands, thereby completing the communication transaction.

referent power Power through personality or influence.

Rehabilitation Act of 1973 Banned discrimination against qualified individuals with handicaps who can perform the essential functions of the job with "reasonable accommodation."

reproductive freedom Freedom to plan child-bearing future through the use of birth control devices.

resumé Written summary of your credentials, including educational and professional experience, awards, and related information designed with the objective of getting a job.

reward power Ability to confer rewards or positive reinforcement on employees, based upon their performance. Reciprocal of coercive power.

rigidity Success factor in which the leader ignores the possibility of failure under stress, perseveres toward final goal.

ROI (return on investment) Formula used to compare either the increased income or increased value of an investment.

$$\frac{\text{Amount Received}}{\text{Amount Invested}} = \text{ROI}.$$

role models Someone whose behavior, attitude, and/or performance sets an example that we want to emulate in our lives.

rote memory Method of learning by repetition.

saving face Win-win strategy that allows the negotiator's opponent to choose from a range of choices that all provide a favorable outcome for the negotiator and in which all agree to the decision.

scanning Futuring technique to collect all available information, including newspapers, newsletters, census reports, magazines, journals, and best-selling books.

secure investments Have a low degree of risk; pay lower but more consistent dividends over a period of time.

selective perception Communication block in which the receiver hears what he or she chooses to hear based upon past experiences, attitudes, or beliefs about the message.

self-esteem Success factor whose value we place on ourselves. Persons with high self-esteem expect to do well and are highly resilient to the ups and downs of business cycles.

sender Transmits messages, choosing the type of channel, choice of symbols, and words to convey a meaning that can be understood by the receiver.

sensitivity Ability to recognize and respond to other's needs.

setting goals Futuring technique involving long-term goals to define Utopia; the way we want the world to be, not necessarily how it will be.

situational leadership Leadership varies, depending upon the situation, leader, and followers.

soft assertion Express affection or sympathy using your own feelings as a basis for communication.

staff Managerial activities that contribute indirectly to organization's output. Advises and supports line personnel.

stereotypes Beliefs about a group's predictable characteristics that allow us to categorize the group and generalize about its behavior without looking at the individuals as individuals.

stockholder's equity Difference between total liabilities and assets; the presumed dollar value assigned to stock owned by stockholders.

stress Condition of strain on one's emotions, thought processes, or physical condition.

stressors Internal or external, real or imagined events or factors that cause stress.

style Way in which a manager approaches the five basic functions of management; how a manager plans, organizes, staffs, directs, and controls.

subliminal learning Takes place at a level beyond our usual perception, outside the visual limits of the senses, such as listening to tapes as you sleep.

success factor Collection of traits enabling you to use your intelligence and personality. Sidney Lecker identified eight basic success traits: rigidity, organization, self-esteem, tough mindedness, introversion, health, intelligence, and creativity.

success strategies Principles or guidelines to help ensure professional development and promotability.

supervision A subfunction of control that refers to the overseeing of subordinates' work activity.

supervisor Oversees work of two or more persons and completes work significantly different from their employees.

systems theory All parts of a system are interrelated and a change in one part affects all other parts. An event that appears to affect one individual or one department may have significant influence elsewhere in the organization.

technical skill Understanding and ability to perform a specific activity or task or to utilize specialized knowledge. Most important to first-level management.

telling style Situational directive leadership style that defines roles, sets goals, gives instructions, and tells people who, what, when, where, and how to perform.

theory X   Autocratic and traditional set of assumptions about people.

theory Y   Human and supportive set of assumptions about people.

theory Z   Model that adapts elements of Japanese management systems to United States culture and emphasizes cooperation and consensus decision processes.

things-to-do list   A list of activities that you want to accomplish within a set time frame.

time as money   View that time is a business resource, an asset to change the way we view time.

time bonuses   Common sense tips that simplify some tasks to give you more time for your important goals.

time management   Effective use of allocated time.

Title IX of Education Amendments of 1972   Bans sex bias in institutions receiving any federal money.

top-down budget   Top management sets financial goals and determines the amount of revenue to reach these goals and distributes the figures to department heads who develop a budget for their group that leads to the revenue amount.

tough mindedness   Success factor characterized by persistence and the ability to conceptualize and solve problems in novel ways.

trade-out   Win-win negotiation strategy in which one or both parties give up something to gain something else, usually tangible assets such as money, titles, equipment, office space, or employment benefits.

transition   Period of change resulting from new or different situations, positions, career, employers, or related events.

tunnel vision   Single, focused; unable to see another's point of view. Unable to see the big picture.

type A behavior   Grouping individuals according to personality type; people who are competitive, lack patience, are overachievers, worry, feel guilty when relaxing, and are preoccupied with achievement.

type B behavior   Grouping individuals according to personality type; people who are patient, calm, and have balanced their professional and personal lives.

upper-level managers   Top level of administrative hierarchy. Coordinates work of managers but does not report to manager.

upward pressures   Organizational pressures that originate from within the organization, filtering from top entry-level employees upward.

value   Personal view of the desirability of certain goals.

variable costs   Costs that give the buyer greater latitude in making spending decisions.

visibility   Being noticed by others.

visualization   Practice of seeing yourself achieve goals; mental rehearsal to prepare your mind for the coming success, to become comfortable with the idea of success.

win-lose mentality   Negotiator interaction in which the participant views the negotiation process as a winner take all, loser take nothing situation; often producing resentment.

win-win mentality   Negotiator interaction in which the participant views the negotiation process as a situation in which both parties compromise, trade-out, save face, or collaborate, so that both parties complete negotiations in a better position than they started.

withdrawal   Flight reaction to stress by pulling away and suppressing feelings or concerns.

"women's work"   Jobs for females according to the sexist, stereotypical traditional classification based upon sex or role rather than abilities or qualifications.

workaholic   A compulsive worker; one who is addicted to work as the only way of life, can and does work anywhere and anytime; prefers work to leisure.

working capital   Current assets minus current liabilities.

work-oriented leadership   Authoritative approach that emphasizes task completion.

INDEX